THE SPORT MARRIAGE

SPORT AND SOCIETY

Series Editors
Aram Goudsouzian
Jaime Schultz

Founding Editors
Benjamin G. Rader
Randy Roberts

*A list of books in the series appears
at the end of this book.*

The Sport Marriage

WOMEN WHO MAKE IT WORK

STEVEN M. ORTIZ

UNIVERSITY OF ILLINOIS PRESS
Urbana, Chicago, and Springfield

© 2020 by the Board of Trustees
of the University of Illinois
All rights reserved
Manufactured in the United States of America
1 2 3 4 5 C P 5 4 3 2 1
♾ This book is printed on acid-free paper.

Library of Congress Cataloging-in-Publication Data
Names: Ortiz, Steven M., 1952– author.
Title: The sport marriage : women who make it work
 / Steven M. Ortiz.
Description: Urbana : University of Illinois Press,
 [2020] | Series: Sport and society | Includes
 bibliographical references and index.
Identifiers: LCCN 2020017312 (print) | LCCN
 2020017313 (ebook) | ISBN 9780252043161
 (hardcover) | ISBN 9780252085031 (paperback) |
 ISBN 9780252052040 (ebook)
Subjects: LCSH: Wives—Effect of husband's
 employment on. | Professional athletes.
Classification: LCC HQ759 .O74 2020 (print) |
 LCC HQ759 (ebook) | DDC 306.872/3—dc23
LC record available at https://lccn.loc.gov/
 2020017312
LC ebook record available at https://lccn.loc.gov/
 2020017313

*In loving memory of my mother, Rose Marie Ramos,
whose life of sacrifice and support I will never forget*

CONTENTS

Preface ix
Acknowledgments. xv

Introduction: Lifting the Veil of Silence 1
1. Influences on the Sport Marriage 17
2. In the Public Eye 46
3. Traveling with the Team 77
4. Star Power. 99
5. The In-Laws 128
6. A World of Groupies 154
7. A Closer Look at the Culture of Infidelity 180
Conclusion: The Final Score 201

Appendix A. Research Methodology 211
Appendix B. Participants. 218
Notes. 221
Bibliography 239
Index 251

PREFACE

THE SPORT INDUSTRY reflects the longstanding value Americans place on athletic achievement, dramatic entertainment, marketable sex appeal, and economic success. In today's global society, an increasing number of cultures are adopting these values, creating new markets that escalate the industry's influence on national and international policies. Many male professional athletes[1] enjoy celebrity status and a select few become cultural idols. Babe Ruth, Jackie Robinson, Muhammad Ali, and Michael Jordan are some examples of iconic professional athletes who have profoundly influenced and inspired generations of Americans, and whose fame transcends sports. Even sport heroes with far less recognition impact myriad aspects of contemporary society and modern consumerism. Despite such public acclaim, we frequently glimpse something not quite right in the high-profile world[2] of professional sports. A good many of these venerated men have generated unwanted public attention by exhibiting selfish and sometimes violent behavior in their private lives, thus becoming the center of widely publicized sex scandals and court cases involving violence against women. Their exploits often serve to feed the public's fervent curiosity. Unfortunately, our scholarly knowledge about their marriages and their relationships with women in general has been quite limited. The public's lack of understanding about the roles women play in a social institution that props up today's $1.3 trillion[3] global sport industry is unacceptable. My own awareness about this deplorable state of affairs came slowly.

I was raised in a sport-oriented family. My two younger brothers participated in organized youth sport programs and what became a lifelong love of sports grew as I became an interscholastic athlete, junior college runner, and intercollegiate runner. I developed a strong interest in sport sociology as an undergraduate student, and as a graduate student I conducted a quantitative study[4] that focused on surfers and their attitudes about the sport. As I considered topics for further research, I was specifically interested in the occupational issues in the careers of male professional athletes. I strongly resisted when it was suggested that I focus on the families of these men, even after it was explained to me that I could pioneer a new area of sociological study. Eventually, I began to see merit in the recommendation, and I committed to conducting a qualitative study that examined how women married to male professional athletes responded to the occupational stressor of geographic mobility. It became evident that this would not be an easy topic to research when I encountered numerous anticipated and unanticipated difficulties in finding participants. With perseverance, however, I was able to interview seven wives[5] of National Football League (NFL) players and one wife of a National Hockey League (NHL) player. This qualitative study,[6] which I now think of as a pilot study, was my empirical introduction to the heteronormative sport marriage.

From a conceptual point of view, women married to professional athletes are members of a social world that is essentially invisible to the public and intersects with the highly visible occupational worlds of players. By virtue of marriage, the players' wives are members of subworlds within the players' occupational worlds and within the larger social world of players' wives. As I was drawn into this private world of women, I was taken completely by surprise. With each successive interview, I learned that there was much more to the lives of these singular women than I had anticipated. Thankfully, once they agreed to participate in my research, they were eager to share the thoughts, emotions, and stories they had bottled up, sometimes for decades. I was flabbergasted by how little scholars know about them and the integral roles they play in their husbands' careers.

When selecting the direction of future research, I once again wrestled with the decision. As I contemplated immersing myself more deeply in this world of women, who insulate themselves and whose lives are fiercely protected by their husbands and their sport organizations, simply gaining a foothold seemed like a monumental task. By then, however, I believed that someone needed to tell the women's stories,[7] and I finally committed to being that someone. Part of my decision to move forward was the chance to combine my interest in the sociological fields of sport, family, gender, and emotion with symbolic interactionist theory. Despite numerous obstacles and challenges, I successfully conducted an extensive qualitative study[8] that examined numerous aspects of the sport marriage. The foundational knowledge for this book is based on that first major study, which I conducted between 1989 and 1993. My research on the sport marriage has strongly influenced my writing, teaching, and views of sociology and microsociology ever since.

Even though I was initiated into cross-gender fieldwork during the pilot study, I became concerned that my gender might work against me with female participants.[9] It became clear to me that the fieldwork process might best be served by adopting specific strategies for gaining the women's trust and developing rapport. For example, to distance myself from the hegemonic masculinity[10] the women were accustomed to, I purposefully managed a personal front[11]—through the use of language, physical appearance, and behavior—that I came to think of as *muted masculinity*, which luckily was more authentic to who I am as a person. I maintained, but didn't emphasize, my male identity in the fieldworker role. This was suitable to the wives and seemed to be consistent with their meanings of the "right" masculinity. In addition, my unfamiliarity with their gender-specific world seemed to be a factor in their opinion of me as an "acceptable incompetent."[12] Listening to and interacting with them provided ample opportunities for me to see men and masculinities in new ways. My knowledge and understanding of the women steadily increased and contributed to my awareness of their lived experience in ways that may not have been possible otherwise. Although they seemed to prefer what might be interpreted as a more feminine approach, I was still put in the hot seat and asked to answer for the actions of all men. Searching for solutions to their marital issues, more than one perplexed wife asked me, "You're a man, aren't you? Why does my husband do these things?" I had to somehow deal with their projections amicably and without being defensive. Perhaps they felt that I was safe to confide in because they didn't define me in the same way they defined the hegemonic men with whom they frequently came into contact in their husbands' occupational world. Their willingness to accept me as a trusted confidant also may have something to do with their perception of me as a male authority figure, which I was not initially aware of and certainly did not encourage. Subsequently, the women gradually accepted me into their exclusive world as a male insider. This became evident in several ways, for example when they seemed to view me as an expert on men, a man who was critical of male entitlement and a professional who was all-knowing, impartial, unbiased, and nonthreatening. My other experiences in the field constitute an enlightening story in their own right,[13] and interested readers can find details about it in appendix A.

After completing my long-term[14] fieldwork, I carefully explored my findings and continued to collect related information. Several of my conclusions were published in scholarly sources. After presenting one particular paper at a national conference, I was caught off guard when the media coordinators informed me that representatives of national and international media outlets were clamoring to interview me about my research. Since that time, reporters from regional, national, and international news organizations frequently contact me to request interviews, primarily when fast-breaking news stories involving male professional athletes are being reported, but also when journalists are writing feature stories about the sport marriage and various sport-related issues.[15] Soon the public became aware of my research, and numerous prospective, current, and former wives of male professional athletes contacted me with requests for copies of my scholarly publications. It became clear that the research touched on a topic of personal, national, and international interest. Many people, especially women, were eager to learn more about the realities of the sport marriage and were curious about whether my research could help them better understand their marriages and themselves. I received frequent requests to write a book that would answer their questions.

As time passed, many people also asked me what had become of the women who had participated in the first study. I, too, wondered about whether they were still married, what happened after their husbands retired, and how certain aspects of their lives had unfolded. My continued correspondence with players' wives, close observations of the social world of professional sports, anecdotal evidence, and discussions with other scholars led me to believe that the sport marriage has not really changed since I began my first study, but as a dedicated sociologist, I knew that a follow-up study was the only way to get a clear answer to the questions that emerged as I developed my previous work. Consequently, I decided to conduct a second study in 2015–16. That study consisted of follow-up phone interviews with several of the women who had participated in the first study and interviews with an entirely new group of women whose husbands or ex-husbands were more recently retired (see appendix B).[16] Among the new group of women, the husbands had retired from their careers four to seven years prior to the women's participation in the study, with the most recent retirement occurring in 2012. Finding new, willing participants was a more lengthy and difficult process than I had anticipated, and I believe that today's unprecedented transparency could explain many women's reluctance to participate. Today's omnipresent media exposes wives of professional athletes to considerably more intense scrutiny and invasions of privacy than the participants in the first study experienced. This became evident when many of the women who participated in the second study told me how glad they were that their husbands' careers had ended or were close to ending before the internet, sport media, and social media reduced privacy and heightened accessibility to players.[17] A few of the wives were married to men who transitioned from their MLB careers as players to MLB careers as coaches, so their perspective was invaluable in understanding the issues players' wives confront today and how it compares to the early 1990s. In the end, I was thankful to interview the seventeen women who were willing to participate in 2015–16. To my knowledge, this constitutes the first and only longitudinal[18] qualitative study on the sport marriage.

We have witnessed major societal changes since I conducted the first study. Most strikingly, the ongoing evolution in electronics, particularly communication technologies, dramatically impacts nearly every aspect of our lives today. It has helped to create a trend toward egalitarianism and away from patriarchal influences, and this is reflected in today's marital relationships. Cohabitation between unmarried heterosexual partners has become normalized, and lesbian, gay male, bisexual, transgender, intersex, and queer (LGBTIQ) distinctions are increasingly recognized. Same-sex marriage is now legal throughout the country. Millennials are delaying marriage or choosing a single lifestyle, and women are gaining leadership status at all levels of our society. These and other social trends are reflected in the world of sports, including the increased presence of women as athletes, coaches, and executives. Despite these trends, however, findings from the second study confirmed my educated belief that the fundamental nature of the heteronormative sport marriage has not changed as a marital institution, even when the husband is nationally or internationally celebrated.

Although labor and work-family changes have occurred over the years in most occupational worlds of professional sport, including the NFL Plan B free agency, the MLB paternity leave policy, and the NFL concussion protocol and player safety rules, the demands on players—and thus their wives and families—continue to shape the structure and overall nature of these marriages. If anything, the escalation of performance demands on players and increased transparency of today's society have resulted in more stress in the sport marriage, especially when the husband is a celebrity. Today's astronomical salaries have fueled performance expectations of sport organizations and fans in general.

Although the traditional heteronormative sport marriage has been the focus of my own research to date, numerous other types of sport marriages exist, such as those involving Olympic competitors, triathletes, boxers, surfers, skiers, marathoners, track and field athletes, auto-racing drivers, golf players, tennis players, soccer players, and rugby players. These marriages also may involve males married to female professional athletes, LGBTIQ partners, partners who are both pursuing a sport career, and so forth. For ease of reference, in this book the term sport marriage specifically denotes heteronormative marital relationships in the four major professional team sports, simply because these relationships have been the focus of my research to date. I eagerly anticipate future research that will expand our understanding of the nature of the sport marriage in general.

Until the group of women in the first, immersive study welcomed me into their homes, their hearts, and their lives, scholars and most members of the public knew little about the realities of the sport marriage. Readily available, substantive, well-researched knowledge was extremely limited. My research projects allowed me to absorb and examine the fundamentals of what the sport marriage is really like, and this book is an attempt to fill a long-neglected gap in our understanding of this marital institution and begin to correct some widely held misperceptions. In response to their heartfelt requests (see conclusion), I use the following chapters to lift the veil of silence for the fifty-four women[19] who shared their experiences, opinions, and insights with me. Because this detailed analysis is rooted in the women's narratives, it provides a rare opportunity to "listen in" as they explain to us in their own words what their marriages have been like. We learn how couples in the sport marriage construct their relationships and how the women try to fulfill their basic personal needs while coping with multiple stressors in the high-pressure, high-profile, media-infiltrated occupational worlds of professional sport. They tell us what they learned about how to make their marriages work, and how and why many of these marriages fail. In short, this book explores the lives of women who fulfill crucial roles in making it possible for married male professional athletes to succeed in their careers. As we shall see, this work also can help us understand the experiences of women in other types of marriages.

It's time to set the record straight. The voices of these women have been silent for far too long, and the realities of their lives deserve our attention. They have earned our respect and our gratitude for what they have done and continue to do to support their husbands in service to professional sport.

To protect the privacy and identities of the participants, their spouses, families, friends, and sport organizations, all names are pseudonyms. All identifiable information in direct quotes and references to individuals has been changed, but the essence of the women's stories has been preserved.

ACKNOWLEDGMENTS

FIRST AND FOREMOST, I offer my wholehearted appreciation to the women who participated in my studies and shared with me countless stories and insights about their lives as women who are married to male professional athletes. This book would not have been possible without their openness and willingness to talk about themselves and their marital experiences. They were the first to share the vision of setting the record straight about the realities of the sport marriage and to debunk prevailing stereotypes with the hope that other women might benefit from their hard-earned wisdom. I am also deeply thankful to the other individuals who participated in my fieldwork, generously contributing their time and their knowledge about the sport marriage.

Many in academia supported me throughout the various research and writing stages that culminated in publishing this book. Many thanks are due to Jonathan Brower, who was instrumental in guiding my early career toward the sport marriage as a relatively unexplored field of sociological research. I am particularly indebted to Arlie Russell Hochschild, who could not have been a better mentor while I was at the University of California at Berkeley. She had the gift of making the impossible seem possible. Arlie graciously offered her sociological insights and continually reminded me to "listen to the data" and "write it down and file it away for later." She helped me to think like a microsociologist, and I will forever be grateful for many years of unflagging encouragement and guidance. Her research on work-family issues and key contributions to the sociology of emotion have profoundly influenced ideas applied in this book. I express my sincere appreciation to Harry Edwards for his sociological guidance during my Berkeley years, especially his unique insight into the paradoxes of sport as a social institution. I also want to thank Lucia Torres-Simon, Elsa Tranter, Jean Margolis, and Kristi Larson Bedolla, all of whom made my time at Berkeley productive due to their continual support. I am grateful to Isaias Forbes for the excellent technical skills he applied on my behalf. Finally, my research and analysis would not have been completed without the financial support of the University of California at Berkeley and the American Sociological Association.

The faculty in the Sociology Program at Oregon State University have given me invaluable support and friendship over the years, and a few made special contributions to my career. My treasured friend and colleague Lori Cramer has been consummately generous with her wise counsel about my research, writing, and teaching. During uncountable hours of fruitful discussions, she offered valuable suggestions and steadfastly encouraged me when I felt overwhelmed or discouraged. Mark Edwards read drafts of my earlier work and provided extremely constructive feedback. Rebecca Warner shared perceptive ideas that helped me with my writing. Kathleen Stanley helped me navigate various obstacles in our profession. In addition, I extend my genuine thanks to Cindy Huddleston and Robin Fifita for their administrative support.

Completion of this book would not have been possible without Oregon State University's institutional support. The university allowed me to take a sabbatical leave and provided a Faculty Release-Time Award to conduct the longitudinal study for this book. I am also grateful to Jim Spolerich and Joe Defilippis for their brilliant technical assistance and expertise during the second study.

I reserve special and heartfelt thanks to Marie Oliver, who has been my editor for many years. My writing has greatly benefited from Marie's editing skills, inspiration, and patience. She has the knack of keeping me focused and has worked with me during the development of this book to make my scholarly findings more accessible to the general reader. As I have said to her too many times to count, I could not have done it without her.

I am exceedingly grateful to the University of Illinois Press and to Willis Regier, former director of the press, who recognized the potential in my book proposal. Many thanks to Jennifer Comeau and Drew Bryan for contributing their copyediting expertise to the final stages of the manuscript. It also has been a delight to work with Daniel Nasset, senior acquisitions editor at the press, who shared Willis's enthusiasm and shepherded the book to the finish line.

Finally, my deepest thanks go to my family. As a first-generation college student, my family's support meant everything to me. These most important people in my life have always cajoled and motivated me to finish whatever I started. Their moral support and financial assistance made this book possible. Words will always fail to adequately express my particular gratitude to my late mother, Rose Marie Ramos. Her unconditional love and unflinching support sustained me as I earned five college/university degrees and was tested in my career, which included a lengthy search for a tenure-track faculty position. I could always count on my late stepfather, Abraham Leos, for his sage advice and perceptions of life. Michael and Linda Ramos have supported me at all times. Mike is an inspiring role model whose invaluable intuition has been more than a nephew could hope for. My brothers Ruben Ortiz, Daniel Ortiz, and Victor Ortiz; my sister Victoria Ortiz; and my sister-in-law and second sister Mimi Ortiz have been there for me in more ways than I can say, giving me the strength I needed throughout my journey as a student and a professor.

THE SPORT MARRIAGE

INTRODUCTION

Lifting the Veil of Silence

DANA

One beautifully clear November morning, Dana got in her car to go grocery shopping at her favorite store. As she drove the familiar route in her neighborhood, she was hardly aware that she was driving faster and faster down a quiet side street. Making a sudden, almost unconscious decision, she pressed the gas pedal to the floorboard and steered her late model car directly toward a very large oak tree. At the last second, she swerved and just barely avoided the tree.

Dana was an outgoing, thoughtful woman in her early thirties who seemed to have everything going for her. Her husband Matt was an extremely successful Major League Baseball (MLB) player who had just finished one of his best seasons, and the couple lived comfortably in a fashionable neighborhood in a small, picturesque East Coast city. Outer appearances suggested that they had a reasonably fulfilling marriage.

Dana had worked hard to establish her own career before marrying Matt and continued to do so early in the marriage, but she soon learned that the all-consuming nature of Matt's MLB career made it difficult for her to juggle the responsibilities she had accepted. She eventually decided to postpone her personal ambitions and career aspirations and give herself wholeheartedly to supporting Matt and becoming a "good player's wife." Despite her own considerable efforts, however, she believed that she wasn't fulfilling her own and others' expectations.

Dana never talked to anyone except Matt about how close she came to crashing into that tree until she shared it with me many years later. "You feel abandoned," she told me, explaining how overwhelmed and neglected she felt in that moment, and how she could see no way out. "I was angry. I was furious. You could not have put one more drop of water in that boiling pan. I mean, I was just ready to boil over and that's what I did. And it was like, 'Who's there for me? I'm there for everybody else.'"

Dana's story poignantly illustrates a sad reality faced by many women who feel trapped, neglected, and personally unfulfilled as they attempt to give all they possibly can to make a sport marriage work. We will learn more about Dana and many women like her throughout the chapters of this book as we examine in detail what the stakes are for women who decide to marry a professional athlete.

A Career-Dominated Marriage

As mentioned in the preface, many contemporary heterosexual marriages are trending toward egalitarianism and away from traditional relationships that are steeped in a patriarchal ideology. It is increasingly expected that women will have their own careers regardless of their marital status, and in a growing number of two-paycheck marriages the husband rather than the wife is the trailing spouse.[1] Despite these cultural changes, the sport marriage continues to resemble the traditional 1950s marriage Betty Friedan brought to light more than fifty years ago in her groundbreaking bestseller *The Feminine Mystique*. At that time, the institution of marriage referred to a committed relationship between a man and a woman, and female domesticity and male dominance were not only expected but strongly reinforced through societal pressure.

In the years since Friedan's landmark book was published, scholars have consistently noted that women take on roles in the family that make men's careers possible and that a husband's occupation can structure a woman's life and involve her contributions to it.[2] Several concepts appear in studies seeking to identify how women support or become directly or indirectly involved in their husbands' careers, including "wife of" identity, vicarious role, husband-oriented wife, incorporated wife, career wife, two-person career, and spousal career support.[3] As my research progressed, I realized that the single most defining characteristic of a heterosexual sport marriage is the absolute prioritization of the husband's career success, and so I came to conceptualize it as a *career-dominated marriage*. This concept fuses and builds upon these other ideas and offers a useful work-family framework that allows us to comprehensively apply them. In a career-dominated marriage, a husband and his career are prioritized, and his wife and family are subordinate to both, whether or not the wife has an occupation or career of her own. In certain cases, such an arrangement may result in the husband's neglect of his marriage and family as he builds and focuses only on his career. This type of marriage remains embedded in numerous male-dominated occupational worlds besides professional sport.[4] Large segments of our society, including the partners involved, take such marriages for granted. In male-dominated occupational worlds, most women are relegated to subordinate status, whether they are wives, unmarried female partners, coworkers, or members of the public. Although the sport marriage brings distinct challenges to women, it also shares similarities with many other career-dominated marriages. For this reason, my findings led me to think of it as the prototypical and possibly the most extreme version of the career-dominated marriage, embedded as it is in occupational worlds that normalize and glorify hegemonic masculinity, institutionalize female subordination and male infidelity, and assume that women will provide the necessary domestic and career support to their husbands in pursuit of the men's goals. These and other influences converge to create complex emotional issues for women in the sport marriage, and these will be discussed at length in the following chapters.

To strive for marital manageability and family stability, a professional athlete's wife may hope for a work-family balance, but she might realize early on that she must learn to accommodate considerable work spillover,[5] much of which is negative or astonishingly demanding. If these women want their marriages to succeed—and all the women I talked to did—they knowingly accept a subordinate role and try to adapt to the multitudinous demands and pressures of their husbands' careers. The women I interviewed were committed to doing their best to make their stress-filled and career-driven marriages work, and they understood that it would involve some level of self-sacrifice. They chose to create a valuable and consequential team with their husbands by working on their marriages while their husbands worked on their careers. A wife's willing contributions and personal sacrifices help him to succeed and, for this reason, I think of these women as *marriage workers*.

Like the wives of military personnel, ambassadors, transnational professionals, and corporate executives, these women lead lives characterized by geographic mobility and instability as they deal with anticipated and unanticipated moves across the country or the world because of trades, cuts, free agency, and other job-initiated changes. They are expected to be trailing spouses when their husbands relocate to other countries to resume or resurrect their careers. More than one woman told me about receiving a call from her husband saying that he was unexpectedly traded and was on his way to a new team, or that she learned about the trade from what she saw or heard on the news. Relocation events can become emotional crises for the wives, especially if a false sense of security had previously permeated their lives. Players' wives also must deal with their husbands' routine and extended absences from home because of job-related activities and travel. After these separations, families must make adjustments in their seasonal lives as the husband/father transitions back into family life, and all aspects of the relationship can be affected. If the marriage lasts until the husband retires from the game, any lack of useful relational skills in discussing and resolving the marital issues inherent in the seasonal cycles can make the retirement transition and the initial postretirement years quite challenging.

Like the wives of politicians and entertainers who are in the public eye, these women must cope with star-struck fans, persistent groupies, annoying privacy invasions, unwanted media scrutiny, and other consequences of their husbands' status as celebrities. Like the wives of politicians, ambassadors, clergymen, and entertainers, a player's wife takes the role of diplomat in public life. Without exception, the wives in both studies constructed some version of a "wife of" identity, meaning that they publicly displayed their support for their husbands and their husbands' careers. They are fully aware of the responsibility they have in representing their husbands in a positive light and avoiding any negative images, so they diligently monitor their public behavior and use of social media. Like the wives of police officers, clergymen, and politicians, they may be expected to follow the moral codes implied in the public's image of professional athletes as positive role models.

Like the wives of physicians, academics, and military personnel, these women's wholehearted support for their husbands exposes them to considerable occupational and organizational influence on their personal lives, including becoming part of a status hierarchy. For instance, throughout his career, a player occupies a position in a status hierarchy defined by his team and his occupational world. Rookies have less status than veterans, and high-scoring or star players outrank less accomplished players. Mirroring her husband's status, a wife is ranked in a hierarchy of players' wives based on interpretations of seniority and imposed by and reflected in the husband's organizational status. It is clear that her status directly reflects her husband's achievements, successes, failures, and abilities, which can have significant implications for the woman's own identity. She may not initially claim her own identity or be publicly recognized as an individual apart from her husband's identity as a professional athlete.

Like the wives of police officers, firefighters, and military personnel, these women must deal with the threat or reality of their husbands' job-related injuries, including life-threatening or career-ending injuries that cumulatively can have long-term consequences. Unfortunately, when a husband/father suffers, his wife and family suffer too. Occupational injuries go beyond the physical and can gravely affect these men's emotional and mental health as they and their wives deal with unexpected or unaccustomed physical or mental limitations, physical disabilities, and lifelong pain. NFL players are particularly susceptible to debilitating health issues. They are at risk for brain disorders and progressive neurodegenerative diseases, such as amyotrophic lateral sclerosis, chronic traumatic encephalopathy (CTE), Parkinson's disease, and Alzheimer's disease and other types of dementia. These neurodegenerative diseases can result from recurrent traumatic brain injuries (TBIs) (i.e., concussions). Second impact syndrome (postconcussive symptoms after two consecutive head injuries) and successive TBIs can have long-term consequences.[6] Although the wives seemed to grudgingly accept the inevitability of the various injuries their husbands sustain during their careers, it was only after the husband's retirement that they became painfully aware of the long-term implications. Several wives told me during the second study that they hadn't known about the long-term consequences of TBIs. It wasn't until the beginning of the 2013 NFL season that the league officially acknowledged these health issues, after a lawsuit initiated by more than 4,500 former NFL players was settled.[7] The settlement tentatively approved a $765 million NFL payout that enabled more than 18,000 retired NFL players who were suffering from the long-term effects of TBIs to become eligible for medical benefits. The NFL wives I interviewed in the second study were aware of the settlement and the new NFL concussion protocol, but they had not yet received any financial support and were not aware of any families who had. They were happy that current and future generations of NFL players and their families will benefit from the new NFL rules, but they insist that they should have been established and implemented much sooner.

Postcareer non-TBI-related depression, suicides, and parasuicides related to CTE are far too common among professional athletes.[8] The routine use of painkillers and recreational and performance-enhancing drugs also can become a serious and potentially life-threatening health issue. This was the case in Lisa's marriage. Shortly after her husband Raymond retired from his NFL career, she noticed that his behavior had become increasingly erratic and his personality was changing in ways that made her uncomfortable. She later discovered that he had developed a dependency on painkillers during his career that carried over into the early stages of his retirement. As Lisa learned more about the extent of Raymond's opioid addiction, she became deeply concerned about his health and alarmed that his deteriorating condition may be harmful to her and their family. She strongly encouraged him to seek help and supported him in his eventual recovery.

Like women in most other career-dominated marriages, a player's wife becomes, by necessity, the primary parent. The nature of a career in professional sport makes it difficult for these men to be the kind of husbands and fathers they might wish they could be, and a player depends on his wife to provide the caregiving labor required to raise the children. It's common for the fathers and their families to live virtually separate lives during the season. The wife uses *gender work*[9] to adopt traditional notions of gender and perform whatever role is necessary to attempt to maintain marital and family stability. In so doing, she enables her husband to enact a prolific occupational/public role without losing face[10] by surrendering his identity or public image as a "family man," even though he may be only marginally engaged in family life. She makes the family as stress-free as possible for him and, as a result, his career becomes "family-free." As the marriage progresses, the woman learns that she must develop and apply abundant organizational, relational, parental, and coping skills as she performs her domestic/marital responsibilities while also providing meaningful occupational support both at home and in the workplace. Her marriage, then, is really a commitment to partnership in a two-person career and the challenges and sacrifices it required. In both studies, whether or not a woman was employed outside the home during the husband's career, they had some level of engagement in his career. Some were more deeply invested than others, but a wife's employment or unemployment didn't seem to be a deciding factor in her decision to participate. Her husband relied on her to perform this gender work, and she normalized it as a result of her marital, parental, and emotional experiences.

As in Dana's case, it is common for women in the sport marriage to decide before they are married or early in their marriages to set aside any occupational or career plans they may have while their husbands are actively pursuing a career in professional sports. Most of the women believed it would eventually be their turn to follow their own dreams and aspirations. Twenty-seven of the women who participated in the first study were college graduates, and five had earned postgraduate degrees. Among the majority of women who were employed outside the home during the husband's career, their means of employment was relatively unstable, primarily because of the all-consuming nature of their husbands' careers and the women's commitment to marital and family functioning. Adding their own employment on top of their domestic responsibilities and the husband's occupational demands and stressors was just too much for many to contemplate. Some women did finally enter the labor force or start a business, but only after the husband retired. In other cases, however, by the time the husband retired, the roles and patterns that were established during his career were so ingrained that they were either no longer interested in establishing their own careers or their finances didn't require them to seek employment. If a wife is employed outside the home, domestic life can be intensely challenging for couples, because a player's ability to meaningfully share household responsibilities is limited by the demands of his career or his lack of interest, and this can create friction in the relationship. MLB marriages are exceptionally difficult because of seasonal relocations and the players' grueling schedules.

The public is aware of the enormous salaries most players are paid, and they may incorrectly assume that all players' wives have the resources to employ a nanny or other domestic helpers. The couple may not be able to afford such support early in her husband's career or if he struggles with establishing a career. Even if she can afford it, she may be aware that his career will be time limited and changeable, and as the family's financial planner she may keep this in mind as she tries to supervise expenses. She also may be reluctant to admit that she can't "do it all," or she may feel worried about allowing a stranger into her home. She or her husband may believe that domestic helpers will be a disruptive rather than a positive influence on the family, and a potential privacy issue.

In addition to the list of issues players' wives share with other women in career-dominated marriages, they encounter other emotionally challenging situations that I suspect are exclusive to the sport marriage. A player's single-minded focus on his career is expected in his occupational world and is considered essential to his ability to successfully establish and maintain himself professionally, so it's not surprising that these high-performing men adopt a workaholic approach to their careers.[11] For some, this approach borders on obsession. Salary increases, physical durability, and athletic skill level are the primary measures of a player's success, and his pursuit of winning requires his wholehearted commitment to his team and the "right" work ethic. He has little, if any, control over his unpredictable and demanding career. Sport organizations tend to view most players as being only as good as their last game, and despite the level of his athletic talent, fame, and marketability, a player knows that he is expendable, even disposable. He is susceptible to injuries and can be traded, cut from the team, or benched at any moment. For example, training camp can be a major occupational stressor for NFL players and their wives, and fear of an injury tops the list as a common camp stressor. If a veteran player has a history of injuries, has not fully recovered from a serious injury, or is older or has contract issues, he is more likely to be replaced by a highly motivated rookie player. This nerve-racking ordeal is described as "sitting on the bubble," knowing that it's always ready to burst. A wife constantly worries about this situation, dreads the phone calls after practice to let her know how bad things are, or copes with this persistent stress by escaping: frequenting a preferred bar, digging deeper into her job, shopping almost anywhere, rearranging her house, or traveling to visit family or friends. Even when escaping, she realizes that she is never truly free to enjoy anything or to be completely distracted until she knows her husband's fate. Even if a husband enjoys some amount of stability in his career, all players know that they must retire from the game at a relatively young age and transition into one or more new careers, and this situation can provoke a host of personal, marital, and family issues. It's worth noting that after some of the husbands retired, they transitioned into other male-dominated occupations, such as firefighting, law enforcement, and coaching, which preserved and extended their career-dominated marriages.

As previously mentioned, most of the women in the studies didn't anticipate before they married the extent to which their husbands' careers would affect their lives. Even if a player's wife was an athlete herself, or was part of his life when he participated in high school or university/college sports or played in the minor leagues, she wasn't necessarily aware of what was required of her as he built his professional sport career. She developed this understanding over time, discovering as the marriage evolved that a career in professional sport has an enormous impact on marital and family life. Much of what occurs in the public and personal lives of these men is brought home to their wives and families and can negatively affect their primary relationships. Wives and children may not always be happy when their husbands or fathers are glorified as legends, celebrities, or role models. When a player is the recipient of public adulation and the focus of media attention, his wife and family often share part of the spotlight. In their attempts to maintain some sense of normalcy, they can become socially isolated as a result of the husband/father's fame.

For these and many other reasons, I suggest that a player's wife is devoted to and greatly influenced by two greedy institutions:[12] her husband's occupation and her marriage. She learns through her marital, emotional, and personal experiences to work on her marriage by developing and relying on numerous self-management strategies. These strategies may be entirely internal, but they usually also involve interactions with others. Self-management includes two major interrelated processes: "management" and "work." "Management" describes the general strategy of constructing, establishing, and enforcing appropriate interaction and behavior with others in various situations. Management is put into practice through some type of "work," which involves the specific methods that are defined as necessary in the use of selected strategies. In this context, "work" is the actual, visible, and practical ways they manage their appearance, interactions, behaviors, and emotions. Unless otherwise noted, each type of work is a conceptualization based solely on my analysis of the findings. A woman's self-definition and her expectations of herself affect the type of work she chooses to use, and her self-management empowers her to cope with stressors so she can fulfill the specific roles, demands, and expectations of her husband, his sport organization, the public, and the media. As the stories unfold, we will discover the many forms of self-management she uses, including those previously identified by other scholars. These ideas provide us with insight into the reality-constructing behaviors the wives deem necessary to achieve or avoid certain outcomes in their marital relationships and their lived experience as wives of professional athletes.

Although male professional athletes captivate fans and the public and it may seem like we know a lot about them, today's media consistently misleads its audiences about their private lives, their families, and the women who marry them. Even if a player isn't rich and famous, the public tends to hold a one-dimensional view of what his personal life and his family's life must be like. As a society, we tend to judge a book by its cover, and this is often the case with perceptions of the women who support these publicly visible men. Mass media is replete with idealized or unflattering images of the wives and unmarried female domestic partners (commonly called WAGs, "wives and girlfriends") of male professional athletes. These women are—for the most part inaccurately—depicted as "Stepford wives," "gold diggers," "eye candy," "fashionistas," and worse. Television, notably reality television, has probably contributed the most to the abundance of prevailing misinformation by providing anecdotal information as factual, reinforcing caricatures, and endorsing distortions of the sport marriage and the players' wives and ex-wives. It may even set the stage for a backlash against these women. Decades of close observation and discussions with these women make it clear that it's time to debunk these prevailing myths.

As part of fourth-wave feminism,[13] the Me Too movement has raised awareness to a new level regarding the prevailing patriarchal ideology that has traditionally devalued women, stifled their voices, and normalized all forms of sexism and oppression. My findings on the sport marriage are wholly pertinent to this sensitizing movement and to feminist ideologies in general. The wives taught me what it means to be a woman in an exceptionally patriarchal and demanding occupational world, where female behavior is stringently managed through formal and informal rules and codes, and where opportunities for self-fulfillment and social support are minimally available. The women's stories revealed to me the complexities inherent in their life choices and the decisions they make in their everyday lives. They explained how they unintentionally became trapped in a marital institution that led them to accept, normalize, and play a role in their own subordination while making significant—usually unacknowledged—contributions to their husbands' careers. Their unflinching narratives revealed how the choices these resilient, courageous, capable women made seriously hampered their ability to become self-empowered over the course of a lifetime, primarily because of how they interpreted their marital and family commitments and the roles they were expected to perform. As a quintessential representation of the career-dominated model, the heteronormative sport marriage offers a wide lens through which we can view the many ways career-dominated marriages can collectively subordinate, dominate, and exploit women while the women provide foundational and integral contributions that prop up the social and economic backbone of American society. We learn through close study of these wives' lived experience how the career-dominated marriage can affect women when they perform and normalize the expected roles within it.

My understanding of the complexity of the sport marriage and these women's lived experience truly began with my first interview in the first study. Haley, an outgoing woman in her mid-thirties, was married to an MLB veteran. When she accepted my invitation to participate in the study and consented to an interview, she explained that because the season was over, she was in the middle of preparing to move her household back to the family's permanent residence. When I arrived at her modest, tract house in a typical suburb, I noticed that several partially filled cardboard boxes were scattered around an otherwise tidy living room. All the same, she was eager to make time for an interview. I'm glad she did, because I gained two important insights that day that were consistently confirmed as my fieldwork progressed. At the end of our interview, I posed this question: "If a woman who was considering marriage to a professional athlete asked you for advice, what would you say to her?" Haley paused for a long, thoughtful moment. Speaking slowly and softly, she told me that it takes a strong woman to make a marriage to a professional athlete work. She said that if a wife doesn't remain flexible (or "go with the flow," as she put it) and isn't able to cope with the demands, pressures, and stressors that come with her husband's career, the marriage will fail. A substantial number of the other wives I interviewed echoed this belief.

The second insight occurred when I realized that Haley had normalized certain things in her marriage that most people might consider unusual. She told me that players' wives learn about and are expected to follow a certain set of attitudinal, behavioral, and interactional guidelines that emphasize conformity. Marsha, another wife of an MLB player, later called this the "unwritten rulebook." By establishing boundaries around a wife's behavior and identifying the roles she's expected to perform, numerous unwritten rules encourage her to be a "good wife" in private life (specifically as it relates to her husband's career) and a "good player's wife" in public life. The following pages will help us learn more about this unwritten rulebook and how the wives internalize and normalize the do's and don'ts of marriage to professional athletes.

As I left Haley's home that day, I gave more thought to her two revelations and wondered if she might be exaggerating. As my research in that first study progressed, I realized that she absolutely was not. In fact, I soon discovered how deeply influenced these women are by the ever-present unwritten rulebook in their husbands' occupational world. We will learn much about the nature of the sport marriage through their interpretation of these rules, which involve the expectations these women have of themselves and the expectations others have of them. The rules revolve around three significant issues in the sport marriage: coping with stressors, providing multiple levels of support, and maintaining a physically attractive appearance. These issues will be examined in the following chapters.

The unwritten rulebook exposes the direct and indirect power of husbands, their sport organizations, and their occupational worlds. The players, the husbands' employer(s), and older, experienced wives on the team implicitly and explicitly impose the rules through verbally or nonverbally communicated sanctions or corrections for rule infractions. A player's wife typically will attempt to comply with as many of the rules as possible because she wants to avoid damaging her husband's career, values her marriage and family, believes she has a stake in building her husband's career, and loves her husband. A rookie wife normally will make the effort to comply with the rules early in her marriage and her husband's career. If she's dissatisfied with her marriage or less interested in her husband's career, however, she may be reluctant to comply with them or even completely disregard them. A veteran wife also may, for various reasons, be less inclined to follow the rules; as she gets older, she may feel more secure about her husband's lengthy career and develop a "rules don't apply to me" attitude. Therefore, rather than reflecting the occupational consequences of following or not following the rules, the extent to which a wife follows the rulebook is a testament to the value she places on her marriage and her ability to make it work. Her compliance signifies how much her marriage means to her, how much she loves her husband, or how much she feels validated by her compliance.

Wives typically communicate this rulebook by word of mouth in the form of subtle suggestions or obvious advice, or by sharing their own experiences. Newcomers to the occupational worlds of professional sport may or may not take their wisdom to heart, but most of the women I interviewed had eventually normalized these rules. They may have occasionally questioned or challenged them, yet most tried to adhere to them regardless of whether they agreed with them or liked them. Husbands, sport organizations, and fans assume that wives will learn to follow the rules, which can be slightly different depending on the individual husband's standing on the team, the expectations of his sport organization, or other factors.

Other sources of stress for these women can include conflicts in managing multiple roles (marital, family, public), her husband's public visibility and possible celebrity, the distinct possibility that her husband will be unfaithful, and various power struggles with her husband and an overinvolved, controlling mother-in-law.

The following chapters examine the inherent complexities of the sport marriage and the nearly insurmountable challenges confronted by the women who were able to share their stories with me during my time in their world. Throughout the book, I explore how these women make difficult decisions and excel in performing the roles demanded of them as a result of their choice of life partner, and what it cost them.

Overview of the Book

The book is organized into seven thematic chapters and a concluding chapter. Each chapter begins with a vignette, a woman's story that is particularly relevant to the analysis in that chapter. Chapter 1 examines some of the major personal and occupational realities that strongly influence the sport marriage in general and the wives' lived experience in particular. It applies key concepts that emerged from my research, which are identified as the *spoiled athlete syndrome, motherization, boundary work,* the *virgin-prostitute syndrome, organizational dominance,* an *institutionalized brotherhood,* and a *culture of infidelity*. It discusses the wife's internalization of a *"we" partnership* and the couple's construction of *marital teamwork*, an arrangement that usually benefits the husbands rather than the wives. It describes a hierarchy of players' wives that mirrors the husbands' team and occupational status and focuses on an institutional brotherhood of teammates that strongly influences the husbands' interpretations of masculinity, normalizes male dominance, and sanctions the husbands' extramarital activities. The first chapter concludes with an examination of the implicit marital bargain between couples in most sport marriages.

Chapter 2 explores how these women confront the challenges of public life in their attempts to avoid damaging their husbands' public image and their husbands' employers' public image. It applies the concept of *image work* to examine how they try to manage their physical appearance and conduct, and how the concepts of *game etiquette* and *quasi-celebrityhood* help us to understand how they use the unwritten rules to perform public roles. It discusses the responsibilities of being married to public figures or celebrities and describes how the women learn diplomacy, how they come to terms with and negotiate a secondhand identity, how they interact with enthusiastic fans seeking autographs or other personal contact with their husbands, and how they otherwise struggle to establish and maintain personal and public boundaries while their husbands are involved in a highly visible career.

Chapter 3 focuses on the lived experience of the wives who travel with their husbands during the MLB season. It identifies an unspoken code of conduct that dictates how the wives are expected to behave and establishes their subordinate status by ensuring their social invisibility. It describes how the players, sport organizations, and the wives themselves use *code work* to construct, apply, and reinforce the code, and how couples who question the code—called code busters—can reap negative consequences even when the husband enjoys high-level team status. It discusses the importance of code enforcement as a means of maintaining the husbands' standing among teammates, establishing the expectation that teammates will cover up each other's sexual activities, including the extramarital relationships of married players. Finally, it explores how traveling wives, who are also expected to keep the men's secrets, become aware of an implicit competition for their husbands' loyalty.

Chapter 4 provides insight into the use of power and control in the sport marriage. It introduces the idea of *control work* and uses this idea to discuss the differences in the partners' motivations for and styles of using it. It explores how the husbands rely on aspects of their occupational lives to try to control their domestic lives, and how the wives rely on aspects of their domestic lives in their attempts to have control in their marriage and family, cope with what they can't control about their husbands' careers, respond to their husbands' efforts to control them, or gain a sense of personal empowerment. It examines how the sexual subordination of wives is achieved through the husbands' control work and how the husbands' control tactics ensure that the wives perform their "wifely duty." It discusses the women's use of manipulation and other control tactics, and the *domestic control* they rely on to cope with marital or occupational stressors. It describes how the wives' upbringing influences their orientation toward power and control, and the potential costs for wives who rely on control work.

Chapter 5 examines power and control issues that emerge in the marriage as the result of the relationship between the wives and their mothers-in-law, and how the husband, wife, and mother-in-law use control work in various types of power struggles. In an attempt to move beyond negative stereotypes, it offers a more realistic interpretation of the origins and construction of in-law relationships in the sport marriage, including the origins of a durable mother-son bond and its effect on the marital relationship. It introduces the idea of *subordination work*, which allows for an insightful evaluation of how the wives manage their subordinate status as they try to preserve their marital relationships and avoid offending their mothers-in-law. It also calls attention to a distinctive role reversal initiated by some mothers-in-law, which can be the outcome of a particularly strong mother-son bond.

Chapter 6 offers greater awareness about a previously undocumented, complex world of groupies that inhabit the occupational worlds of professional sport. Based on the wives' explicit and richly textured narratives detailing their perceptions of and experiences with individuals they define as groupies, it provides a typology of groupies and introduces the idea of *groupieism*. The typology identifies an unexpected and eclectic range of both visible and invisible groupies, many of which contradict prevailing stereotypes. It explores how the wives use boundary work in public interactions with various groupies and examines why the pervasive presence of female groupies is deeply troubling for the wives, how they cope with these women, and how the existence of this world of groupies can negatively impact the marital relationship and the wives' emotional lives.

Chapter 7 takes a closer look at the culture of infidelity that pervades the occupational worlds of professional sport, examines how it is constructed and reinforced, and discusses how it affects the wives. It explores why wives share a universal fear that their husbands will be unfaithful and how they are affected by the possibility or actuality that their husbands will engage in sexual or emotional relationships with other women. It identifies three patterns of infidelity in the context of the sport marriage: the one-time encounter, the short-term affair, and the long-term affair. It explores how the culture increases the opportunities for husbands to be unfaithful and introduces the idea of *suspicion work* to examine how the wives try to manage the fear that their husbands may succumb to temptation. It describes re-entry routines and communication methods some couples use when husbands return from travel and the boundaries of fidelity and forgiveness wives establish as they attempt to cope with the realities of their husbands' lives on the road.

The concluding chapter wraps up by making some final observations about the longitudinal research itself and its short- and long-term effects on the women involved. It identifies the few areas of the sport marriage that have seen improvement in the past few decades, discusses the conscious decisions the women make to continue normalizing the career-dominated marriage, and reports on how the marriages fared over time. It describes the women's experience of personal empowerment as a result of their participation in the research and passes along some of the advice and suggested keys to a successful sport marriage that the wives in both studies offered, based on their lived experience. This overview essentially describes how and why the wife of a male professional athlete must adapt to realities if she wants her marriage to survive her husband's career and retirement.

The appendices provide a discussion of some of my fieldwork experiences and the ethnographic methods used in collecting data for both studies, and a list of the participants and their husbands.

You're the mother. You're the father. You're everything. You're the handyperson. You're the controller. You're the secretary. You're the receptionist. You're the agent's assistant. Another thing, too, people don't understand that the wives do so much behind the scenes, and they think it's so glamorous. It's not glamorous at all. The only glamorous part is dressing up and going to the games, and out to dinner. It's definitely not a reality program. You don't have a makeup artist. You don't have all that. You're home alone with your kid and you're multitasking. All I can say is that you're just working your ass off with just being a supportive wife. . . . A wife should always think of herself as being a support system. . . . And you're not really paid. He's the employee. He's being paid, but you're being paid in other benefits if your husband has a very lucrative, exciting career. Very challenging. Very stressful. Very unstable. I don't think fans understand how unstable it is.

—ALAINA

CHAPTER 1

Influences on the Sport Marriage

RHONDA

They had just won the World Series! Rhonda stared in disbelief as Brent's teammates ran out of the dugout and rushed to the pitcher's mound, hugging, laughing, jumping, and piling on each other in wild happiness. It had been a dramatic event filled with heroes, records, and incredible plays, everything a baseball fan could ever hope for or dream about. Bathed in bright lights on a balmy October night, Rhonda was glued to her seat as she tried to make sense out of what just happened. Despite her excitement, she couldn't help but think about all she had been through during the eleven years of "living for his career." She knew she had been instrumental to Brent's success on this historic night.

In the next hours, days, and weeks, mainstream and sport media directed their attention to Brent and some of his teammates. Although she had anticipated this reaction, it was more overwhelming than she could have imagined. Brent was inundated with requests for coast-to-coast interviews and appearances, including various television talk shows. She was surprised when, unlike his teammates, Brent declined all media requests.

His refusal to engage with the media didn't really bother Rhonda; she could live without the television appearances and media hype. She knew that Brent was more comfortable playing baseball and less comfortable being in a spotlight of this magnitude. But she also thought he was being selfish. Amid the turmoil and excitement, his team and their families were invited to the White House to meet the president, a traditional practice in certain occupational worlds of professional sport. Without consulting her, Brent declined the invitation, later explaining to her that he "wasn't into that kind of thing." The possibility of meeting the president meant more to Rhonda than she could say, and she was furious. "To him, it was no big deal," she said. "But to me, it was a great privilege. But he didn't look any further than his view of it, and he wasn't willing to make the sacrifice for me." In her mind, she was more than willing to support and sacrifice for him and had done so for years, but he was unwilling to do the same for her. "He took away an opportunity of a lifetime, and believe me he was made aware of the fact he took that chance away from me."

After initially expressing her anger to Brent, Rhonda continued to suppress her feelings.[1] She built a wall of silence around the incident over a period of a few weeks. She interpreted the incident as proof of Brent's complete disregard for her, proof that he didn't care for her as much as she had believed he did. Her resentment occasionally flared up whenever the White House was mentioned, but she gradually came to terms with it. "It was not only because I didn't get to go to the White House, but because it exposed something there that brought it all out into the open," she said. "It told me he wasn't willing to sacrifice a day in his busy schedule to accommodate something that I really, really wanted to do. I wasn't even considered when the decision was made. It was that 'he' was tired and 'he' didn't feel like going, so 'we' weren't going. I get really, really angry and resentful. But I can't change him. That's the toughest part of being married to this person. There are so many things about him that just drive me crazy, and I try. I try, but you can't change him. You just have to learn to live with it."

Rhonda learned what other wives of professional athletes usually learn at some point: no matter how much her husband depends on her, no matter how much he loves her, and no matter how much her marriage work contributes to his career success, the final score always puts her in third place behind her husband and his career. In this chapter, we will explore in detail some of the defining fundamental and influential characteristics of the modern sport marriage that drive or contribute to this outcome. I identify factors that distinguish the sport marriage from other career-dominated marriages and discuss several personal and occupational influences on these couple's lives. Influences include the family patterns that shape male athletes from an early age, the complex occupational terrain they navigate, and the explicit or implicit agreements between the partners that affect how they construct their relationship.

Personal Influences

The women in the first study consistently identified and discussed three characteristic patterns in attitude and behavior on the part of their husbands. Not all professional athletes express these patterns, but a majority of the wives in the first study reported them to some degree, and many in the second group confirmed aspects of the original findings. These patterns, which we might think of as personal influences, greatly affected their marriages. I identify them here as the spoiled athlete syndrome,[2] motherization, and the virgin-prostitute syndrome.[3]

SPOILED ATHLETE SYNDROME

Sharing a booth in a crowded pizza restaurant on a breezy spring afternoon during my fieldwork for the first study, Samantha and I were discussing our views about the egotistical behavior of certain professional athletes that is frequently reported through all forms of media. She casually used the term "spoiled athlete syndrome" as a way of describing these men, and I immediately realized how well this term captured the types of behaviors we were discussing and that I had observed, behaviors that couples in sport marriages seem to take for granted. Neither study specifically focused on the husbands,

> They're as much a victim of it as you are, because they've been the spoiled, pampered athlete. I mean, it's ingrained in them, and then we feed into it some more, and so you just don't break the cycle.
> —ARISA

but much can be gleaned from listening to the women who presumably know them better than anyone else. Samantha was certainly not alone in her assessment of the kinds of personality traits expressed by many professional athletes.

The spoiled athlete syndrome describes what we might think of as an eternal boyhood, and it is one of the most significant personal influences on the sport marriage. Many professional athletes begin to adopt the syndrome when participating in organized youth sport programs. Athletically gifted players are singled out, catered to, continually praised, and even glorified. Pampering by coaches, male peers, female partners, cheerleaders, fellow students, family members, and community members is meant to encourage a young male athlete's effort, but it also can cause him to develop the expectation that he's entitled to this special treatment. As a gendered characteristic of the syndrome, a young athlete's early interpretations of certain qualities involve his understanding of hegemonic masculinity, and this is expressed through his early gender work. His understanding of power and control also is shaped by sport participation and interactions with teammates and opponents. Seeking respect from others—most importantly, his teammates—he begins to value aspects of hegemonic masculinity, and this gradually becomes evident when he uses intimidation, aggression, and violence on the field or off the field. He works to manage the right masculinity by becoming a tough player and to convey the impression[4] that he is an exceptionally talented athlete and, therefore, deserving of special treatment.

Even in sport-oriented families with the best of intentions, various forms of adult domination[5] can become problematic. Parental "overinvolvement" can include criticism, interference, unrealistic hopes, verbal abuse, a strong emphasis on winning, and arguments with the umpire, the coach, and the spouse.[6] Whether or not they are coaches, controlling fathers may be the most familiar figures in this role. According to the wives in the first study, however, the mother rather than the father was a stronger presence and influence in her son's athletic life, and this resulted in a durable mother-son bond. As an extension of her idea of motherhood and parenting, the overinvolved mother encourages and at times pushes her son to participate in organized youth sport programs, supports his involvement, dotes on him, pampers him, and vicariously lives through and feels validated by his athletic achievements.[7] As her son grows up, she becomes excessively concerned about him, and she may believe that nothing is too good for him. She's a fixture on the sidelines or cheering for him in the stands during his games. She nurses his injuries, prepares his favorite or required meals, disciplines him for missing practice, provides emotional support when he doubts his athletic skills, intervenes on his behalf, and attends or participates in team functions. Rhonda spoke for many of the wives when she described her husband's mother's part in this pattern and how it continued in his MLB career: "Brent's mom had four boys, and she catered to them on hand and foot, and then he got into baseball. Even in his college sports, he always had this real awesome job to pay his way through college. Every step of the way it's been that way. My biggest and most common complaint about the system is that these guys are babied, spoiled, and pampered—totally. In my mind, they lose a sense of reality. They have no responsibilities and, for the most part, they have no cares."

Intentionally or not, an overinvolved mother becomes an enabler and plays a pivotal role in how her son normalizes the spoiled athlete syndrome. Her pampering, and possibly the pampering of an entire overinvolved community,[8] may lead the young athlete to become narcissistic at some level. He learns to control others by influencing, pressuring, or manipulating them to accept his wishes or views, or to acquiesce in some specific way. At its most extreme, by the time he becomes a professional athlete, he carries a deep sense of male entitlement, a strong perception of occupational power, a lack of accountability for inappropriate off-the-field activities, and a diminished sense of responsibility for marital and family functioning. He has developed what can be fairly described as a "God complex."[9] Regardless of race, ethnicity, or social class, he has a "rules don't apply to me" attitude, believes that the world revolves around him, publicizes employment grievances through the media, and thinks that his status as a star athlete should open doors, impress others, excuse his offensive behavior, and explain his inappropriate activities. He assumes that others will take care of things like hotel accommodations, travel arrangements, complimentary tickets, entertainment perks, personal appearances, or mundane tasks, and this "take care of me" attitude is inherent in his relationships with intimate partners. He may surround himself with his own entourage that supports or encourages this self-indulgent attitude. If he's famous, a spoiled athlete will welcome and covet his celebrity status and most likely will try to use it to his advantage or to take advantage of others. The syndrome may allow him to conceal or compensate for his insecurities or low self-esteem.

Sudden mood changes and inappropriate emotional outbursts, excessive sensitivity, rash judgment, emotional or verbal abuse, acts of hostility, and violent behavior are relatively common among those who exhibit the syndrome. Star athletes with the syndrome are well aware of their value to the sport organization and often exploit their status to excuse their errant behavior. Depending on the circumstances, a conspiracy of silence may protect them, especially if they're star players. The justice system may not always enforce accountability, either, largely because of the public adulation these men enjoy.[10] The syndrome can become a shield, serving to insulate and protect them from the consequences of their exploitative or violent behavior.

By default, husbands who internalize the spoiled athlete syndrome seem to take their wives' contributions to their marriage for granted. As the wives described the marital relationship, they take almost everything else without giving back as much as they receive, and many are unfaithful to their wives. Especially when combined with fame, the syndrome provides an axis of power from which these husbands try to manipulate others to get what they want, including achieving some desired outcome in the marital relationship.

A player's wife can play a key role in or continue to influence how much her husband internalizes the spoiled athlete syndrome. "I think baseball players' wives take care of too many things for their husbands," said Kalyn, whose husband had a lengthy MLB career. "They pamper them, wake them late, keep all the kids quiet in the house because Daddy's sleeping, postpone trips because of Daddy, and induce babies because of Daddy. It's not normal."

MOTHERIZATION

Osten's mother was overinvolved in her son's athletic life. Gwen shared many of her personal qualities but was reluctant to admit it: "A lot of people say, 'Oh, Gwen, he saw a lot of qualities of his mother in you.' And I'm like, 'Oh god, please don't say that.' But that's what it was. 'You are strong and he isn't. So he thought you were going to be just like her.' I'm like, 'Yeah, I can see that now.'"

Craig's mother, on the other hand, worked outside the home and was relatively unavailable as Craig was growing up. "His mom worked two and three jobs," Jill said. "Maybe I'm the way he wished his mom could be. Maybe I'm the mom that he didn't have."

Although their upbringings were different, both men relegated their wives to the role of mother in their marital relationships. I refer to this process as the motherization[11] of the wife, and it consistently emerged as a pattern of marital interaction. A player's wife becomes a replacement for his over-involved mother, or she gives her husband the mothering he never had. Motherization begins early in the relationship, before the couple marries, as he becomes dependent on his fiancée to take care of numerous domestic and occupational details. As will become clear, the woman happily fulfills this role in the beginning, but she can feel trapped by it later on. Motherization secures a husband's power in the sport marriage.

Owing to the nature of the husband's career, players' wives typically favor the organizer role and, as an extension of that role, they may initially prefer a nurturing, supportive, protective, and controlling way of interacting with their husbands. Marsha's husband Glenn struggled to sustain an MLB career as a pitcher, and she explained it this way: "I like it because I'm a controlling person. I mean, I'll admit it. I like to control, and Glenn comes from a controlling mother. It's something he's always lived with, so it's an easy way for him. He doesn't have to change. It's how life has always been for him. So it was just really good for him to fall into that role and let somebody else control him, because it's the best thing for our marriage." By taking this role, however, Marsha became a parent to her husband and therefore vulnerable to his insistence that she behave like a mother to him. Many wives are fairly comfortable in this maternal role, and this may be rooted in their early childhood experiences, or they simply may find it easier to be a mother to their husbands because it avoids unnecessary conflict and helps to preserve stability by providing some semblance of continuity in their hectic seasonal lives. This is especially true when the husband is on the road most of the time. Motherization limits a wife's ability to relate to her husband as a whole person.

> Whether it's basketball, baseball, football, or hockey, you're their psychiatrist, nanny, teacher, and housekeeper. You're all of these things. You have made this beautiful cradle for them to lie in and you take care of them like a baby.
> —DANA

A player's wife most routinely acts as a mother to her husband when he needs emotional or esteem support or when he suffers a crucial setback in his career, such when he's unexpectedly traded, loses his position in the starting lineup, or experiences a serious injury. Most wives will support their husbands in these and other occupational situations regardless of whether they have been motherized, but the motherized wife slips into this role because it has already been defined and realized as integral to the relationship, and because she believes it benefits his career and their marriage. "I was mommy when he was down," Arisa said. "We're convenient. We're there when needed."

Once this pattern is established in the marriage, a woman's deference[12] to her husband and his career can become habitual and, in this case, it plays a part in a husband's dependency on his wife. Because she's married both to her husband and his career, and perhaps because she needs to feel needed, she depends on his dependency on her to manage family life so that he can concentrate on his game and deal with occupational stressors, failures, and crises. "I think it's because you're on your own so much, especially if you've got kids," Marsha said. "You get so used to doing everything that it just takes over. I mean, it's hard to change for two weeks on, two weeks off. So you just learn to take care of everything, and you just keep going when he comes home because it's easier than changing your way of life." A wife tries to demonstrate domestic mastery, and she may feel guilty if she fails to do so. Her hesitancy to compromise her gender work, however, can take an unfortunate toll on her. Skylar recalled a point in her life that required her to re-evaluate her need to take on so much: "I developed really severe IBS and depression, and I wasn't well at all," she confided. "Our youngest was maybe four or five, and then I had the baby, and then we had been traded and moved and new team and all of that stuff, and I was just really sick a lot. And that off-season I came home, and I pretty much—I mean, Carter will tell you, I basically laid on the couch, and he was scared because I just couldn't function, and so he knew that something had to change."

A wife's dependence on her husband's dependency may backfire on her and benefit him by giving him more power in the marriage. She shields him from any distractions that might prevent him from staying on top of his game.[13] She recognizes that if he succeeds, she succeeds, and thus she feels validated for her support and sacrifice. By running interference and minimizing distractions, however, the wife unintentionally plays a part in her own subordination. Her support makes it possible for her husband to succeed, but it also provides him with the power necessary to exploit her.

Motherization allows the husband to use his occupation to more effectively get his wants and needs fulfilled. Sharon talked to me about her marriage to Walt, a thirteen-year NHL veteran:

> We were so codependent and dysfunctional because I was all wrapped up in Walt's life. In other words, I took total control. I cut all his wings—he had no control. Yet I was frustrated because the end result was on how much he scored and how much he made. In other words, all of my work saw no results. So I felt extrinsically controlled and intrinsically totally out of control of my life. It was total frustration. Walt gave everything to me and became the latent adolescent. He never took any responsibility for anything. I did the bills. I did the taxes. I did the investing. I had my babies on my own. I did everything. You know, the whole routine, and with tremendous anger, with tremendous anger; and the more I did, I

literally cut his balls off more, and more, and more, in my own eyes. The joke among sports wives is we're so masculine because in our own eyes we've de-balled them; and you have, physically, emotionally, intellectually, and socially, because we've become so controlling. We're just as much at fault as they are for letting it happen because they buy into this maternal take-care-of-me mentality: 'I'm on the road. Cook for me. Screw me. Have my shirts clean for me.' We do that. So what we literally do is clip their wings and we're the man-woman at home. It's almost like we don't need them because the paycheck comes in and they're gone so much. The scary reality is you learn to totally live alone and he's a guest in his own home!

Even if she initially agrees to it, a wife may get tired of being in the maternal role and may try to change it. She may verbally or nonverbally discourage her husband from defining her in this role—mostly where child care and the division of labor at home is concerned—and encourage him to redefine her in the role of wife. Robyn explained her efforts to discourage her husband Tyler's attempts to motherize her:

I get tired of being mommy and I'll say, "I don't want to be mommy today; you do it." So sometimes he'll take over. But he tries to finagle me to do things. He puts on a little baby act to get me to do particular things for him, chores, plane reservations, or anything where you have to call somebody on the phone to get something done. He pleads like he doesn't know what to say. So he wants me to do it. I'm tired of it now. But he's spoiled because he knows I'll do certain things for him.

Practically speaking, any redefinition of roles may be impossible during the season or during an occupational crisis.

Marsha initially preferred the maternal role in her marriage. Later, she realized that Glenn had become overly dependent on her, which was a pattern she had observed in his relationship with his mother and which she had assumed she could avoid in her own relationship with him. She decided it was time to minimize this dependency by discouraging the maternal role she had previously favored. She had become tired of Glenn calling her "Mom" and she wanted him to stop doing it. "Glenn's mom and dad are like that," she said. "His dad always called his mom 'Mom.' I just hate it. So today, when he's talking to our daughter he says, 'Now give that to Mom.' I said, 'Don't call me Mom. I'm not your Mom.'" Marsha's attempt to correct Glenn is a form of what I call boundary work.[14] In domestic situations, boundary work is occurring when women try to correct their husbands by establishing or enforcing their preferred boundaries of interaction and behavior. Marsha and Robyn attempted to de-emphasize their role as "mother" and remind their husbands of their role as "wife." Their dilemma, however, was that their husbands were fairly passive partners and they preferred to be the controller in the relationship, so the boundaries remained ambiguous. Other wives share this dilemma and will attempt to set boundaries in a similar way when they are tired of their husbands' dependence or efforts to motherize them. Jill provided an example: "I'll be cleaning our bedroom and I'll clean up everything except his clothes that are on the floor. Things like that. I'll clean up my side of the bedroom and pick up my towels. But I'll just leave his on the floor, and he's noticed that."

VIRGIN-PROSTITUTE SYNDROME

Like other men who value hegemonic masculinity, some professional athletes tend to view certain women as objects of sexual gratification. But unlike most other men, professional athletes have substantially more opportunities to act on their limiting and stereotypical beliefs about female sexuality. According to the wives, these men tend to make a sharp distinction between sex and love, or they emphasize sex in their expressions of love,[15] an attitude that can indicate a good girl/bad girl duality in their notions of femininity.[16] The good girl—the passive, conservative, pedestaled virgin—is loved, protected, and desexualized. The bad girl—the mysterious seductress—is objectified, targeted for promiscuity, possibly feared, and sexualized or hypersexualized.[17] I refer to this attitude, which is apparent in the ingénue/femme fatale images in film, art, and literature, as the virgin-prostitute syndrome and see it as another pattern in and integral to the motherization process.

The concepts of the virgin-prostitute syndrome and the spoiled athlete syndrome describe a set of common beliefs in the occupational worlds of professional sport. A professional athlete who expresses the virgin-prostitute syndrome believes that a husband's role is to be protector and sole provider for his wife and family,[18] and he expects his wife to act in ways that make her worthy of protection, financial security, and material comfort. He views his wife as the good girl, and in certain situations he may attempt to virginize her by de-emphasizing sex in their relationship and expecting her to sublimate her desire for sex. As an outlet for the sexual energy he must withhold from his wife, he seeks the bad girl, such as an eager female groupie. During the first study, Sheila pointed to this dualistic attitude: "They don't really see their wife as a woman. That's probably one big reason why the guys fool around.

These women they see out on the road, they don't have kids dragging along behind them and they're dressed fit to kill every minute when they see them. They don't think of their wives in that way." Sandy observed, "Most of the guys feel that their marriages are like being with their mothers."

As Sheila noted, a player who motherizes his wife may make a sharp distinction between the wife at home caring for their children, and other women, such as female groupies and sex workers, who are "out there" and sexually available.[19] This attitude points to the belief that motherhood and female sexuality are essentially different and perhaps incompatible. A husband may not always be comfortable with his wife's sexuality and may attempt to desexualize her. The women told me that expressions of the syndrome are more noticeable when their husbands have been on the road. When a player returns home from a long road trip and his wife is delighted to see him, she may attempt to initiate a romantic encounter or sexual interaction. If he has motherized her, he may become confused and discourage or refuse her advances. He may say that he's too tired and instead would prefer to relax and have a good home-cooked meal. Rhonda experienced this type of rejection when she tried to step outside the role of mother and into the role of sexual initiator. She had become frustrated by the lack of intimacy, so she attempted to try to recapture some semblance of love in her marital relationship by booking a surprise romantic getaway in a beautiful historic hotel near their home:

> We went there with the premise that we were supposed to meet some friends for dinner. I called ahead; the staff knew what was going on. They seated us at a table for four. As we were waiting for our friends to show up, there was a phone call. I came back and said, "Well, they can't make it after all." Halfway through our dinner, I said, "I'm going to the restroom. I'll be right back." I gave a note with the room key to the waiter to deliver to him, and went up to the room. A few minutes later, Brent knocks on the door, walks in, and here I am: I'm in this gorgeous negligee, the champagne's chilled, the candles are lit, the stage is set. And he got mad at me!

In this type of situation, a husband may believe that he is the target of a joke, and a wife may think that her husband has rejected her, lost interest in her, or is having an affair.

Regardless of how love is defined in the sport marriage, and whatever meanings are attached to love,[20] the motherization process seems to limit romantic expressions of love, which many wives have learned to accept. Conceding that these expressions are scarce and less realistic in their marriage, they learn to value masculinized or practical expressions of love,[21] such as when a husband gives his wife a spontaneous hug in the kitchen, voluntarily performs household tasks, carries out parental duties, picks up some needed items at the store, provides game tickets for friends or guests, or makes time for "date nights." Interestingly, the women in the first study reported that these practical expressions of love were quite scarce, but the women in the second group enjoyed them more commonly. We might speculate that this is because in the past couple of decades, mass media, self-help information, and the care-oriented professions have attempted to make couples more aware of the need to work on their marriages.

As Rhonda's story about her attempt to recapture romance with her husband illustrates, a wife may believe it's up to her to initiate, plan, or nurture other expressions of love if it's important to her. Unfortunately, husbands can sometimes have trouble interpreting their wives' sexual interest as an expression of love, and this can leave a woman feeling neglected and devalued. In this case, he fails "to keep the home going," as Olivia observed. Wives will normally avoid any such effort during the season, to keep their husbands' focus on the game.

All of this isn't to say that a husband who expresses the virgin-prostitute syndrome doesn't expect his wife to be ready for sexual activity with him on his terms. He does. For certain husbands, a potential wife has to "have that sleaze about her," Tanya said. This husband makes a distinction between the image of his wife as the virgin and his wife as the prostitute, and he favors one or the other depending on the situation. In essence, he wants the good girl and the bad girl in the same woman. Some of the power and control issues that emerge as a result of this dichotomy are discussed later.

Occupational Influences

In our many interviews, the women in both studies consistently identified and discussed four occupational influences that had a distinct impact on their marriages: organizational dominance,[22] a hierarchy of players' wives, an institutionalized brotherhood,[23] and a culture of infidelity.

ORGANIZATIONAL DOMINANCE

Professional athletes are rigidly ensconced in enormously competitive sport organizations with a distinctive culture that demands loyalty and total commitment from its players. Even though sport organizations are unique in some ways, they also share certain characteristics. In addition to valuing the "sport ethic,"[24] they share certain features that are consistent with "total institutions."[25] Examples of total institutions include prisons, military boot camps, and religious cloisters, places where people live and work together and are strictly controlled by administrators. Sport organizations enforce strict boundaries with the public and tightly control activities such as practices, physical conditioning, skill development, meetings, and road trips. Team events and functions are routinized, regimented, inflexibly scheduled, and governed by organizational policies and procedures. These activities focus solely on fulfilling institutional goals, and the primary goal, of course, is winning. Winning symbolizes success and substantially increases revenues and profits. To ensure that the players concentrate on developing their athletic skills and improving their competitive performances, sport organizations place a high value on privacy. Organizational management typically protects the players' occupational and personal lives, including their marriages and families. Activity disruptions and privacy invasions can clash with organizational ideology and impede team goals, and thus are vigilantly monitored. Administrators try to keep secrets,[26] most notably when dealing with members of the media.

> We're not their employees, but our spouses are. But we are associated with the team by default, in an employer/employee capacity. It just comes with the territory. It's a package deal.
> —ALAINA

Like organizations in the world of the military,[27] sport organizations have certain institutional beliefs about the roles players' wives should perform. These roles include providing support and carrying out responsibilities on behalf of their husbands and the sport organizations. A set of formal rules for players' wives may not exist, but many implicit rules directly benefit the sport organization and indirectly benefit the husbands. Emma, who participated only in the second group, talked about some unwritten rules for wives: "Well, you were expected to look good at a game. Show up; always had to be on your best behavior for the front office. You had to always pass the test of being attractive when you walked into the stadium. Everyone knew where you sat, so they knew who you were."

Even though the wife of a professional athlete is integral to her husband's ability to succeed and is under considerable occupational and organizational influence, she's an outsider in several ways. She can be an outsider in her marriage because of her social and emotional isolation, her husband's relative lack of support, and her husband's family. She's regarded as an outsider in her husband's occupational world because of her gender, and her husband's teammates, his sport organization, and female groupies and fans reinforce her outsider status. This becomes apparent in her dealings with certain sport organizations, such as when administrators minimize the importance of the players' wives and families by specifically excluding them in various ways and are not as family-friendly as they could be. For example, because of her husband's commitment to a seasonal schedule, the expectation is that even childbirth can be managed. Inducing labor has been a fairly common practice, for instance, in the MLB world. "Oh, that happens all the time," Sheila said during the first study. "Yeah, I have to have this baby on time. (Laughs.) . . . When you're wanting to have a baby, you've got to try and have it born in the offseason. . . . When we had our first child—you know how pitchers and catchers start their training early—she was born four days after my husband was supposed to report [to spring training], but he didn't go until the baby was born. And he had the worst year of his life and it was blamed on the four days of spring training he missed." Parental leave during the season in the major professional team sports has not been a routine procedure.[28] It wasn't until 2011 that the MLB adopted and granted an official paternity leave policy, but it can still be problematic for a player's career if he chooses to use it. Such a policy has yet to be initiated by sport organizations in the other team sports, and many would insist that it is long overdue.

HIERARCHY OF PLAYERS' WIVES

Two major classifications define a player's status on his team: rookie and veteran. The basis of this status hierarchy is his status as a rookie or veteran player, but his athletic ability, fame, longevity, successes, and failures can also affect it. Depending on the sport organization and specific sport, there may be finer gradations or distinctions within the two classifications. Players who are in their first year of employment are called rookies, and those who have been employed for more than a year are referred to as veterans. Star players have more status than journeyman players, marquee players have more status than those with average talent, and so forth. The hierarchy serves to announce a player's identity and status among his teammates, those in the sport organization, fans of the team, and the public. It affects interactions among teammates and their wives, affects how organizational management treats individual married couples, and permeates the wives' private world.

As mentioned in the introduction, wives become ranked in a hierarchy of players' wives. They are ranked, influenced, and guided by unwritten rules that are sanctioned by the husband's employer, veteran wives, and married players. A wife's status in her husband's sport organization and among the other wives may follow a progression based on longevity ranging from the *rookie wife*, *apprentice veteran wife* (a younger wife of a journeyman/bench player or a rising star with two to five years in MLB or the NBA, or two to three years in the NFL), *tested veteran wife* (an older wife of a journeyman/bench player, starting player, or marquee player with six to nine years in the MLB or the NBA, or four to nine years in the NFL), and *senior veteran wife* (an older wife of a journeyman/bench player, starting player, or marquee player with ten years or more in a professional sport league).

As we can see, movement to the top of this female hierarchy usually depends on the husband's occupational success or longevity, but it can change if her husband becomes a star player or has a serious setback in his career. In the MLB world, for instance, rookie wives are led to understand that they must "earn their stripes" or "pay their dues" (such as the years spent in the baseball minor leagues) before gaining respect and seniority among the other wives on the husband's team. The highest status is normally accorded to a veteran wife whose husband is the franchise player on the team. He commonly has the highest salary, enjoys celebrity status, is acclaimed for his athletic prowess and many awards, and has had a lengthy and fairly durable career with the same team or other teams in his occupational world. If a player leaves one team for another and the former

> You had rookie wives and veteran wives. The veteran wives had the money, they were seasoned, and a lot of them, I think, had been through their own trauma with being rookie wives. I think they always felt the need to make sure you knew your place. But as we played longer, we became the veteran group, then the people that were younger were coming in with money. The pecking order is different than it was when we first started out.
>
> —SKYLAR

team was prestigious, a player's elevated status—and consequently his wife's status—undoubtedly follows him. If the husband was a much-admired star athlete in college or a first-round draft pick, the couple arrives with elevated status. Depending on how this wife interprets her status, it can affect her relationship with the other wives. Alaina, a participant in the second group, observed, "We were happy that this particular couple came to our team—marquee player, All-American, everything, just famous. But we never saw his girlfriend or his wife. She never came into the family lounge [at the stadium]. She never associated with us. . . . We just knew not to associate with her."

Should a wife want to participate in the social circles[29] of players' wives, this hierarchy influences the likelihood of her joining or her ability to join certain social circles (for example, the husband's veteran/rookie status or his playing position can affect her acceptance by other wives in the circle). For many wives, social circles serve as a basis for support, friendship, mentorship, sharing interests and activities, or bonding based on occupational, marital, or life circumstances (for instance, expectant mothers). They provide the women with a sense of belonging, and a way to cope with stressors, dilemmas, loneliness, and alienation. Social circles can exist separately, or intersect or overlap, creating other social circles. Whether they are close-knit or loosely structured, these circles typically include face-to-face and social media interactions. If the circles are close-knit, some can become very exclusive and serve as inner circles for certain wives.

Unmarried female partners have yet to qualify for status in the hierarchy of players' wives. The wives in the first study referred to these women as "girlfriends" and identified four social types:[30] the *revolving-door girlfriend*, the *steady girlfriend*, the *cohabiting girlfriend*, and the *fiancée*. These distinctions were influential in determining how the other wives on the team regarded these partners and if the wives accepted them, primarily because veteran wives are unsure how long the relationship with a teammate will last and whether including them will be worth the effort. For this reason, a fiancée would be more likely to achieve acceptance than a cohabiting girlfriend, and those considered to be revolving-door or steady girlfriends are least likely to be accepted into the wives' exclusive world.

In her husband's first year with a team, when it's uncertain whether her husband will sign with the team, a rookie wife is essentially in a waiting period and her status is marginal. If he does join the team, she may still need to earn the veteran wives' approval and acceptance, and she will likely subordinate herself to them until she achieves it. She's fully aware that her husband is in the beginning stages of his career, and she will almost certainly make every attempt to comply with any unwritten rules and avoid doing anything that might impair his reputation or standing on the team. She seeks to earn but not presume acceptance and learn her place among the other wives. On certain teams, for example, veteran wives are given better seats, and when a rookie wife attends a game, she should not assume that she can sit with the veteran wives without a friendly invitation. "You don't just come in as a rookie wife and just take over," Alaina said. "You really just have to understand who is who, make good friendships, and let people know that you're friendly. If you're friendly and you have a good personality, you're not going to have any trouble making friends. But if you're stuck up, and you're caught up in being so-and-so's wife because he's a 'rookie of the year' and all that, you're not going to be treated well."

Becoming a veteran wife is a transitional process. It can depend on the ongoing development, advancement, and achievements of her husband's career in addition to his longevity as a player and the salary he can command. The disparity in MLB salaries has increased dramatically, for example, and differences among wives have become accentuated in the hierarchy. Wives whose husbands earn the highest salaries tend to have more affluent lifestyles and may have greater power among the wives.

As rookie wives transition to veteran status, they become aware of other unwritten rules, some of which their husbands initiate or encourage. For instance, a husband can influence a wife's decision about who she should or shouldn't associate with on the team. She may learn that she's expected to get along with her husband's teammates and that she should make an effort to become friends with the wives of his close teammates.

Many veteran wives claim and take great delight in their elevated status, believing that since they have worked hard and sacrificed to attain it, they deserve it. Their very survival speaks volumes. In certain situations, it isn't unusual for rookie wives to feel slighted or intimidated by veteran wives. Thinking back to her rookie experience during the second study, Beth remembered how much she liked the other rookie wives, but also how much stress the veteran wives were capable of creating:

> Each team was different, and it really depended on the dynamics of new players and wives that came to the team, and what level they were at. So there were young wives when I first became a baseball wife. Most of us were pretty close in age or, even, they were a little bit younger than I was. But it felt like there was more camaraderie because we were kind of all in it together. Once the veteran wives were more involved in the

team, then there was definitely a pecking order and things became more stressful in our marriage. It was really just that you avoided being in any situations with veteran wives because you just didn't want to deal with some of their baggage that they brought along with them.

Veteran wives will include rookie wives in various social events, community activities, team functions—such as promotional events, fundraisers, celebration parties, holiday parties—or more private wives' activities—such as baby showers, bridal showers, and Bible study meetings—but certain veteran wives may express a cordial coolness, an aloof friendliness, or superficial sincerity in their interactions with rookie wives. On one MLB team, both rookie and veteran wives refer to such a wife as the "queen bee." "The ones that were really old school were wives of husbands that played for twenty-plus years," Emma said. "They were the boss and they were the president of the club, and what they said went. Their husbands were MVPs so no matter what, they wanted you to know who they were, and that they were the queen. But it was in their own minds. The rest of the team didn't really feel that way. But you had to make them think that they were, because you didn't want to cause a problem, because even the front office would acquiesce to them."

The relationship between rookie wives and veteran wives isn't always difficult, however, and strong friendships can develop among them. Some veteran MLB wives take rookie wives under their wing and act as a mentor, mostly because they remember what it was like for them when their husbands broke into the big leagues, and they believe that rookie wives need their support. Alaina described the isolation rookie NFL wives typically experience and how they can benefit from the support of others: "I feel so sorry for rookie wives, who really come from that college family atmosphere, and then they get sucked into the atmosphere of this business. The dynamics change. This is business; you're alone, and you're in another state without your family and your support system, and you're having to manage all these things and people and strangers, and you're really just on your own until he comes home. . . . You really have to be tough." Likewise, rookie wives may seek guidance from veteran wives. "I knew that they had gone through a lot more, so I looked at them as allies," Skylar said. "I need to ask questions. I need to understand, because they've walked through this longer than I have."

In most cases, veteran wives simply don't have as much in common with rookie wives as they do with other veteran wives. Keira said, "The rookie wives have their own set of things in common because they're newly married or they're younger. But the veteran wives, they've been there longer. They might appear to be more intimidating, because they walk around with an air about them." Veteran wives are entirely conscious of their public image and elevated status among the wives on the team. For some, this is evident in their conspicuous display of status symbols, such as always showing up fashionably dressed and accessorized, maintaining a sleek physical appearance, driving expensive cars, and living in an impressive home. Although it may seem superficial or ostentatious, such displays announce their husbands' success and may be a way of communicating the benefits of being a loyal and supportive wife. It also serves to emphasize their position in the hierarchy to other wives, fans, and the public.

INSTITUTIONALIZED BROTHERHOOD

To avoid distractions and encourage a single-minded focus, sport organizations isolate the players from the public and most outsiders, strictly control the men's schedules and activities, and encourage them to strongly bond with each other. Whether the teammates are at home or on the road, they are restricted to private places like clubhouses, locker rooms, weightlifting rooms, practice facilities, and training camps, and this sequestration encourages what I came to think of as an institutionalized brotherhood. Membership in this exclusive brotherhood isn't limited to players on the same team, but can include fellow players on other teams. This brotherhood emphasizes strong support, mutual respect, feelings of solidarity, an inherent loyalty, and sharing of meaningful confidences, contributing to a feeling of "we"[31] among teammates. Traveling together in close quarters, competing together in games, and participating in bonding interactions gives special and gendered meaning to their teamwork both on and off the field, court, or rink. The men may socialize together after practices, games, and on other occasions, and some of these activities routinely exclude most outsiders. As an example, even the hotel where teams stay during local and away games is typically off-limits to the public and, in many instances, even to the wives (see more about these exclusionary practices in chapter 3).

> They're together so much that it's like an extended family. . . . They're your close-knit family, because every aspect of what you do they're going to try to get involved, because they're looking out for you.
>
> —GWEN

In what can be a supportive and cooperative but also an undeniably competitive environment, the men engage in bonding interactions and team-building activities that include minimizing pain and injuries, swapping and embellishing stories of sexual conquest to try to "one-up" each other, and playing pranks on each other. These and other types of interactions and activities can strongly influence the ways teammates follow the sport ethic and interpret and express solidarity, loyalty, or masculinity on the playing field, such as playing with pain and injuries and declining to report injuries. They also may be used to express or reinforce homophobic, misogynistic, and sexist attitudes[32] and to normalize marital infidelity and violent behavior off the playing field, including violence against women.[33] Their gender work includes attempts to avoid any form of subordination among teammates that might result in criticism, stigmatization,[34] or losing face. Some form of leadership by one or more teammates can set the tone of the institutionalized brotherhood. Callie, a member of the second group, discussed the significance of a team leader and how flexible it can be:

> There was a strong figure, who was quarterback for the first team we were with, and he was a strong Christian man and he didn't push his beliefs on anybody, but he set the precedent of "This is how I expect the locker room to go. This is how we'll host family barbecues and everybody's welcome." But, then, that next year after he left, the next quarterback, and I think of the quarterback as the leader of the offense, he was out partying and the party scene went way up. So it really depends on the structure of your team makeup, and I think it also has to do with who is the leader in the locker room.

Various implicit team rules preserve and enforce group boundaries and exclude most outsiders, and teammates and wives understand that there can be serious consequences for violations of these implicit rules. Teammates cooperate in collectively managing the boundaries of their solidarity and loyalty to each other, and this leads them to exclude women such as the wives from various areas within their occupational worlds, guard their clubhouse or locker-room secrets, and protect sexual privilege with female groupies and other interested women. Teammates relax or violate these boundaries only when it's in their best interest and when it works to their advantage.

The institutionalized nature of the brotherhood is evident when interpretations of elitism emphasize male dominance and female subordination. These interpretations become deeply embedded in the team culture and provide a source of personal empowerment and occupational privilege for the men. Teammates may develop a strong sense of superiority over others as they share meanings in their male-specific, occupational experiences. As a characteristic of their solidarity and loyalty, their gender work becomes an extension of their masculine identities as they distinguish between themselves as insiders and most others as outsiders. The inner sanctums of the locker room or clubhouse provide privacy and freedom from public scrutiny, providing settings for the men's gender work that conforms to hegemonic masculinity.[35]

As members of the brotherhood, teammates often think of each other and their team as a second family and the clubhouse, locker room, or organizational facilities as their home away from home. Because the brotherhood is so influential, meaningful, and deeply rooted in the teammates' occupational lives, it can greatly affect the sport marriage. Despite the women's belief that their marital relationship is close and intimate, the men's occupational relationships may be closer, which confuses the women and can lead them to strongly resent the brotherhood. More than one wife said that when her husband was at home during the season he would completely avoid or delay resolving family issues or taking care of family responsibilities or tasks in preference to team-centered activities. Some MLB wives told me that their husbands left for the ballpark hours before the game—much earlier than was necessary—telling their wives that they had to prepare for the game when, in reality, they simply preferred to hang out with teammates in the clubhouse rather than resolve a pressing marital or family issue.

Many wives felt that they were in direct competition with the brotherhood. During the first study, Alyssa described an incident in which a young rookie player on her husband Douglas's team was invited to join his teammates for "team spirit" night, a time-honored tradition during the NFL season that included barhopping, clubbing, or hanging out at a favorite nightspot. The rookie player was surprised to discover when he arrived at the nightclub that he was the only teammate to bring his wife. He soon learned that these exclusive teammate-bonding activities were meant to provide opportunities for the teammates to meet with female groupies or other interested women. The next day, he found a note taped to his locker specifying that his teammates had imposed a "fine" of $600 for violating an implicit team rule against wives attending these team-only nights.

Many players may be said to share in a "fast-food sex mentality." The personal and occupational influences on the marriage and their specific nuances, when combined with the persistent presence of female groupies and other sexually available women, converge to set the stage for players to be guided by and participate in a culture that perpetuates and normalizes marital infidelity.[36] This entrenched culture would undoubtedly not exist if the institutionalized brotherhood didn't support teammates who individually and collectively take advantage of sexual opportunities with female groupies or other interested women and who actively guard secrets.

> Whenever you hear player's wives describing men they'll always say, "They're all dogs, and if their mothers would lay down with them they'd go to bed with them, too."
> —LISA

According to the wives, the culture of infidelity exists because of the assertive actions of women in the players' occupational world (see chapter 6). They also said that the players share the blame because they condone and encourage the presence of these women. In this culture, most women are considered prospective partners to unfaithful husbands, and male infidelity is so common that it's institutionalized. Extramarital activities can include casual one-night affairs, spontaneous trysts, short- and long-term relationships that occur "on the road," encounters with strip-club dancers, and sex parties involving multiple female participants. Many of these sexual escapades may result in public scandals involving paternity suits, legal problems, broken families, and other repercussions.

Basic Marital Understanding

In light of the many challenges required to make the sport marriage work, an astute reader may be wondering, "Why would a woman get involved in such a marriage?" It's a fair question. After Beth and I had spent many hours in conversation over a four-year period, we were discussing whether women decide to marry a professional athlete because of the financial security, the material comforts, and the perks his occupation offers, or because they fall in love with the man himself. Beth suddenly stopped midsentence, became visibly upset, and said, "I married the player, and I wished I hadn't." After a long, contemplative silence, she explained to me what she meant. Initially, she had high hopes for her husband Cliff and his fledging MLB career, but as the years went by it became clear that he wouldn't achieve the success that he envisioned. She was terribly disappointed in Cliff, and her participation in the study finally empowered her to admit this to herself, even though it was a difficult emotional moment.

When one type of woman marries the professional athlete, she marries the material comfort his high income provides or might provide, or the fame he enjoys or she expects him to achieve. This woman may have a history of financial insecurity and, as a result, may have developed lofty ambitions of future abundance. She confronts and copes with the occupational and marital demands of the sport marriage because she's willing to trade what she hopes are temporary personal inconveniences for fame and financial security. She tries to advance his career when she can because if her husband benefits from her efforts, she also benefits. She agrees with the "wife of" identity and the two-person career partnership in her marriage because she benefits from both. She worries about potential career setbacks and failures, or painful chronic and serious injuries, not necessarily because of how they will affect him, but because of how they affect her. If her husband successfully establishes a career, she takes charge of their finances and enjoys her enviable lifestyle. "I've known wives that bought a house without their husband knowing it. I don't know how they pulled that off, but they had their whole other life set up and then walked out, and he had no clue," Sheila said. She may have knowingly married the spoiled athlete and, in this case, she will make an effort to ignore her husband's shortcomings, including his efforts to manipulate her. If he becomes an unfaithful husband, she will try to overlook his extramarital relationships. She doesn't want to lose the things his career might provide or has provided for her. If the woman married the substantial income, the affluent lifestyle, and the celebrity rather than the man, he's probably aware of it, and this mutual understanding between the couple informs how they relate to each other. In an effort to preserve the marriage and the personal, marital, or social benefits his career provides, she may be more willing to accommodate, support, or condone his efforts to advance his career, his extramarital indiscretions, his reluctance to perform parenting responsibilities, his disproportionate influence in the marriage, his role of spoiled athlete or heroic icon, and other uncomfortable realities. This wife is the basis for the public's stereotypical view of these women.

Another type of woman marries the man because of who he is, not what he does for a living. She may have met her husband in high school or college and fallen in love with him before he became a professional athlete. This woman is also inclined to agree to the "wife of" identity and become a partner in a two-person career. She accepts their challenges because she loves her husband in spite of his occupation, not because of it. Family is her priority, so she's willing to shoulder the burdens and responsibilities of the marriage and do whatever it takes to maintain relative stability. She isn't always comfortable with her husband's fame and doesn't enjoy the spotlight his fame brings to her and their family. She worries about her husband's occupational setbacks or failures because she's concerned about how they will affect him and their family. She may or may not accept the spoiled athlete pattern in her marriage. She may accept it because she values her marriage and family, but if she believes he's using it to exploit her, or if she becomes tired of it or angry because of it, she may try to minimize it or end it. She fiercely protects the family's privacy, yet she understands that her husband must pay attention to his public image, which may cause her to feel trapped and in need of establishing her own identity.

Many of the wives in the first study thought they married the man, not fully realizing that he would become a professional athlete or what that would mean for the marriage. Some of these women thought they "lost" the man as his career engulfed him. Some "lost" the man after his career ended and he had difficulty shedding his identity as a professional athlete. Even if he didn't exhibit extreme signs of a workaholic attitude or the spoiled athlete syndrome or exploit his celebrity during his career, he may have done so after retirement. In Alyssa's case, Douglas began drinking heavily, hanging out at bars and nightclubs, and reliving his glory days with others. In so doing, he neglected her. Alyssa suspected that he was unfaithful to her.

Some women believed that they had married the man but discovered at some point fairly early in the marriage that they had actually married the professional athlete.

A woman who consciously marries the professional athlete may have unrealistic hopes, may tend to be selfish and insecure and perhaps spoiled and pampered in her own way. The woman who marries the man may be more concerned for others and more willing to put the needs of others above her own. Even though both types may view the husband's career as a means of upward mobility with aspirations of personal happiness and material comfort, the wife who married the professional athlete seeks affluence and desires to maintain her lifestyle. The woman who married the man may not expect or be accustomed to affluence and may be more realistic about her husband's financial prospects.

The combined majority of the women in both studies believed that they married the man rather than the professional athlete. The distinction can be ambiguous, however, and as Beth's revelation indicates, the woman herself may not be clear about why she married her husband. Kaylee mentioned that she had previously asked herself the same question:

> I think we're both pretty intense, passionate people, and I think that the fire of professional athletics seems to intensify things a lot. So I think everything was just intense. I think we loved each other intensely. I think we fought intensely. I think we just went through everything with more of an intensity because of his job. I think it's hard to divorce the two, because his personality is part of what made him a professional athlete. So, because he's passionate and he's driven and motivated, that's part of what I love about him, and that's also part of what made him able to succeed at such a high level. So it's hard to say. I think I would still love him if he wasn't a professional athlete, but I wouldn't be surprised if he was doing something else that was a high-level type thing. So I love who he is as a person but, like I say, it's hard to divorce the two, because that drive made him be someone who was going to be great and be in the spotlight.

Whether a woman married the professional athlete or the man, the language players' wives regularly used in our interviews demonstrates an internalized "we" partnership[37] with their husbands. They saw themselves as part of a consequential team, and they closely associated their own identity with their husband's occupational life and his professional successes and failures. This "we" partnership is evident when a wife says, for example, "we just got traded," "we are ready for the season to start," "we can't wait for the season to end," or "we have just been called up to the big leagues." Not surprisingly, one of the major drawbacks of the "we" partnership is the emotional demands placed on a woman when she watches her husband perform during a game. "When I'm watching him pitch, I feel helpless," said Stacy, whose husband Dennis was an MLB relief pitcher. "I get real nervous in the pit of my stomach. I find myself wishing he wouldn't even pitch. But, then, I think, 'Well, if he never pitched that wouldn't be good, either.' So I have real mixed emotions." Stacy, in fact, internalized the "we" aspect of her marriage to the point that she believed that she was part of her husband's performance. When Dennis was announced into the game through the public-address system, she tried to avoid jinxing him by not acknowledging his appearance as he emerged from the bullpen and jogged to the pitcher's mound. Instead, she continued conversing with her friend until he was ready for the batter. She believed that if she stopped what she was doing, she would bring him bad luck. These types of superstitions are not limited to MLB couples or wives.

A wife's expectations of her husband's performances, whether they are overly optimistic or unflinchingly realistic, is an integral characteristic of the "we" partnership. When her husband disappoints her, his teammates, or his coach during a game—such as when he doesn't start or get in the game, is benched, or makes an error at a crucial part of the game and his team loses—a wife views these occupational failures as "our" failures. But, given her allegiance to the unwritten rules and her support for her husband, she will conceal her dissatisfaction or embarrassment.[38] In the context of the marriage, he has not only failed his team and himself, but he has failed her and broken their unspoken understanding. Nora, who was part of the second group, discussed this expectation as an agreement that each partner must respect:

> I'd say that when the ego started coming out again, it's almost like a mother-to-child relationship there, where they start complaining about those things and you say, "Listen, you know your job is to get these stats. Stop complaining about the ref, stop doing this, be accountable, do your job, take care of the family." It's not spoken out loud, but I think that's ultimately what the message is. But if you're supporting them in every regard, where all they have to do is walk onto the court and perform, then you suck it up for that time that you're going to do that, because twenty-four hours out of the day I'm doing all the work and one hour out of that twenty-four hours you're doing the work. So that's definitely the serious aspect of playing; you know, stop complaining, be accountable, and do your job.

Because a young wife values the support role, viewing herself and her marital contributions as normal and necessary, she's absorbed or incorporated[39] into her husband's occupation early in his career. By providing both domestic and occupational support as a partner in the two-person career, she teams with her husband to contribute to his career through her behind-the-scenes direct and indirect involvement,[40] and these directly and indirectly benefit the sport organization. She attends his games, makes appearances at various civic events (with or without her husband), participates in community fundraisers and philanthropic activities on behalf of him and his employer, runs important errands for him when he's traveling, manages the relocation process with little support or completely on her own, prepares a diet and meals that are consistent with and complement his seasonal training and weight-watching habits, assists him with contract negotiations for his current team or a new team, trains with him or contributes to or facilitates his offseason training program, gives him rubdowns after his games, supports his rehabilitation from various injuries, and, as Arisa explained, "You know, just the general psych thing—keeping him up all the time, emotionally, because you can get down when you're not playing or when you're injured." For most wives, providing some level of care work[41] is expected and normalized during the husband's career. It may even be a crucial factor in prolonging his career or determining his success, and he may come to depend on her care work to help him get back in the game. Anticipating, learning, and performing the role of caregiver during his career is a rehearsal, a preparation for caring for him in his retirement. When her husband Nathan suffered a potentially career-ending hip injury during his NFL career, Arisa provided all the care work she was capable of. "I mean, from there on, I had to dress him. I had to do everything for him," she said. "I was the nurse, psychologist, mom, dad, trainer—everything for quite a while." During his lengthy rehabilitation, Nathan depended heavily on Arisa to embrace the role[42] of caregiver. Many of the wives in the second group said they viewed this as a form of teamwork. "I would describe it as being very supportive in the marriage, but that's what you do when you have a growing business," Nora said. "You support that business to grow and do what it takes. So, yeah, initially, I really believed that it was a team effort. He was the product and I was selling it."

Keira, a participant in the second group, recalled the origin of teamwork in her marriage: "When he was trying to learn his plays when he finally went to a different team and needed to learn the system, I would quiz him on his plays, that type of thing, and took care of the family, so that he could devote his time to what he needed to do with his career." A wife like Nora also contributes her business acumen: "My contribution was meeting with and deciding which agent to hire, helping negotiate contracts, managing a camp. My background was in public relations and I also had a business emphasis, so managing the finances and accounting, and doing the PR for events, and blogging, and really promoting the image of the profession." Jessica basically agreed with Nora, but she expressed it another way: "I'm better at promoting somebody else, pumping them up, giving them ideas, or getting them into it. I don't have what it takes to be a world-class competitor or the guts of steel."

In Alaina's case, this "we" partnership included extending herself to others on her husband's team. "I engaged myself in charitable activities, coordinated team-related activities, such as special events, and we had dinner parties and get-togethers and we invited the players to our homes or to venues," she said.

"We had different team functions at venues so that we could bring the team together as a family, and to get the players involved so that they could also get to know each other. . . . You have to do everything to sacrifice yourself for the sake of the team and the sake of winning."

A married player depends heavily on his wife's teamwork, sometimes to an extreme degree, because her efforts allow him to concentrate on his career with minimal domestic responsibilities, such as those involved when the family is relocating to another residence. "All he had to do was just jump on the plane," Alaina said. "You pack everything up, call the movers, call the storage, all by yourself. He is gone. Well, he may help out some, like decide who's going to ship the car. He's going to be responsible for that. Or he may help pick out a mover or something like that but, for the most part, he's gone. You have to coordinate all of that." Numerous wives in both studies echoed Alaina's experience.

Notwithstanding her belief that she's part of a marital team and that it's a productive arrangement for the couple, the situation can backfire on a wife, especially if her husband is a spoiled athlete. Emma recalled, "I remember one time Mason had a great game, and we'd come home, and I said, 'Oh, honey, the garbage needs to be emptied.' And he looked at me and said, 'I just had a great game. You're asking me to empty the garbage?' And I was thinking, 'Are you kidding me? Seriously? This is part of our household chores.' And he's like, 'Yeah, and I'm not emptying the garbage right now. I'm on a high. I'll deal with that tomorrow.'"

In reality, this type of teamwork is an unequal arrangement from which the wife most likely doesn't benefit. Her husband may begin to take her sacrifices for granted, lack appreciation for what she does, or manipulate her feelings for him, and certain power and control issues can emerge in their relationship. Her efforts to support her husband in these ways may hold their marriage together during his career, but they may no longer be required after he retires. If this is the case, the marriage will likely be troubled or dissolved. It may be surprising and frustrating for a wife to realize that her husband has learned to value the importance of teamwork in his occupation yet has not learned its importance in his marriage. She also may discover later in her marriage, or after her husband retires, that because she was so deeply committed to her role in the two-person career that there are certain unintended consequences and a high cost for her years of sacrifice and her participation in their teamwork. She may deeply regret redefining her identity, delaying employment outside of the home, or shelving her own personal aspirations. Borrowing a metaphor from Washington Irving's celebrated fictional short story *Rip Van Winkle*,[43] she "wakes up" years later and realizes that she lost those years.

Initially, a player's wife likely won't question her involvement in the complex interdependencies of her career-dominated marriage. Irrespective of the reasons she married the man she did, the women in both studies valued their marriages. Her husband's career success likely validates a wife's teamwork and her sense of who she is in the world, even though the lifestyle she chooses can inadvertently contribute to her exploitation. This might at least partially explain why she can sometimes become jealous or resentful of her husband's career; the very thing she supports takes him away from her and her family and may even alienate her from her husband.

My research focused on the experiences of women married to professional athletes, and certain challenges appear to be unique to this type of marriage, but my findings shed light on any career-dominated marriage in which the husband's career comes first.

CHAPTER 2

In the Public Eye

OLIVIA

Flashing bright lights and excited reporters with microphones greeted Olivia and her daughters as they stepped off the plane at a crowded international airport. Olivia's husband Lewis, who had already been playing baseball in another country for some weeks,[1] had agreed to meet them at the airport gate, but he was nowhere in sight. "Typical," Olivia thought.

It was Olivia's first time in the country. She didn't speak the language and knew little about the culture. Not knowing what do, she grabbed the hands of her two daughters and they all bowed their heads to avoid eye contact as they walked briskly toward the security gates. All the same, the reporters aggressively followed them as they walked faster and faster. When they made it through customs and finally spotted Lewis, Olivia saw that the flashing bright lights and eager reporters had also engulfed him. Reporters wanted photos, and they asked him to embrace Olivia and their daughters, separately and together, and then pose with civic dignitaries and executives from Lewis's new team. Afterward, Olivia and her family were hustled into a taxicab waiting outside the terminal and a police motorcycle escorted them through traffic. Throughout the experience, Olivia felt a range of unpleasant emotions, including embarrassment, confusion, fear, and vulnerability. She was also annoyed with Lewis because he failed to prepare her for the media reception, but she suppressed her irritation and didn't bring it up later.

Olivia and her daughters became the targets of intense public curiosity in a country that loved baseball. In the United States, Olivia had become accustomed to being treated as "just an MLB wife," she said, and this celebrity-style treatment caught her completely off guard. Her past interactions with the media during Lewis's MLB career had given her some measure of exposure, but none of it had prepared her for the level of visibility she was experiencing. "If you were at the game they were always there," she explained. "There was a cameraman behind home plate. There was one to the left of me, one to the right of me, and one behind me. So they always knew where I was. Their expectations of you as a person are real high. It's not like you're really a person. You're supposed to look a certain way. You're supposed to act a certain way. You're better than everybody else."

Living with this level of visibility was like living a nightmare for Olivia, and she felt ill-equipped to cope. "People were clapping while you're walking down the street," she said. "They would jump up and down and they would grab hold of you, and hug you and shake you. They would pick up the kids and hug them." Even though most street behavior of baseball fans was fairly innocuous, on certain occasions interactions with fans could be perilous. In one frightening experience after a game, Olivia sustained physical injuries at the hands of overly enthusiastic fans.

Hopes for Lewis's performance were exceptionally high, but early in the season he didn't perform well, and in a short while he and Olivia became the target of negative publicity. Olivia discovered that it was important for her and Lewis to have a shared understanding of certain issues that might emerge in the media. She learned that if they had different points of view or any disagreement, the media would seize the chance to take sides or emphasize their differences. The couple's reliance on interpreters further complicated things.

At one point, Olivia returned to the United States for a brief visit, and during her absence the media blamed her for Lewis's lackluster performances. Given the importance of the family and the media-created drama, Lewis advised her not to grant any more interviews after she returned home, and she agreed. When Lewis ended his slump and had a great game, it was attributed to Olivia's return. As she framed it, "If he got a hit, he's doing better now, his wife's in town." Lewis's attempts to restart his career were proving to be less than successful. Moreover, Olivia had difficulty adapting to the new culture and the policies of his sport organization. So she was more than happy when they decided to return to the United States with high hopes of resuming his MLB career.

Not all professional athletes are national celebrities, but they may be famous in their hometowns, the cities where their teams are headquartered, or in the cities where they keep a primary or secondary residence. Mass media establishes and maintains the public's positive image of those they define as celebrities. We put these men on a pedestal and lavish them with praise, and we expect them to live up to their media-created images, including making good on the promise of athletic excellence and fulfilling our desire to view them as cultural heroes. Unfortunately, mass media can shift our perception in the time it takes to click a mouse or announce a headline in a fast-breaking news story. In our current era of information and communication technology, the boundaries of privacy for professional athletes are diminishing,[2] and this trend has significant implications for the sport marriage.

Unwanted media scrutiny and privacy invasions have always led these couples to try to maintain two personas: a public self and a private self. A player's image as a celebrity can become an important part of his public self, and he may lack identity apart from this self. Aspects of his public self can spill over into his personal life and affect his marital and family life, and if they do, this public self can provide him with power and control within the family system.

Before marriage to a professional athlete, a woman ordinarily has certain ideas about life in the spotlight, but the realities of her marriage may differ greatly from her preconceptions. She may enjoy sharing her husband's celebrity and the advantages it has to offer, yet she may find it difficult to accept things such as sharing her husband with star-struck fans or not being able to take her privacy for granted. This is understandable when we consider modern society's idolization of celebrities and the existing celebrity culture,[3] which is driven by all forms of media. Few women who marry professional athletes are prepared for public life or the roles they are expected to perform. "Public appearances, or being in the spotlight, or whatever, are totally foreign to me," Rhonda said. "I had never been in those circumstances before. But you just wing it."

A player's wife develops a keen awareness of the responsibilities involved in representing her husband and his sport organization in public. Entering public life often begins with appearances at civic events or team-sponsored events such as "fan day" or "family day" at ballparks or stadiums. Wives may be expected to attend all or most home games and may be asked to appear at charitable events such as celebrity roasts, celebrity softball games, fashion shows, food drives, benefits, luncheons, blood drives, silent auctions, walk-a-thons, and telethons, with or without their husbands. They also may be expected to engage in volunteer work in the community. The sport organization may expect or insist on these types of appearances, and most husbands assume that their wives will comply. Learning to participate in and manage these and other public situations sensitizes a wife to the presence of the media. She may be expected to give interviews or have pictures taken of her, sometimes with her children. Participation in these and other activities associated with her husband's profession can affect her ability to create and maintain her own identity apart from his public identity.

Presenting the Right Image

A player's wife understands that it's in the best interest of her husband's career for her to present the "right" image of herself to fans and the public. Fulfilling the public's expectations of this image requires an emphasis on and display of a traditionally appropriate form of femininity.[4] I came to think of this as image work[5] because it involves managing her physical appearance—her body shape, weight, makeup, clothing style, hairstyle, and so forth—and also how she conducts herself and interacts with people she encounters in public life. "You need to look a certain way and you need to act a certain way," said Paula, who was a young rookie MLB wife during the first study. Likewise, Rhonda became aware of the need to use image work fairly early in Brent's career. "I was real, real conscious of trying to project the image of the 'good wife,' the 'supporter,' the 'rah, rah wife,' and that type of thing, because that's what I saw as the correct role," she said.

Although the wives in the first study told me that sport organizations may encourage or have opinions about a dress code for attending team functions or home games, they indicated that most often it's the wives themselves who collectively do image work by establishing an informal or formal dress code, which is guided by unwritten rules and enforced through peer pressure.

Wives in the second group confirmed this finding. Conformity to a dress code frequently involves a wife's self-induced pressure to "fit in" and meet various expectations. The women mutually agreed that the image preferred by fans is one that represents tradition, morality, femininity, and beauty. "There's this whole idea that you represent your husband, of being attractive, taking care of your body, looking attractive at games—I felt like that was a huge unwritten rule," Skylar said. "You didn't want to be like the fat, unattractive, unhealthy wife who didn't care about the way she looked. So that was a level that was really challenging." Nora, like all the other wives, was aware of an implicit dress code. "There was an unspoken dress code as far as you're representing the image, so you have to dress according to that image, so you're not going to come to a game in your sweat pants. But you dress professional, based on game behavior," she said. Dressing in poor taste or in a "sleazy" manner (as some wives described it) must be avoided. Dressing too casually, even if the outfit shows support of the team, isn't considered acceptable. "Glenn would shoot me if I showed up in a team T-shirt. That's like an unwritten rule of baseball wives. You don't dare show up in a jacket or a T-shirt with the team's name on it. It's just not done," Marsha said.

In many cases, it's a wife's personal taste and fashion preference that matters most. "I like to dress," Keira said. "When you're going to the game, I think you're representing your husband, you should look nice." Whatever the reason may be, the shared goal of most wives is to positively represent their husbands and their teams. They are expected to dress tastefully, fashionably, and perhaps expensively.

> I governed myself. I know how to act amongst the public, because you never know who's looking, and you don't want to be in the newspaper or radio or TV and somebody talking about you—his spouse. You always have to be aware; at least you should, because you shouldn't be a distraction to the team. This is not written anywhere; you just have to know this. . . . [It's] so mentally draining. I can even imagine what the First Lady goes through, because you have to be everything for everybody. You have to just act a certain way here, act a certain way there, don't say this, don't do this. You're just like a robot.
> —ALAINA

Among NFL wives, for example, this emphasis on physical appearance begins as a rookie wife.[6] When rookie wives attend preseason or early-season games, they may dress as though they were still attending a college football game. If they're fortunate, veteran wives will coach them about acceptable styles, and by the end of their rookie season most will have conformed to the styles of dress, hairstyle, and accessories that the other team wives, their husbands, his sport organization, and fans seem to expect. NFL wives also may be expected to conform to a dress code distinctive to their husbands' team. The NFL season (16 games) includes eight home games, and many wives shop during the week before a home game to work on their image. An agreed-upon theme determined in advance by veteran wives or an unwritten rule about never wearing the same outfit twice during the season may cause them to dress in a different outfit for each home game. In contrast, the MLB season (162 games) is considerably longer and therefore the number of home games is much greater. Still, dressing appropriately for home games and "looking like an MLB wife" isn't taken lightly. With the exception of team functions or certain home games, MLB wives tend to dress more casually than NFL wives, but appropriately. "In the minor leagues, I don't dress up as much. But in the major leagues, it's really different," Paula said. "You better have on your designer sweaters and all that." Rhonda recalled a significant moment as a newly minted MLB rookie wife:

> When Brent first got called up, I'd never seen a major league ball game at all. I was just living from paycheck to paycheck and had virtually nothing. I had to borrow a bunch of clothes from my roommate and get my little outfits all coordinated for the games. I can remember coming to the ballpark early with him, the first day that he came to the ballpark, at three o'clock in the afternoon, and sitting in the stadium and watching it fill up with thousands of people. I was just totally overwhelmed and awed by this whole thing, and here I was in my little coordinated outfit that I had to borrow from my girlfriend to look the part.

Susan, on the other hand, wasn't aware of a dress code before attending her first National Basketball Association (NBA) game as a rookie wife:

> I definitely felt like I didn't measure up. You know, I didn't have the right clothes, I didn't have the right shoes, and I never had. I definitely improved my wardrobe after that first game, when I was just absolutely mortified, where I'm looking like I did in college, when I went to a ballgame in just jeans and tennis shoes. I mean, it was a little bit better than

that, but not much, and I get there and these women are all dressed up for a ballgame. I'm like, "What the heck is this?" I just was very surprised. It was like a contest to see who could look the best. Not my style, but I definitely spruced up my wardrobe, so that I wasn't embarrassed anymore.

Dressing tastefully is partly an effort for the wives to set themselves apart from other women in public life, such as female fans or female groupies. Whether a formal or informal dress code is observed or more relaxed fashion trends are generally popular, most wives still believe (and may be pressured to believe) that they have to fulfill each other's expectations and those of their husbands, friends, fans, or the public regarding how they should appear in public. If it were up to the wives, most would dress more casually than they do. Image work, however, may be so deeply ingrained in a wife that if she fails to look "just right," she may feel guilty. Emma shared this story with me:

It was snowing, and we were tired of being housebound so we went to a mall, and we were in a bookstore, and I remember I had barely put on any makeup and had on the wrong clothes. I had boots on, and not stylish boots, but snow boots. It was like we just threw on stuff and we went out. . . . We were in a bookstore and, all of a sudden, this man and his son walked up to Mason and I was standing next to him, and he says, "Hello, Mr. X, do you mind if my son gets your autograph?" I'm really thinking, "Oh, my god, are you kidding me?" I walked away, and Mason stood there and spoke to him for a little while, and then he came and found me. . . . That was the last time I left the house not looking my best.

As another part of their image work, players' wives pay close attention to what they say and do in public, recognizing that they are essentially representing their husbands and the sport organization. They know that their husbands are the center of media attention and public scrutiny, and this knowledge is normally sufficient to compel a wife to feel a sense of responsibility to manage her emotions. She knows that public misbehavior can have consequences, so she will try to comply with the primary rule of public life: never do anything that might reflect negatively on a player or his team. Wives conscientiously avoid saying anything or engaging in any behavior that might discredit either one. A wife will strive to manage herself in public life to establish, preserve, and express what she believes to be an appropriate "face" in her interactions with others in public life. Using face work[7] as an integral aspect of her public image, she tries to project pleasantness, respect, and dignity and to avoid any interactions that would lead to embarrassment. Naomi called this her *wife face*, and it may or may not be genuine. "I put on my wife face when the reporters call and ask me stupid questions like, 'What do you think about this coach being fired?' And I have to be diplomatic," she explained. "Other than that, that's Naomi's face being nice to people and taking a minute to say 'hi' to the girl in the wheelchair who thinks Todd's great. That's not a wife face; that's a Naomi face. The wife face is when I have to be diplomatic, because that's not me." Other wives talked about putting on a wife face when attending formal occasions where diplomacy was required. "You can be nice. You can be cordial and still be quiet and still be there. That's a wife face," said Kellita, whose husband Donald was a seasoned NFL veteran. In this way, wife face can lead to a form of social invisibility; wives may strive to be seen but not heard. The attentive management of wife face is a necessary part of public life, and wives look forward to removing it in private life.

PRACTICING GAME ETIQUETTE

When attending her husband's games, a wife becomes acutely aware of a form of image work I call game etiquette: the unwritten rules she follows to govern her behavior, interactions, and emotions at her husband's games. A wife is expected to express support for her husband and his team by applauding and cheering for him, but only at the appropriate moments during the game. She's expected to be excited for her husband when he performs well, but she must not display too much excitement. "You do get happy, but you don't get too happy, because you don't want to draw attention," Gwen said. "You're supposed to be low key. You're a professional's wife." Alaina also said, "You don't have to keep jumping up and showing up and acting the fool when your spouse is scoring. You know, have fun, cheer, but don't be obnoxious." Displaying the "wrong" emotion at the wrong moment may reflect negatively on a wife, her husband, and other wives. Emotional outbursts such as fist pumping, jumping

> If someone makes an error behind your husband, we don't ever say anything about that. You don't show any emotion about that. . . . I learned that the hard way in the minor leagues, trust me. By the time we got to the big leagues, I pretty much knew what to do and what not to do.
> —SHEILA

up and down enthusiastically, giving high-five slaps, fist-bumping everyone seated around her, or cheering too loudly or uncontrollably may be acceptable if a particular play is deserving of a legitimate or emotional response, but such animated outbursts are typical among fans up in the nosebleeds and should be avoided in routine play. "No jumping, unless it was something very spectacular," Gwen explained. "If we were down, down by whatever, and it was the last seconds of the game and his basket could be the winner, that's when you get excited. If it's just a basket, you just clap."

A wife may follow the rules of game etiquette to try to influence or affirm her husband's status on the team and her place in the hierarchy of players' wives. "You're not cussing and spitting, like the fans up in the nosebleeds," Nora said. "You are clapping normally, you know there are times when the camera's going to be on you, and so you're aware of your presence and posture."

If a player's wife becomes jealous of a teammate's performance during a game (because it could affect her husband's standing on the team), it's in her best interest to avoid expressing it in any way. "You would never criticize a player," Nora said. "That would be the fans' role, to criticize the players. But, as far as the families, you didn't criticize. . . . If an up-and-coming player was on the cusp of making it big, there was obvious jealousy there; especially when they're sitting behind you and their husband's not getting the playing time that your husband's getting. There's definitely some unspoken jealousy going on."

A player's wife will be understandably concerned if her husband is seriously injured; nonetheless most wives believe that it isn't a good idea to express too much fear or distress or to emotionally "break down" or "fall apart." This is challenging, for example, during an NFL game, when her husband is injured badly enough to stop the game. It can be intensely difficult for her to watch with the rest of the crowd as the medical staff determines the extent of his injuries and whether he is ambulatory. If he is not, he may be carried off the field on a stretcher or in a cart, indicating a more serious injury. His wife knows that cameras are trying to capture her reaction, and that fans, the sport organization, and the sport media are curious about her response: will she display strength or stoicism in the face of adversity? She may not know the severity of her husband's injury until she is informed that he has been taken to a hospital.

Conformity to game etiquette is also sorely tested when a wife has to deal with unruly spectators. Verbal and emotional displays of approval and disapproval are customary and even expected among fans, but sometimes their actions can get out of hand. In addition to verbal heckling, spectators have been known to throw snowballs, cans, bottles, and heavier objects at the players or onto the field, court, or rink. Although raucous behavior is typically directed at visiting teams, it can be directed at the home team and their wives when the team is performing poorly. In this case, wives initially will try to avoid any confrontation, particularly if the spectators are visibly intoxicated and belligerent. A woman in this position understands that her actions can only encourage the continued barrage of inappropriate language and behavior and can only lead to trouble. On certain occasions, however, a woman may be sufficiently upset that following the nonconfrontation rule has ceased to be an option, and she may decide to challenge a spectator. "I'll say something to them like, 'Can you keep it down, because there's children behind you.' I try not to let them know that I'm a player's wife, because some of them will get all over you. That pushes them further," Dana said. When all else fails, a wife may send for stadium security, either openly or discreetly. Sheila confided, "I have had people removed from the game. They didn't know it was me. [This was] mostly when my kids were little. The constant swearing, it's like, 'Okay, I don't have to listen to this.' I would usually ask them to stop, nicely, and they just continued. Now you can text and they'll just come and get them, and they don't even know."

Because of the depth of her investment in her husband's career and their marriage, and the "we" partnership, a player's wife likely has definite expectations about his performances. If he performs poorly, she will have a strong and complex emotional response. Like other wives, however, Kathleen believes that if she's disappointed in her husband's performance during a game, she shouldn't express it. "Doing his job, he has to have such a high self-esteem. You know? I think I'm careful not to chisel away at that. I make him feel good about himself so he can go out there on the pitcher's mound and feel good about himself. If he does blow a save, I shouldn't be disappointed," she said. Wives like Kathleen carefully bury their feelings and avoid any display of disappointment in their husbands' less-than-stellar performances. To do otherwise could imply to other wives, those in the sport organization, fans, and the ever-present cameras that they don't support their husbands.

A player's wife also will always try to avoid disparaging comments about her husband's teammates, even if she believes a teammate deserves such criticism. "You didn't bad-mouth another player while watching the game, whether you knew they made a mistake or not," Callie said. "So, for example, one time my husband forgot to go out on a play he was supposed to be out there on, so we got a penalty for it. Nobody said anything to me." Discussing the importance of this rule, Skylar said, "An unsaid rule is you don't trash someone else's husband's performance. Like, if Carter's pitching and the shortstop misses a play, I don't want to have a conversation about that in the stands, because that's somebody else's spouse that's right next to me and that's a teammate. So that kind of stuff is very frowned upon." Game etiquette calls for offering a kind word of encouragement or support to the wife of a husband who made a major error by saying something like, "Oh, we'll get it back." Regardless of any envy she may feel, she also should congratulate another wife on the same team when the woman's husband scores the winning basket, run, goal, or touchdown, especially if it results in winning a crucial game.

These women feel responsible to not only follow game etiquette themselves, but they also realize that the failure of family members to follow the rules can reflect poorly on them, and thus on their husbands. "I had to tell my father-in-law not to get too emotionally involved in a game, because you never know whose family he's sitting next to," Callie said. To avoid the possibility of violating game etiquette, some wives will take the initiative to monitor their in-laws' behavior. Skylar explained, "I've had family members that are not allowed to go. If they do, you're going to have to sit them someplace else, because they cannot keep their mouths shut in the family section."

The last thing a wife wants to do at her husband's game is to create a scene. This can call unfavorable attention to her, which defeats the purpose of image work and can have negative repercussions. One of the most important rules is to avoid consuming too much alcohol or using other substances that could alter her behavior in public situations. The consequences can be damaging when mainstream media, sport media, or social media become involved. During the first study, one of the wives shared a story with me about the rookie wife of a promising running back who became intoxicated during an NFL exhibition game. When the rookie wife stood up and her loud behavior became obnoxious, a female spectator seated behind her asked her to please sit down so she could watch the game, but the woman wheeled around and called her a derogatory name and pointed her middle finger up in the air. A shouting match and fistfight with another spectator ensued. Yellow-jacketed security guards quickly intervened and the rookie wife was escorted from the stands. Many of the wives on the team, who had watched the scene with disbelief, were disappointed, offended, and angry. They believed that the woman's behavior made them and the sport organization "look bad" in front of hometown fans, and they anticipated an apology from her. None was forthcoming. Some wives gave her the benefit of the doubt, reasoning that she was relatively young and inexperienced, but others were less forgiving. Some thought it was a really awkward way for her husband, who had a promising future, to begin his NFL career. Her standing among the wives changed for the worse, and she and her husband left the team shortly afterward.

A player's wife will try to avoid any confrontation with spectators that might involve disclosing her identity. For a variety of reasons, a player's wife ordinarily will go to great lengths to conceal her identity at games. Calling unwanted attention to herself may not only make her feel uncomfortable, it may meet with her husband's disapproval if he finds out. When the behavior is potentially dangerous, however, she may believe that she has no choice, as Alaina recalled: "Once, oh, my gosh, I remember when we played one team, we got cursed at and things thrown at us and we had to literally—I think it was during an ice storm—have our umbrellas out like machetes, to poke them to keep them away from us until we got security to help us get out of there. It was terrible. It was frightening. I thought to myself, 'These fans are nuts.'"

Over the course of his career, a player becomes accustomed to the presence of hecklers during games, and he simply regards them as occupational hazards. He learns to tolerate unreasonable criticism, and he expects his wife to do the same. Wives find this disappointing, believing that their husbands fail to understand their position. It irritates some women that their husbands are trying to compare their own occupational situation to their wives' situation. "He feels I should just walk away, ignore it, because he would just think, 'Oh, Robyn, I hear that all the time. They're always calling me a bum,' and this and that," Robyn said. A woman may believe that her husband is insensitive to her feelings and critical of what he defines as her inappropriate behavior. He may reprimand her for letting the heckler "get to" her. If he displays a lack of concern, trivializes what occurred, or fails to support his wife and her response to stressful situations, it may upset her further.

ENCOUNTERING AUTOGRAPH SEEKERS

Awe-struck fans like to take advantage of public events to try to meet their favorite players, take "selfies" with them, ask for autographs on memorabilia, and so forth. Even if these events are scheduled, they can be an ordeal for players' wives, who are often shoved, jostled, elbowed, pinched, or squeezed by eager fans who are trying to interact with their husbands. Although a woman may have learned to "grin and bear it" in these public situations, she may find it impossible when fans treat her rudely and she can't extricate herself from the situation. Initially, she may try to altogether avoid autograph-seeking fans (the wives call them "autograph hounds") in various public situations. She may rely on a form of boundary work that Susan described as the "walking-ahead" strategy. "I will usually walk ahead," she said. "I typically won't stand around and wait. A lot of times, depending on the situation, Bill will do it on the move. He signs everybody's. But if you stand there, then you could be there forever."

I had an occasion to experience the walking-ahead strategy during my fieldwork. One hot summer night after a game, Olivia and I went to meet Lewis so we could all walk together to her SUV in the players' parking lot. As Lewis emerged from the visitor's clubhouse, fans seeking his autograph immediately surrounded him. Two of his teammates, who needed a ride, soon joined us. As we left the ballpark and walked to the player's parking lot, the eager fans followed us. Lewis led the procession with Olivia and I following close behind him. The two teammates were behind the three of us. In their attempt to maintain for us some distance from the fans, his teammates autographed memorabilia, first stopping to sign and then signing while they continued to walk. Even though this provided some space around us, I knew that if we stopped walking we would be hard pressed to disengage from the fans. Sure enough, as we reached the players' parking lot and found our way to Olivia's SUV, the fans immediately surrounded us and pressed us against the vehicle. I could that see that Olivia was upset, yet she tried to smile and appear friendly, maintaining her composure. Finally, one of the teammates distracted the fans long enough for us to get the door open and jump in. Lewis, who was also slightly alarmed, good-naturedly asked the fans to step back so he could get in the vehicle. They did, but they continued to hang around the vehicle as we slowly drove away. These types of situations allowed me to better understand the nature of the expectations and demands placed on the women and the issues they confront as they attempt to do all they can to support their husbands in this very public occupation.

If a wife's boundary work fails, she may step out of the way as the fans rush to greet her husband, trying to keep a manageable distance between her, her husband, and his fans. At times, she may abandon any effort at image work and express her disapproval verbally or nonverbally through facial expressions, tactful body language, or eye contact. "I will usually let them know I'm irritated," Marsha said. "I'm obnoxious about that. I'll say, 'Excuse me.' I couldn't care less how I look. If you're going to roll over me, who the hell are you? If you're that obnoxious, I couldn't care less." As in other situations, when a wife like Marsha loses her temper and her husband witnesses it or otherwise finds out, she may incur his disapproval or anger because he's uncomfortable with public displays of the "wrong" emotions. He may be more concerned with the feelings of his fans than his wife's feelings, and this can further upset her. If a woman gets angry with her husband in public, however, she may feel obliged to suppress it while trying not to appear submissive or passive when the opposite may be required, such as in situations with female groupies.

A husband's reluctance to confront overzealous fans and support his wife in these kinds of situations is a constant source of stress for some couples. Stacy talked about this issue. "I've been pen-marked, pushed, stepped on.... I just look at him and think, 'Why can't [he say], 'Excuse me, you're stepping on my wife. Do you think . . . she's nobody?' . . . But Dennis would never think of doing something like that. He'd be more apt to glare at me if I were to say, 'You're stepping on me,' or whatever I would tend to say. He'd look at me like, 'Stop it,' because he's upset at me. That's a real sore spot." If a wife is angry with her husband in a public situation, she will typically suppress it and wait to express it privately.

Despite a wife's feelings about adult autograph seekers, she will almost invariably help children who flock around her husband. These situations may be less about the necessity of image work and more about a sincere effort to support children who want autographs from their sport heroes, as Beth explained: "Sometimes, I'll stay there to help the smaller ones, or the ones that are shy. I push them along, or tell them to put it up there, or give it to Cliff, or say, 'Cliff, don't miss this one over here.'" In these situations, most players' wives refrain from almost any use of boundary work, although they screen out much older children who attempt to cash in on signed objects or baseball/football cards by trading or selling them for a profit, and this can involve direct confrontation. "There's this one kid who's always there every day. I think if he had a hundred bats of Cliff's . . . the kid would always want more," Beth said. "People like that really irritate me and I'm not very nice to them, either. I usually don't hold my tongue. I will say, 'Haven't you asked him already for enough things?' There comes a point in time where you don't have to be nice to those people anymore."

When a player realizes that autograph seekers are surrounding him, finding ways of disengaging from the situation isn't always easy. He may not be able to simply walk away, such as when it involves what Marsha called the "talkers." In these cases, he might rely on his wife to initiate a getaway strategy that will allow him to leave as politely as possible. But he may be reluctant to leave or his fans may try to keep him engaged, and in these cases he still needs her to initiate the disengagement process. Unfortunately for her, if fans realize that she's the reason he's leaving them, she may be perceived as the "bad guy."

The women I interviewed exhibited varying levels of image work, ranging from giving it a minimal effort to becoming totally absorbed. "I think that a lot of wives get carried away with the image of the wife," Rhonda said. "They take themselves and the responsibilities, or the unwritten codes, too seriously." But whether a wife takes image work too seriously or too lightly, she attempts to convey a standard of respectability.

Married to a Celebrity

During his career, a player may achieve local, national, or international celebrity. Even after he retires, his name and reputation may still have value, and he may endorse commercial products, participate in major fundraising events, broadcast games, or serve as a sport analyst. Fans continue to revere their sport heroes long after the players' careers are over, and their overt adulation doesn't necessarily diminish over time, as Alyssa observed. "I mean, they're old and they've been out of the game for thirty years, and these people act like they're some type of demigod or something," she said. "It's just crazy. So, you know, once a player always a player." Of course, the more famous he is, the more special treatment he receives. When we think of celebrities, we commonly focus on the advantages rather than the disadvantages, and we may even believe that the advantages will always outweigh the disadvantages. But star treatment can be a double-edged sword, especially for the players' wives.

The advantages to couples of the husband's fame range from exciting gifts like ocean cruises to simple perks in daily life. "At the cleaners they throw in that extra shirt for free," Naomi said. Donna explained, "When you go to the grocery store to buy meat, they'll save the best cut of meat for you. We can get limos at a discount. Whenever we have to go to the airport, we can just take a limo and people probably think, 'Gosh, they pay so much for this,' when we really can get it cheaper than anybody else."

Like Naomi and Donna, most wives appreciate these kinds of everyday perks, but because they know the special treatment can end at any moment, they try to avoid taking them for granted. Some couples, however, share what some MLB wives called a "big-league" attitude. This sense of entitlement involves having an inflated sense of self, trying to impress others, and expecting star treatment from others. Although this might sound like the spoiled athlete syndrome, in this case the husbands and wives share this tendency, believing that they have paid their dues, realized their dream, and are entitled to the advantages that come with the husband's career. A wife who has a big-league attitude tends to see herself primarily as a player's wife, shares her husband's identity in public life, and most likely married the professional athlete rather than the man.

Another advantage wives fully appreciate is "getting out of things." Marsha recalled an incident when she was late for a game and sped through the ballpark's main parking. After she parked her car and got out, she saw a police officer sitting in his car with the lights flashing. He asked her if she was a player's wife, and she said yes. "That's ingrained in me," she said. "I'm guilty of saying, 'I'm Glenn Doe's wife.' Rather than say, 'Marsha Doe.'" The officer let her go, saying, "We all have bad days." As we will see later, there may be consequences for wives who use the "wife of" identity in this way. Using or borrowing her husband's public identity may contradict a woman's need or ability to carve out an identity apart from her husband's public identity.

Like Marsha, a player's wife may grow accustomed to the benefits of her husband's status, but she also becomes aware of the many drawbacks. The women I interviewed were initially unprepared for the personal costs of their husband's fame. "For everything you get, there's a price you pay," Rhonda said. "You go somewhere and the manager of a restaurant will buy you dinner. But, by the same token, he comes over and he chitchats with you for a while, and then he asks for autographs for his seventeen nephews." As they learn about the strings attached to the husbands' stardom, wives recognize the ambiguous nature of celebrity. "You go to the grocery store and you get the best cut of meat, and then you go home and you find out you got traded to another team," Donna said.

Violation of trust is one of the most serious and troubling issues for a woman married to a professional athlete. She may be reluctant to trust or confide in others, including friends, neighbors, family members, and media representatives, because she fears being taken advantage of in some way. This happened to Skylar on more than one occasion:

> Well, there were situations in my life where people would initiate relationships with me and take me out to lunch and we'd get through the lunch, and really what they wanted was to see if they could get Carter to speak somewhere or get him to do a function for them. They were taking me out as a way to get two steps closer to him. I think that was probably the most painful thing about him being in the public eye, is that people would use me because they were trying to get to the person that they wanted to know.

In an effort to avoid being taken advantage of, a woman may try to anticipate and clearly understand what others want from her. "You know how much you're prepared to give, and where to draw the line," Rhonda explained. "If somebody says, 'I need seventy-two tickets for tomorrow night, is that okay?' You can say, 'Sure,' and then kick all the way home, or you can say, 'I'm sorry, but if you want four, no problem.' You have to be aware of the limitations and enforce them." Using boundary work to draw the line in this way can be more problematic with her husband or family than it is with the public. "With John Q Public or Joe Fan, I find it much easier to enforce the boundaries or draw the line," Rhonda said. "It's a vicious cycle. The more you give, the more people expect, and the boundaries are gone."

LIVING WITH QUASI-CELEBRITYHOOD

Professional athletes are regularly asked to make special appearances to promote specific activities or products or to attend events sponsored by sport organizations such as "fan day" or "family day," with or without their wives. These public events provide opportunities for fans, families, and children to meet the players. The players shake hands, have their pictures taken, and sign autographs. Apart from these types of events and scheduled game days, husbands are not always accessible to the public, and they take steps to guard their privacy.

Aside from these planned events, star-struck fans might define a player's wife as a substitute for her husband and treat her as the next best thing—a quasi-celebrity—and interact with her accordingly. If her husband is unavailable, strangers may be anxious to meet her, shake her hand, and talk to her, and they may ask for her autograph, request a photo with her, and so forth. Depending on the situation, some women might enjoy this attention. "Sometimes the limelight is fun," Stacy said. "It's not something I would want to live in all the time, but just to feel it once in a while is nice. It's fun to be named off to people and watch their reactions, and watch how different they treat you. I love to play games with that."

Strangers may ask a woman about her husband if he or the team is performing badly. Sometimes, however, that's not even the point. They may or may not be concerned about the team, the player, or the woman, but instead are interested only in being close to someone who is close to someone famous. On the other hand, if a player is sidelined with a serious injury or another issue that prevents him from playing the game, concerned fans may approach a player's wife to console her. Marsha said, "With Glenn's injury, I've had a lot of people that I've never seen in my life come up to me and wish him the best and say nice things, and I think that's nice. It means a lot, even though I don't know who they are and I'll never see them again in my life."

But in all these situations, the woman seems to be defined both as a substitute for and an extension of her husband. She may feel that she's on display and thus approachable, but she may resent being viewed only as a player's wife, which may result in conflicting feelings. She struggles with the belief that it's in her husband's best interest to engage in some form of image work, but she may detest being on public display as a physically attractive woman who is perceived as vain, superficial, or materialistic. In either case, she may be challenged to resolve this dilemma. It may become more complicated for her when, for example, her image work backfires. Believing that there is a great deal more to her than being a player's wife, she may wish to remain anonymous in public situations, and perhaps even become socially invisible. Social invisibility can allow her to accept the obligations and demands of public life without deep involvement in public roles, but it also can reap consequences.

Fans typically experience a "we" partnership with their favorite player or team (which is often expressed in absolutist attitudes such as "us against them") and, in their effort to identify with their favorite player or team, they may attempt to include a player's wife in this "we" experience. They may congratulate her for a win or for her husband's excellent performance, or they may complain and reprimand her for a loss or for her husband's abysmal performance. Without any prompting or encouragement, they may provide a detailed analysis of her husband's or his team's performance, whether or not either did well. Recalling an incident with the team's owner, Robyn said, "He'd walk through the wives waiting area and say, 'Good game, ladies.' Like we were the ones that did it. Or they say, 'What are you feeding that guy? Everything must be great at home. You must just be treating him like a king.'" In a situation like this, a wife might be led to believe that she's somehow responsible for her husband's excellent or poor performances. Situations like this reinforce her belief in subservience to her husband's needs and emphasize the place she has in her husband's career.

Some women may allow themselves to be viewed in this way because they believe they should support the fans' expectations of them as players' wives. Even if they don't accept this publicly held "we" partnership, the expectation that they will accept it can create another dilemma for them. As we have already seen, they do play a pivotal role in their husbands' ability to be successful. The emotional support and marriage work a player's wife provides affirms her belief in the "we" partnership. On the other hand, a woman may want to believe that the "we" partnership is specific only to her private relationship with her husband, and she may be reluctant to include public adulation as part of this partnership. She may resent the fans who individually or collectively identify with her husband in their version of a "we" partnership and who try to include her in it. For some wives, however, public or media interest can be important because her support is publicly validated or because she enjoys or feels entitled to the public attention her husband's fame provides. She may be flattered or surprised to learn that she's featured on television or a website or is the object of social media attention. But another wife considers such media attention as "weird." It makes her uncomfortable because she knows the only reason she's the focus of this media attention is because of her husband's reputation, rather than what she does or who she is.

ACCEPTING A SECONDHAND IDENTITY

Even though a wife may take the unwritten rules to heart in her effort to present a decidedly positive image to the public, she may feel constricted in public roles, and perhaps even trapped in them. She may be comfortable sharing her husband's public identity if it results in her inclusion in certain public events or social opportunities that may not otherwise be available to her, but even if she prefers not to claim the "wife of" identity, others may still define her as an extension of her husband's public identity and treat her accordingly, as Donna discovered: "It bothers me, but I have realized that there's nothing you can do about it, because that's how people identify you. People will ask, if you're at a certain function or at the stadium, 'Who are you? What's your name?' I'll say, 'Donna.' I've had people actually say, 'But who are you really?' Meaning, Donna Smith, Donna Jones, Donna Doe. 'Who do you belong to?' People say that all the time, 'Which player do you belong to?'"

Whether a wife prefers to share her husband's public identity or accepts it and resigns herself to the way things are or tries to make the best of it, she still makes an effort to convey the right wife face, to make the best possible impression, and to complement her husband by looking attractive. "I try to look as nice as I can, so if nothing else, they can remember me," Donna explained. "They will, at least, remember he has a really nice-looking wife, because they're not going to remember anything else. . . . It would be nice if people would stop to find out more about you, but if it doesn't happen—and it probably won't—there's nothing you can do."

Even if the public defines a wife as a quasi-celebrity, she may still be snubbed, ignored, or excluded. "Normally, I'd go to a party, and I'd have just as much fun talking and doing whatever as my date would. Whereas now that I'm married to him, you become a wallflower in your own way," Stacy confided.

When a wife is continually defined as an extension of her husband, it may adversely affect her self-esteem. She may resist this perception and try to establish her own identity apart from him. "It's important to me," Marsha said. "That's part of my self-confidence and my self-esteem—to know who I am." In her effort to do this, a wife may try to manage her own identity or, if desired or necessary, a public identity consistent with her husband's public identity through identity work.[8] "When I first got married, I did the baseball thing in winter league with Cliff," Beth confided. "I sat through every baseball game, even though he never played. But in spring training it was like all of a sudden I felt, 'Wait a minute. Who am I? I just feel like I'm not doing anything for myself, for who Beth is.' It was like I had to do an identity."

A woman's struggle to establish her own identity will often involve another type of identity work in which she seeks to establish her own sense of self in an occupational world that would rather ignore or exclude her and in a marriage where she may be primarily valued for contributions that support her husband's career. To be acknowledged as an individual, a woman may say and do things to get others to treat her as someone with her own identity. She's keenly aware of the widespread expectation that players' wives present themselves as "eye candy" at games and various civic events, fundraising/charity activities, and team functions. As Donna told me, "You're just there to look nice on his arm while you walk in." In this situation, a woman's identity work might include politely and with civility asserting her own identity when she's introduced, when she introduces herself, or during conversations with others. Emma

> This is the thing that I remember mostly, which really would irritate me: every time I was introduced, I was introduced as, "This is Mason's wife, Emma." The next time I saw anybody that I was introduced to, they would say, "Oh, hello Mrs. X." And they always said to me, "I don't remember your name. I just remember who you're married to."
> —EMMA

recalled one of the ways she used identity work: "I remember when we got married, because of that I never changed my name; I hyphened it because I felt like I didn't have an identity without having my name part of my married name. I remember when they would pass balls through our section, people wanted autographed balls with all the wives' names on it, I would never put Mrs. X; I would just put my name. I remember one time one of the wives saying to me, 'Well, they're not going to know who you're married to.' I said, 'I don't care.' . . . I thought, 'It doesn't matter to me if they know who I'm married to, that's the only reason why they want the ball, anyway.' So I never signed it with his name, I just signed it with my name."

Attempting to establish her own identity can be challenging and, at times, frustrating for a wife. Several of the women I interviewed had made the decision to focus on other areas of their lives and were able to establish an identity that was more relevant and fulfilling. Some focused their energy on their children, some developed friendships outside the husband's occupational world, and some pursued their own interests and participated in favored activities that didn't include the husband's team or the other wives on his team. Some maintained their distance from the other wives, and some avoided joining any of the wives' social circles. Such activities allowed these women to be defined as individuals rather than as extensions of their husbands. In this way, private life wasn't only a respite from their identity work in public life, but a haven for expressing their own identity as an essential part of self.

Identity work requires wives to construct their own personal identity as they cultivate their own friends, interests, and activities or to have their own careers or businesses. This isn't easily done in the sport marriage, given the demands of the career-dominated marriage. Before finding full-time employment, Beth decided to do volunteer work in her community. Being a "giver," as she described it, was rewarding in itself. Donna became a successful entrepreneur toward the end of Keith's NFL career. Unfortunately, establishing an identity apart from their husbands can be an insurmountable challenge.

In many public interactions, a husband may be reluctant to support his wife, and he may even exclude her in certain situations. If she feels angry with her husband for not supporting her right to be seen as an individual, she will suppress her feelings in public and bring the issue to his attention privately. Even if a woman is successful in her own occupational pursuits, her husband may not recognize her worth beyond her utility as his domestic partner. When Alyssa's local business community selected her for a prestigious award, she was invited to an evening banquet and ceremony, where she was to receive a plaque honoring her accomplishments. When she proudly and excitedly shared the good news with Douglas and asked him to attend the event with her, he was amazed to learn at the banquet that she was so well-known and respected. He had no idea that she was so active in their community, let alone that she had operated a thriving business.

As a wife gradually learns what it means to be in her husband's shadow, she may realize that it can be a blessing or a curse. She may prefer to live in her husband's shadow because it allows her to live a more "normal" life or because she's uncomfortable in public life and has no inclination to be in the spotlight or to interact with fans, strangers, or the public. She may believe that she doesn't deserve any attention. "It's a lot of work to put up a front, and it's not my front," Kellita said. "I didn't work hard for it, even though I helped him." Other wives may not appreciate living in their husbands' shadows. They want to be defined as distinct individuals. "I don't want to be in anybody's shadow, and I don't want anybody in my shadow. I like to be my own person," Susan said. Donna agreed: "Just basking in whatever success he might have and not really do anything for myself is not me. I enjoy the success he has, but that's not all there is. That's not my sole reason for being."

Wives may believe that they don't have a choice about whether to live in the husband's shadow; the choice has been made for them by the husband's highly visible occupation and by fans and the public. "It's not a situation that we have any control over," Rhonda confided. "Compared to his career, there's nothing that I will do, or am doing now, that will afford the public acclaim that he's getting. They're in the spotlight and so naturally his family is going to be in the shadow. But it's not that we choose to be."

BETH

Beth was raised in a large working-class New England family in a tranquil harbor town. As a child, she sat at home in her small living room and lost herself in the World Series and other televised MLB games, dreaming about an entirely different kind of life. Seeing the players' wives on camera, she imagined that they lived like movie stars and thought about how exciting their lives must be.

Beth was working in a department store and Cliff was in minor league baseball when they met and married. She knew it was only a matter of time until he realized his dream of making it big. They were both elated when he finally made it into MLB. As he struggled to establish his career, Beth did whatever she could to help him succeed. She went to great lengths to work on her public image when interacting with baseball fans. Sharing Cliff's celebrity in public life made her feel good about herself, and she was happy to be the "wife of." "I go home and people say, 'Well, I know you're married but what does your husband do?' So there's a point where I get to feel like I'm the star too, and gloat a little bit and say, 'Well, my husband plays with the (name of team).' You feel that you are part of it because you are married to him. So I think you get to share in his success because then they ask you questions about it. It's exciting."

It wasn't long, however, before Beth discovered that she had to work hard on her feelings at games and other public situations, even when she was disappointed in Cliff or his team. She tried to follow the unwritten rules, but slowly, over time, she grew weary of it all and began to question why she was doing what she was doing. She wanted Cliff to succeed as much as he did. Unfortunately, she felt psychologically and emotionally trapped. She believed that it was her duty to take care of him and she worried about letting him down, but she also wanted to focus more on herself and not feel guilty about it. Combined with the realization that Cliff might never establish a sustainable MLB career, she began to take more of an interest in other areas of her life. Bit by bit, she began doing things that were important to her and didn't always include Cliff or his fledging MLB career. Unlike many husbands in the sport marriage, Cliff supported her decision to establish her own career.

One night, Cliff got a call informing him that the team was letting him go and he was being sent back down to the minor leagues. "I came to the ballpark and I put on my happy smile," Beth said. "But deep down inside you're thinking, 'Dang it. Why us?'" Her childhood dreams were dashed. Cliff's success was all she had wanted for both of them, yet she realized that the reality of an MLB player's wife was much different from what she had imagined as a child, and that fame was fleeting.

As mentioned earlier, Beth was initially attracted to Cliff because of his promising MLB career. She had chosen him out of a profound hope born in an unfortunate childhood, and during the first study she was finally able to reconcile herself to this fact. When we talked during the second study, she told me that Cliff was deeply disappointed about that crucial career setback and similar setbacks that followed, but he gradually accepted them, retired, and transitioned into a successful coaching career in baseball. Beth continued to support him, but she eventually developed a fulfilling career of her own.

Guarding Private Life

After the season is finally over, couples look forward to the offseason with great anticipation, especially if the season was lengthened due to postseason playoffs or championship games. They look forward to having more freedom and some measure of privacy back. Many of the women shared Callie's sense of relief: "I remember, after each season, just having a big sigh of, 'Ah, we made it.' You know, we made it through another season and now we get some time together." As many wives discovered, however, their personal lives weren't always as private as they wanted them to be.

Interpretations of what distinguishes private life from public life are subjective and tend to vary based on a woman's attitude. Some player's wives live permanently in the city where their husbands' sport organization is located, while others maintain a residence in the team's city during the season and return home in a different city during the offseason. Privacy is always an issue, regardless of where the wives live, but they stand a much better chance of keeping their personal lives private during the offseason. "It's weird. During the season you're somebody and in the offseason you're not," Chloe said. Even when wives believe they should have more privacy because they live in a different city during the offseason, they know they can't always escape from public scrutiny. Nora discussed this reality as the "on" and "off" issue of private life: "I didn't have to be 'on.' I could go home and put on my sweat pants and watch TV and didn't have to work and dress the part. . . . So, for me, it was coming home. But there was still some level of expectation from

> A lot of people say they know you, or this or that, and you have no clue. People showing up at your house wanting something. People following you into the bathroom so they can ask you a favor of your husband. Being in public because everybody's staring at you. Coming up during dinner. It's just a fishbowl.
> —COURTNEY

the neighbors and friends in the community. You're the wife of a professional athlete. 'What kind of car is she driving? Oh, you aren't dressed so well today.' So there's definitely some need to be 'on' when technically you should be 'off.'"

Neighbors tend to be well aware of the sport family that lives in their neighborhood, and this may or may not concern a wife. "People drive by and look when I go out to the driveway in my robe in the morning to get the newspaper," Robyn said. "Every time somebody drives by, they stare at me." Gwen agreed, "They're watching you under a magnifying glass. They see everything we do."

Because these women tend to have less privacy during the season and learn to value it, they make an effort to keep their public life separate from their personal lives during the offseason, when they enjoy leaving seasonal pressures behind. Marsha felt lucky that she was able to go home during the offseason and relax into a more normal life. "I like to be a real person in the offseason," she said. "I like to just deal with my neighbors on that level. I don't want people coming up and saying, 'Wow.' I just don't like to deal with people at that level when we're outside of baseball."

Wives who remain in the city where the team is located may have less autonomy and privacy during the offseason, and these wives may be more guarded and less trusting. They are not as likely to reach out to others outside of the husband's sport organization. "Sometimes you think that people want to be friendly because of who you are," Kellita said. "So, in that instance, that's why my husband and I just stay to ourselves. Most of our friends are on the team because they're the most like you. You don't have any friends outside of anything else besides the team. You rely on them for their friendship and that's all that you know. That's the safest and most comfortable way to be."

A wife must work hard to maintain some semblance of stability in her family life while managing the spillover from her husband's occupation, including dealing with the many fans who believe that professional athletes should be accessible to them. Maintaining boundaries in her personal life can be a major challenge. "Maybe it's because I feel, sometimes, that people expect a lot out of me," Kellita said. Lisa realized that she had to be vigilant to maintain a lifestyle that didn't open the couple up to unwanted public interest or invasions of privacy: "He's more visible, and that means your marriage is under the microscope a little more than somebody else. So you try to be a little more on top of it."

The less private life a player's wife has, the more meaningful it becomes. Her experiences teach her that her personal life, and the lives of her children, may be invaded with impunity. When Brent was called up to the big leagues, a beat writer approached Rhonda after a game, and she answered what seemed to be harmless questions about their lives, assuming that their conversation would be confidential. A few days later, she was shocked when much of their conversation appeared in a feature story in a major daily newspaper. Another beat writer interviewed Pam and her husband Lucas and proceeded to tarnish his reputation as an NFL player by misquoting them in a newspaper article. As a result of these types of unpleasant media experiences, it's not surprising that these wives feel vulnerable. They are understandably reluctant to grant interviews with members of the media, particularly in light of how social media can be used. "You become less trusting, and you hate to think that you can't trust anybody, even your mother," Tanya said.

Most wives learn to manage the boundaries of their privacy in an effort to keep people away. "When it's the ballpark, you kind of owe it to them—it's your public," Marsha said. "But when it becomes my private time—no. That's where I draw the line."

A wife may equate privacy with security. The more privacy she has, the less vulnerable she feels, and the more control she has. Marsha described her feelings of vulnerability when she visited her permanent home without her husband during the season: "I think I'm more scared than anything else. Like when we moved into our house. The guy that did our walk-through . . . that was the first thing he told people, and people told us, 'Oh, he told us you're a ballplayer.' So it bothers me to a point, when I leave my home for six months empty. I go back and forth, and visit the home, and check on it. I'm alone when I do go home. So it's scary in that way. I don't want people to know that our house is left empty, and when I'm there I'm by myself." Other people may experience similar feelings of vulnerability in their lives, but because a player's seasonal schedule is required to be public knowledge, the risk of intrusions is relatively greater.

Given social media and today's 24/7 news cycle, persistent and uninvited media scrutiny into off-the-field activities of professional athletes and their families is a constant source of stress, partly because it can provide sensationalist fodder for public consumption that could ruin the lives of all involved. Onlookers can completely misinterpret even an innocuous action, leading to a public scandal. Skylar recalled such an incident: "You know, there was a picture that they took with someone and they got it put on Facebook, and then the wife was so upset because it was like, 'Who is this woman, your wife?'"

Players' wives believe that dining out with their families should be respected as a private occasion, but many people incorrectly assume that because a player is in a public setting, he's open to a friendly greeting and available for conversation. Strangers regularly stop at their table—sometimes presuming familiarity—and flatter the husband, pat him on the back, or shake his hand. A wife like Kaylee, a participant in the second group, typically becomes uncomfortable or even annoyed with such behavior:

> It's an interruption upon our time, because usually when we went out we were going out to eat dinner or whatever, so it just seemed like it always took so much longer. And there I was, trying to keep the kids happy and quiet and they didn't always understand. I can remember my oldest son when he said, "Why does everybody think Daddy's so great?" I said, "Well, because he can put a ball in a hoop so, you know, that's just how it is." He just didn't really understand it, but I could see a little bit of resentment in why can't we just go somewhere and just be able to do something without everybody bothering us.

The women normally define this kind of fan behavior as rude, but many will suppress their anger and present a wife face to mask their annoyance. If this fails, they will attempt to put an end to the inconvenient interruption or the excessive attention given to the husband, which is what Nora often did when she tried to resolve these situations. "Maybe somebody hangs around too long, or they're invading your privacy, and the only thing I could do is turn my head and roll my eyes and say, 'Okay, it's time for you to go now.' I was never intentionally rude, but because family time was so minimal, I wanted my husband to myself." Most women, such as Rhonda, resigned themselves to the realities of public life. "It's irritating, but in my mind you just make the best of it because it's part of the job," she said.

In these and other "fishbowl" situations, it isn't unusual for a wife to feel uncomfortable when people stare at her in public, which typically happens when dining out. "They're looking at you to see what it is you're eating," Donna explained. "Are you picking up the right fork? Are you drinking the right wine with whatever it is you're eating? You just feel that somebody is staring at you through the whole thing. Or every time you look up, there's somebody looking right at you." These unwanted intrusions may not occur every time the family dines out, but they can be irritating when they do.

When guarding against privacy intrusions, a wife is understandably protective of her husband and children. During the NFL season, Tuesdays are "family days" or rest days because it's the husband's only day off. When the neighborhood children drop by to visit with the husband or to play with their children, a wife most likely will run interference and try to intercept the children before they wake or disturb her snoozing husband, and he may depend on her to do this. Marsha used boundary work to protect her own privacy on Glenn's days off. "When we're in our winter home, I don't really want to be bothered," she explained. "When Glenn's working on the yard, he's usually got kids around him. If the kids see him, they'll usually come over. That's good for his ego, that's fine, but don't bother me. When I'm home, I'm home. That's my limit."

Adapting to Exclusion

A player's wife may agree with fans and others that her husband deserves recognition for his athletic talent and achievements, especially if his team is winning. She also may believe that the star treatment he receives can be excessive and lacks proportion to other areas of their lives. She may arrive at the conclusion that he receives more public adulation than he deserves and, whether she married the professional athlete or the man, she may begin to feel jealous or resentful.

A wife's outsider status is apparent not only in public life, which may be assumed, but also in private life, which may not be expected. She's ignored and even snubbed in public situations where her husband is given the star treatment. Neighbors, fans, friends, sport organizations, and many others may purposely or inadvertently exclude her. Her husband may be oblivious to her plight or he may expect her to be his number one fan, which only makes matters worse for her. It was hard for these women to accept that their husbands were unwilling or unable to give them the same support and understanding they offered to their partners, and it left them perturbed or indignant. Nora's husband, Wyatt, for example, had a habit of ignoring her in public. "There would be a game or an event where there were fans and the families also were there, and we would be together as a family, and he would turn his back and, basically, I was overshadowed by him,

> Someone actually asked me if my husband is a normal man! "Does he come home and eat baloney sandwiches, and sit on the couch?" Baloney sandwiches? He lives on baloney sandwiches just as well as anybody else. Who do you think he is? He's not God. He's not someone that does something so much different than you do.
> —TRACEE

he just turned his back to me and that bothered me the most. . . . You're not asking to be involved or have the spotlight to be turned on you, you're just asking to have love and respect, and so it's hurtful when you don't get that." Although his dismissive gesture angered Nora, she suppressed the anger. "I would just put on a smile," she said. After Dennis's team won the World Series, in which Dennis was one of the heroes, the neighbors who lived next door to their permanent residence held a party in his honor. Stacy thought it would be a great opportunity to become more acquainted with them, but when she saw that the invitation was addressed to Dennis only, she knew it would be a challenge. "From the second we entered that door, it was almost like an autograph-signing session," she said. "I was pushed back as people surrounded him. They brought out their kids' cards, and balls, and their hats for him to sign. They wanted Dennis to tell stories about the World Series, and they were just real wrapped up in pretty much everything, men and women, both alike. It was pretty horrifying. The whole atmosphere amazed me." After they returned home from the party, Stacy could no longer suppress her feelings or restrain herself, and she expressed her frustration to Dennis, who had done little to discourage their attention. His attitude wasn't what she hoped for, although his less-than-supportive response didn't surprise her. They argued, and Dennis finally understood that she simply wanted him to acknowledge that the star treatment was excessive and that she had been totally excluded.

We've already learned that a wife may resent being included in the "we" partnership her husband's fans expect to see, but she also may resent it when they don't acknowledge certain aspects of the "we" partnership between her and her husband. She may become irritated if fans take for granted the domestic and emotional support she gives that makes his career possible. "A big disadvantage is not being part of the 'we' that you think there is in the public eye," Chloe said. "I swear they think that every ballplayer is single. If you're in a crowd, you're pushed aside. I think the big disadvantage is that he's a celebrity. People think that he owes them something. They just don't consider that this man is human."

As suggested in chapter 1, in spite of the sport organizations' expectation that wives will do everything they can to support their husbands, the organization may exclude them or treat them as outsiders. For example, one NFL team prefers to introduce the cheerleaders instead of the wives alongside the players at certain team functions. Most wives understand that this is only for the sake of public appearances, but other wives regard it as offensive. Lisa describes this team's attempt to promote a glamorized or sexualized version of the "wifely" role at team functions, where the wives are displaced as the traditional spouse in favor of the "fleshy" spouse: "I'll tell you what makes us madder, though, is when the sport organization would have a function, and they'd bring the cheerleaders in and introduce them with our husbands, and not say a word about the wives sitting there. They couldn't even say, 'And this is the table of the wives,' or something like that.... The cheerleaders would do things like come up to you, and when someone wants to take pictures they'll ask you to move so they can sit next to your husband." The wives are on public display but socially invisible and the cheerleaders are given the roles that wives would customarily perform. "People want to see flesh," Lisa said. "So bring out some of the cheerleaders."

Because a wife enjoys certain privileges or perks, she may assume that she will be included in the many social opportunities her husband is urged to attend, such as prestigious social events, community fundraising drives, celebrity golf tournaments, or entertainment galas, but if her assumptions are incorrect, she may become jealous of his fame and resent her lack of inclusion in these social opportunities because she's "just the wife."

The star treatment a husband receives can become a source of tension in the sport marriage. Although a wife may suppress her anger at fans in public situations, this emotion work[9] may be a short-term solution to a deep-seated relational issue, as Stacy noted:

> It causes a lot of tension when I disagree with how people are acting and voice my disagreement. Sometimes I suppress it, and when I suppress it that's bad, too, because then I just get angry at other things going on with us. But even when I voice it, and he disagrees with me voicing it, either to the person or later to him, he'll complain about me voicing it a lot of times and say, "Why are you yelling at me about it? I didn't do anything wrong." When, really, I'm not yelling at him about it. This comes up constantly.

Stacy's need to discuss the fans' behavior with Dennis may be an attempt to manage her irritation, and his reluctance to engage with her can cause her to shift her resentment to him.

If a wife is resentful, jealous, or feels excluded, it may be because her husband neglects her and their children in favor of his career and the fans that adore him. He may take his wife for granted, believing that he doesn't need her attention and that she may not need his. She may understand his need for fame or the "game" but miss his presence in her life. Rhonda fought with her feelings around this reality:

I'm jealous of the time that he allots to his career, and his fans, and other people. But that's tied into the resentment of not being given equal treatment, equal time, equal devotion. One of the things that I like so much about him is that when we first met, and we were dating, he is the nicest guy to Joe Blow. He would do anything for you. But when you get in his inner circle, you get dumped on, because he's so busy being nice to his fans and to everybody else that there's nothing left for you.

CHAPTER 3

Traveling with the Team

STACY

When Stacy married Dennis, she wasn't working outside the home and the couple had not started a family. Dennis's team was one of the few that allowed wives to frequently travel with the players and had a policy of covering expenses for families. Even so, Dennis was a bit taken aback when Stacy said she wanted to travel with him for the entire season. She was a woman who exuded an air of quiet strength and confidence, and it was easy to believe that she could accomplish anything that mattered most to her. After a lengthy discussion in which she explained to Dennis that she wanted to spend as much time as possible with him, he agreed to her plan.

Unknown to Dennis, Stacy had another reason for wanting to travel with him: to reduce her anxiety. She was aware of the temptations that existed for professional athletes, and her husband's budding MLB fame had gradually made her insecure about his ability to remain faithful to her. He had never given her any reason to question him, but she decided that she would rather not put him to the test.

Stacy knew from the beginning that her presence on the planes and buses and in the hotels would be awkward. Even before embarking on the first trip, she knew that there was an implied code of conduct for traveling wives. Even though she didn't like or agree with the code, she learned to bite her tongue and suppress what she really thought and felt. Although it sometimes took tremendous willpower, she tried to ignore the flirtatious interactions among the players and the flight attendants on the chartered flights. She knew that the single players dated these women, and she often heard rumors about affairs between married men and flight attendants. It was an uncomfortable reminder that Dennis may not be immune to their advances.

Stacy's resolve to have a strong marriage and support her husband's career aspirations enabled her to confront the numerous issues and situations that emerged while she was on the road with his team throughout the years, but she also learned just how much of her own personality she had to alter in order to fit in and how stressful it could be to be continually on the alert to ensure that she did the "right" thing.

The four major professional team sports have travel schedules, but some teams travel much more than others; for instance, NBA and NHL teams travel more than NFL teams, and MLB teams have the most grueling travel schedule.[1] Because the MLB season is so long and players are usually away from their families for six months or more, some MLB wives have a desire to occasionally or regularly travel with the team. This chapter focuses on their experiences. Some MLB teams may restrict or actively discourage this practice, and this is perhaps understandable given the nature of organizational dominance. Individual sport organizations establish their own policies regarding when and how wives are allowed to travel with the team, and most husbands won't challenge the established policy.[2]

Teams that allow wives to travel with the ball club may do so because they believe that the wives are a source of stability for the players, making them more productive on the field. They also may believe that the presence of wives discourages or limits the players' extramarital activities on the road and thus maximizes their ability to focus on the game. "It's the thought that if they have their wives with them, they know where they are," Emma said. "They're not going to be screwing around—they're in the hotel. You know, they're not out way past hours out on the road, basically in cabs, at other bars. They have an eye on them." On the other hand, they may believe that wives belong at home and therefore discourage them from traveling with the team. Some husbands consider the road to be a different and separate life, one that doesn't mix with wives and families.

A wife may decide not to travel with her husband if she believes that it's in the best interest of his career. She may not want to be a distraction, and she doesn't want to be responsible if he fails in some way.

Whatever the case may be, those wives who travel with their husbands rarely do so for the entire season. They may join their husbands for special games during the MLB postseason, such as the World Series, or for special "family trips." Emma was an exception; she joined her husband at a moment's notice whenever he invited her. "Mason would call me and say, 'Hey, I want you to come out,' so I would get on the plane and, literally, in a couple hours be there. I was constantly traveling with him, constantly at every city, constantly at the spur of the moment. In fact, the guys used to say, 'Get her a uniform.'"

Code of Conduct

Inherent in the unwritten rulebook for MLB wives is a code of conduct specifically for road trips. Nearly all the MLB wives I interviewed knew something about this code, and wives in other occupational worlds may have to follow similar rules if they travel with their husbands' teams. Shared beliefs shape the code, which defines acceptable behavior and includes the expectation that the wives will display compliance in interactions with the men on the team. It also supports the imperative to preserve organizational dominance.

Wives who violate the code are predictably reprimanded in some manner. Emma explained how this can occur: "If you did anything to disrupt what happened on the road, or you said anything, it would affect the whole team. You would not be

> We always talk about the unwritten rulebook of being a baseball wife. . . . There's these unwritten rules that you just do and don't do. That's why everybody thinks that every wife should have to go into the minor league system. Wives that marry straight into the big leagues, we're like, "Oh, she didn't get the unwritten rulebook of being a baseball wife."
> —MARSHA

allowed to go on the road anymore; not just you, the wives would not be allowed to go anymore. You would be banned from traveling with the team and banned from hotel bars. So you just didn't do that." Teammates (and husbands) negotiate and enforce the code, and it includes various strategies for excluding the wives or keeping them under control. In an effort to avoid jeopardizing her husband's standing among his teammates, a traveling wife will strive to conform to the code by carefully monitoring and managing her behavior through code work.[3] Both men and women are capable of using code work; the wives use it to follow the road-trip rules, and the teammates use it to enforce them. Within the MLB world, code work is highly influential in structuring gender relations among traveling wives, their husbands, and their teammates.

A wife who travels on road trips is essentially a "stranger."[4] In certain road-trip situations, she's socially invisible, and the expectation is that she will subordinate herself in interactions with the men on the team. Despite the situational pressure to be one of the guys, which we will discuss later, she must present the image of compliant femininity—the "good girl"—in her appearance and behavior. She should refrain from flirtatious behavior or becoming a distraction to the men, and using offensive language while in the company of teammates. Stacy confided: "I would say I'm less apt to cuss in a group like that than I would be with good friends or with Dennis." As they learn to deal with the code, the wives find themselves conforming to male beliefs about female behavior by relentlessly monitoring themselves. When they comply with it, they reinforce their subordination.

So why would a wife want to travel with her husband and follow the code? She may feel lonely and isolated while her husband is away. Also, traveling provides opportunities to visit new cities, sightsee, shop, socialize, dine out in trendy restaurants, and visit with friends and family, activities that are less available to her when she's at home. Or she may simply miss the man she loves. As Stacy's story illustrates, she may not completely trust her husband to remain faithful. A wife is more likely to travel with her husband when they are younger or if they don't have children, in which case she has a greater tendency to make her husband's occupational world her own and become much more involved in it. A rookie wife is more aware of the need to follow the code of conduct, and her husband has more anxiety about her ability to follow it. If her husband has a long career and the couple has children, it's typical for her to weary of the burdens of traveling with the men and decide to travel less or not at all.

A traveling wife soon becomes even more aware of an implicit competition for loyalty between the team and the marriage and how often her husband sides with his team. One distressing characteristic of this competition is that marital infidelity on the part of the men is tolerated or may even be encouraged among certain teammates.

The culture of infidelity can lead teammates to fear gossip among the wives, so a wife who travels with the team all season might feel uncomfortable if she's seen hanging out with the other wives who are also traveling with the ball club. Teammates may try to enforce the code by frowning or may more directly exclude a wife if it appears that she's gossiping. This type of male exclusion may lead a wife to avoid joining with the other wives because of her fear that she won't be allowed to travel with her husband on future road trips or that she might jeopardize his standing on the team. In so doing, she avoids solidarity with the other wives, who otherwise might reinforce her right to be there.

A woman may not wish to know about her husband's activities on road trips, believing that "ignorance is bliss." In this case, she may choose to stay home in an attempt to avoid learning from another traveling wife that married players are having affairs on the road,[5] and this allows her to manage her fear that her husband will be unfaithful while the couple is separated. "I do believe him when he looks me in the eye and says, 'I've been faithful to you all of our marriage,' but there's no way to a hundred percent know that, because you can't be with somebody 24/7," Skylar confided. "You also can't live constantly fearful that he's going to go on the road and something bad is going to happen."

Whether or not a wife chooses to travel, the ramifications of the code provide us with a lens through which we can examine female conformity to male dominance in the context of institutionalized infidelity. As an indication of the organizational dominance discussed in chapter 1, organizational management may seem to condone the extramarital activities of certain husbands on road trips and thus participate in the institutionalization of infidelity. Skylar shared a relevant story with me: "I had a very good friend at one time that worked for a pretty large hotel chain, and she said it really bothered her because when we came into town, or when players came into town, the traveling secretary would call and he would request certain rooms for certain players. So it took her a while to even trust Carter wasn't running around on me, because married players stayed on one floor, single players stayed on another, people that were having affairs stayed here, and the traveling secretary handled all that."

ON PLANES AND BUSES

Paradoxically, group travel on a plane or a bus, where individuals share both physical and social closeness,[6] can actually magnify a wife's social invisibility and heighten her feelings of exclusion. In this and other road-trip situations, the men and flight attendants often treat her as a nonperson.[7] Seating on planes commonly is arranged or assigned according to a hierarchy, although the specifics vary from team to team, as Skylar explained: "There was always a way in which the plane was organized and where everyone sat. So you usually had the head coaches and media in the front. In the middle were the married players or rookies, and then in the back would be the guys whose wives didn't come or the guys who were veteran players." The back of the plane is regarded as a safe region[8] for teammate interaction, and unless a wife is invited or married to a veteran of long standing, she isn't allowed there. From a wife's perspective, it's comparable to the clubhouse or locker room; it's an exclusive male region and it has certain boundaries that define, protect, and isolate teammate interaction. The teammates may even regard other men, such as beat writers and coaches, as intruders. Not all teams enforce this in-flight part of the code, and teammates may not always enforce it individually, but to be on the safe side, traveling wives prefer to stay in the front of the plane. "Basically, you knew that when you got on the plane, you were going to be towards the front, you and your husband, and that's where you stay," Beth said. Based on her traveling experiences, Emma would agree: "I would sit in my seat. If they wanted to chat with me, they would come up and chat with me. If they were sitting back there playing cards or something, I would never interrupt. I would never just go and sit with the guys. That would be stupid." When a wife needs to use the restroom at the back of the plane, she tries to avoid eye contact as she walks down the aisle, staring at her destination and attempting not to look from side to side. "I do that because they pick on me," Olivia said. "I figure if I don't look at them, and don't give them anything, they won't say anything to me. But they do anyway." As Emma and Olivia mention, when it favors the men, teammates may undermine a wife's efforts to follow the code in certain situations. This can occur when the men initiate a conversation with a wife and then quickly exclude her from further conversation.

The importance of this part of the code varies with each ball club, so a woman often takes cues from her husband in deciding when it's appropriate to sit in the back of the plane. In the end, however, the burden is on the wives to become aware of the code; even though a husband supports his wife in learning it, she's ultimately responsible for fully complying with it. On some teams, the exclusionary practices may be minimal and a wife may feel free to hang out in the back of the plane and not feel like she has to avoid the interaction among the teammates. "I don't feel like I couldn't go back there if I wanted to. I just don't want to," Sheila said. "I mean, I've gone and hung over the card game and said, 'How's it going? Who's winning?' and things like that. But it's boring." Not all traveling wives followed this part of the code in all in-flight situations: "Well, they know we're supposed to," Emma said. "But I didn't. I mean, I wouldn't intentionally avoid their eyes. . . . If I saw that they were flirting with a stewardess or something, I wouldn't look."

Some traveling wives thought it best to avoid the back of the plane on general principle because they preferred to avoid creating any problems that could affect the husband's standing among his teammates. "For me, it wasn't so much that I wasn't allowed to, but I really didn't want to go back there, because I didn't want to cause a problem," Skylar said. "I just looked at it as 'this is business,' and so I would prefer to use the restroom in the front because I didn't really want to go to the back of the plane where it was just filled with guys. You know? Just wasn't my thing."

When a wife tries to fit in and follow the code in most situations and she's comfortable with the in-flight situation, she may make an effort to get along with the men on the team even when they are in the air. Robyn believes that interacting with the men is necessary, and she won't purposely avoid it. "I just talk with everybody, especially if I was friends with the guys," Robyn said. "If there were some guys I didn't know very well, I wouldn't say anything. But I wouldn't not look at them. I mean, I figure I'm on the plane too. If I want to go by there and use the bathroom, then I can look at them, for crying out loud." When teammates are discussing certain "hot" topics, such as trade talks, however, teammates exclude outsiders and wives diligently avoid the area. Robyn said that sometimes when she walks toward the back of the plane "they all shut up." Sheila avoided contact with the men in these circumstances because it felt awkward to her. "There was one flight where I don't remember what had happened. They were really upset about something. And they all gathered in the back and it was like all this bad language flying around, and f-this and f-that, and not that I'm such a prude that I've never heard that before, but I don't really want them to know that I'm hearing it. You know what I mean? Not that you could help but hear it, but I don't want to be like standing around listening. I mean, that makes me uncomfortable."

While traveling, wives may be reluctant to initiate or participate in a conversation with the teammates unless they are spoken to first. Stacy told me that she tried to be receptive to the men's nonverbal signals in deciding when to engage in conversation or initiate interaction. Like most wives, Beth waited for an invitation in the form of a teammate's smile or comment directed toward her. Still, teammates may attempt to enforce this part of the code by giving a wife a glaring look of disapproval, as if to remind her of the code or to discourage interaction or conversation.

Most flight attendants also treat traveling wives as outsiders or intruders on charter flights. Flight attendants can be territorial and possessive in their use of boundary work to let the wives know their place, and they may resent the wives because they are in the way. Robyn shared with me some of her experiences with flight attendants:

> When the wives are on the plane, we get the worst service from the flight attendants, and they're bitchy to us because we're on the plane invading their time with our guys. It's like they have this little relationship with the players, and when we're around they can't have that same relationship with them because they are our husbands. You'd ask for something, and they would slam the Pepsi down on your tray, or slide your dinner over to you. Just a couple would do this, but enough to where other wives are noticing it and saying, "Hey, she's got a bee in her butt."

Sheila pointed out that it's galling to wives when the men treat their wives as outsiders and the flight attendants as insiders:

> Sometimes they're pretty snotty to the wives. I think that they're looking forward to having the team on the flight, and then when they show up with all these wives, they just don't think it's going to be as much fun. I don't know why unless—I mean, a lot of guys have slept with flight attendants. Maybe some of them have in mind they're going to get a date with one of them or something, and I don't think they care if they're married. I know of three or four instances where guys have been caught by their wives and the girl was a flight attendant, and he met her on a team flight. I don't think the wives have any particular animosity towards flight attendants. It's just that they're real snippy. Sometimes they're very nice. But they'll ask your husband twenty times, "Can I get you anything?" But then if you ask for something they'll say, "Just a minute."

Flight attendants and traveling wives interpret their femininity differently. In this and other road-trip situations, as part of the code of conduct that expects *muted femininity*,[9] a traveling wife will minimize aspects of her femininity, but a flight attendant will emphasize desirable feminine qualities, allowing her to perform a more provocative role. Flight attendants may encourage the men's flirtatious behavior by exchanging the latest jokes and other intimate banter, and some of the men willingly respond and hook up with a flight attendant after landing. (Flight attendants who develop sexual relationships with married or single teammates could be classified as *visible groupies*. See chapter 6.)

Another part of the code for traveling wives involves a process I came to think of as *mood sharing*,[10] which is also applicable in the private lives of these couples. On planes and buses, mood sharing is a collective expectation and experience. Depending on how the team is doing, a wide range of strong emotions—from excitement to despair—are commonly expressed in various forms of mood sharing in road-trip situations. The brotherhood of teammates sets the prevailing mood, and everyone is expected to be sensitive to it. Players' wives are aware that in this instance, code enforcement should be left up to the husbands, teammates, or coaching staff, and not the wives. The code tells a wife how she should feel, which emotions she should and shouldn't express, and when she's expected to express the "right" emotions to fit in with the team.

Travel is normally comfortable and enjoyable when the team is winning, but if the ball club loses a close or decisive game, the mood on the plane or bus is melancholy and subdued, and a wife uses some form of code work to share in the mood. "It's like a death in the family, because everybody's in mourning," Marsha explained. "You need to be upset, and you have to show that you're upset, at the loss." When the team is in the doldrums, which is undoubtedly the result of a losing streak or a bad slump, tension and stress permeate the plane or bus. In these cases, teammates expect the wives to share in expressing the appropriate emotion. Stacy talked about a road trip she had recently returned from:

> Losing four in a row in one city—right there, it puts a lot of stress on the team. When they're down, like on buses and planes, you're really supposed to show your disappointment. So I have to go along with that too. If you have a funny story to tell your husband, you can't tell it and laugh. If you're going to be on that bus as a wife, especially with our team, because we travel with them on the same bus, you don't start talking to other wives. At least I don't. There are a couple that I've seen do it, and I get embarrassed, because I think to myself, "Oh, no, these female voices. These guys are pissed off, and here they are jabbering about what they bought." And I just cringe, because I think, "Oh, this will be the last trip we get to go on." So I'm real conscious of that and I get nervous.

Sheila recalled a specific incident when she was encouraged to be a mood sharer on the bus after Frank's team lost a crucial game:

> One time I was on a trip with the team—of course you were allowed to travel any time you wanted with the team—and several wives were on this trip and we had just gotten our brains beat out in one city, and something happened on the bus. It was so funny. A couple of us were just cracking up, and one of the coaches turned around and said, "In case you girls didn't notice, we just lost three games in a row." I was like, "Oh." But, I mean, it was still funny. I couldn't help it. I know you're not supposed to do that. But it was just something that was so funny. I thought, "Lighten up." But that's how it is. Whenever we have our family trip everybody says, "Gosh, I hope they win so we can have some fun." Because it's not fun if they don't win.

This type of code busting can result in repercussions that could adversely affect a husband, so wives take the code seriously.

It's important for wives to accurately understand how the teammates are defining a mood-prevailing situation. The collective tension on the plane or bus can shift from a solemn mood to a much lighter mood through the emotional efforts of a team leader, star player, or well-respected veteran who tries to inspire his teammates. Dana described one such incident: "We'd lose, we'd be swept, or we lose two games in a row, and we might fall behind in the standings, and it was just sort of gloomy among the players. And then, all of a sudden, Lucas would holler, 'Hey, I thought we were all still alive, man! We can come back from this!' And it was breaking the mood and everybody started laughing." Wives are undoubtedly relieved when these somber moods are lightened with humor. This antidote often occurs when the teammates tell each other that it wasn't anyone's fault that they lost the game (although it may well have been), and this is often achieved when they joke and laugh with one another about the game. Again, however, it's the teammates and not the wives who are the mood breakers.

Even though the overall mood is lightened in this way, or the team just won a critical game, wives also must be sensitive to other types of job-related stress that permeate the atmosphere. A key teammate may be struggling with inferior pitching or hitting, or teammates may be exchanging trade rumors or opinions about team politics, and these kinds of issues can cause mood swings or dampen spirits.

IN HOTEL BARS AND NIGHTSPOTS

One part of the code of conduct applies to bars in the hotels where the teams stay and other nightspots in the city, and learning about this part of the code can be a complex process for wives. Husbands typically initiate their learning by explaining this part of the code in advance. In Marsha's case, however, it began with her first encounter:

> Our first year up, we stayed at this one hotel. When the guys get called up, that's where you stay. I remember walking into the bar with Glenn to get a drink, and we went to sit down and Glenn looked around and, all of a sudden, he saw a couple of coaches and players. He grabbed the drinks and said, "Let's go." I said, "Well, I thought we were going to have a drink?" He said, "Well, we'll go have them on the patio by the pool." He was so quick to get out of there. I mean, he went white. Sure enough, we went out to the patio and I said, "Why?" He said, "Because I don't think we're supposed to be in there." I thought, "Well, that's ridiculous." That's when it first started for me.

One might assume that teammates hang out in the hotel bar to bond with teammates, unwind from traveling, relax from the pressures of the game, and talk about personal or occupational issues. This may be the case, but it's expected that wives will stay out of the hotel bar, which is also a public place for the men to meet other women. It's common knowledge among teammates and wives that female partners, girlfriends, sex workers, and female groupies hang out in these bars for the purpose of meeting or hooking up with the men on the team. "We're not supposed to go in certain hotel bars because that's where the guys that are married—that don't have their wives with them—are going to be with the groupies, or whatever," Marsha confided. "It's like a groupie hangout. So you don't have the wives in there."

> They tell us when we can go with them on the road, and then they tell us they have all these ground rules. We were not allowed to go in hotel bars. You know, "You can't go in there." Oh, that used to drive me nuts! I hated that.
> —ROBYN

Although this part of the code also varies from team to team and may not exist on some teams, the MLB wives in the second group said it still exists today. It may not be strictly enforced if the husband is an influential veteran or star. On some teams, wives are not even allowed in the hotel lobby. Marsha recalled this rule: "You know, now that I think about it, we're not really supposed to be in the lobby too much. Just in case there's, you know, running into each other in the lobby."

Among some couples, like Stacy and Dennis, this is a crucial dimension of the code. It exists because many unfaithful husbands are indiscreet about their on-the-road sexual activities. As Sheila observed, "I've found that most men end up not being very discreet. They just think no one's going to notice or no one's going to catch them, and they end up getting caught every time." It's an attempt to define the boundaries of exclusion, based on the premise that if a wife sees an unfaithful husband with another woman, she may tell others—even the player's wife—what she has seen. To comply, a wife tends to walk straight from the elevator to the street without lingering near the entrance of the bar. As Sheila said, "You don't even look in there." Women like Sheila know that they are expected to blend in with the surroundings, avoid suspicious definitions of innocent situations, avoid loose talk, and embody a reputation for being "cool." In these and other ways, the wives become conspirators in the sexual escapades of these men—or in keeping other secrets—even though they strongly disagree with and disapprove of their extramarital or sexual activities.

It's also a common practice for an unfaithful husband to meet his female partner away from the hotel bar, or to hook up with other women in the various bars and hangouts he frequents in the cities scattered along the road-trip circuits, so husbands also will tell their wives that they must stay out of specific bars, restaurants, clubs, theaters, or nightspots. This also applies during spring training. Not all wives felt annoyed by this part of the code, but it irritated Marsha: "I always thought, 'This is the most ridiculous thing I've ever heard.' You know? Oh, I get infuriated because I think if . . . they're doing something they shouldn't be, then that's their problem, not mine."

Team veterans initiate and enforce the expected code work for traveling wives, and the restrictions are handed down to teammates from season to season, who in turn pass it along to their wives. As we have seen, the specifics of the code and commitment to enforcing it varies from team to team, husband to husband, husband to wife, and wife to wife, but the code itself always serves the men.

It isn't only the influential and unfaithful husbands on the team who establish and perpetuate this part of the code, but faithful husbands as well. They have too much at stake to challenge it. Regardless of who establishes it, if enough teammates are involved in its creation and enforcement, it will continue. Some wives believe that this dimension of the code only exists because the wives allow it to exist, and these wives are often critical of the wives who comply, believing that they make the other wives "look bad." They believe that following the code implies a denial of the basis for it.

Guardians of the Code

The code has several implications for a player's wife. What does she do if she accidently sees a husband with another woman and he notices that she sees him? This ordinarily occurs near the hotel where the team is staying, and more than one wife has found herself in this predicament. Depending on the wife and her husband's shared understanding of this part of the code and whether she's with her husband, her first line of defense is to ignore the straying husband. This may not be a self-defined requirement for most wives, but it's normally a wife's initial response. In this awkward situation, she relies on her social invisibility. If she sees him before he sees her, she will look away before he catches her looking at him, hoping that he will think that she didn't see him. If she sees that he sees her first, she will quickly look in the opposite direction or pretend that she didn't see him. Such efforts are often pointless when an unfaithful husband recognizes her. She's defined as a threat even if she keeps his secret and maintains her silence.

Attempting to manage social invisibility in these uncomfortable encounters is fairly common for most wives. They may feel trapped and intimidated. "I wouldn't say anything because Tyler would make me leave," Robyn said. "So I'd pretend I didn't see him." Sheila recalled a very unsettling incident:

> There was also a guy in one city. He was just there for one year. He had this girl who traveled with him, and he had a wife and four kids back in another city. I saw them together on the elevator in another city. I got on the elevator with them, and I actually tried to act like I didn't see him. I turned around and I looked at the wall, and he said, "Hello." Well, later on, he asked Frank if I would say anything and Frank said, "Well, no, I don't think she would. It's none of her business."

A wife may find that her attempts at social invisibility are completely ineffective. Her fear of getting caught is realized and she's put on the spot. This happened to Olivia when a husband approached her and introduced her to his female companion. "I have no respect for this man no more," she said. "He can't say shit to me. Look what he did in my face and then introduced her to me. He just didn't give a good goddamn." Another wife may be afraid of getting caught watching a teammate's forbidden behavior, as if it were all her fault. "I'd probably feel terrible," Kathleen admitted. "I'd probably think, 'Why did I walk that way at this time?' I just wouldn't want to see it because then I would feel real funny and I would feel guilty, like I knew something I shouldn't know."

The fear of retaliation can be stressful for a traveling wife, whether the intimidation is directed at her or her husband. Sheila confided, "If you acknowledge the fact, and if you even show any disapproval of it, then you won't go on any more trips because they'll tell your husband, 'Your wife better keep her mouth shut.'"

Dana criticized the code and the necessity for a wife to be socially invisible in these situations. She told me this story:

> There was a rain delayed game and it didn't get over until late. So we found a restaurant. . . . So Matt and I were there and it was about two or three in the morning, and we come back [to the hotel], and there's two other players with two other women that weren't their two wives in the lobby. Now, I've got to walk through the lobby. . . . I've got to look at these other wives. I've got to say, "Tell me, what are we supposed to do? Are we supposed to leap from the sidewalk outside the building, up to our room, on a trampoline and hope we can get hold of the windowsill?" You're going to see it. It doesn't matter. So it's like, "Keep your mouth shut and you don't have to worry about anything."

Many wives try not to jump to the wrong conclusion when they see a husband with another woman. After all, he may be completely innocent of any wrongdoing. Perhaps he's entertaining a visiting female relative, sister, female family friend, or sister-in-law. But other wives who are quick to make assumptions and share secrets—who basically refuse to follow the code—are described as the "blabbers" among the wives on the team. "We've had a situation this year on this team where one wife had blabbed what she saw on road trips, not to the guy's wife, but to everybody else, which I think is the worst," Sheila explained. "If you're going to tell somebody, then tell the guy's wife, don't just talk about her behind her back." These are the wives who, the other wives say, are quick to think the worst of a husband, search for a husband they suspect is unfaithful, and tell others what they have seen. "There are certain wives on certain teams that the only thing they enjoy doing is getting their jollies out of seeing who they can find," Dana said. This intrusive behavior angers the wives because they insist that a wife should know all the facts before saying anything—if anything is discussed at all—or keep it to herself because it isn't her concern. "If someone was in the hotel bar, just talking to another girl, then they don't want the wife to run back and tell his wife that she saw him with a girl," Robyn said.

The women I interviewed in the first study speculated that a wife may spread her suspicions about what could be innocent situations because she's projecting her own fears or compensating for the fact that her own husband is having an affair. They inferred that the women who gossip or spread rumors are insecure about their own marriages or that they have difficulty in resolving their own marital issues. They also maintained that the consequences of such actions are potentially damaging for them and those they gossip about, which is why they sanction each other for gossiping. A woman who stays home may distance herself from those who travel with the team because she's afraid of what she will learn about her husband.

An opinionated wife may talk about what she has seen on the road, but most wives believe that it's genuinely important not to tell the wife of an unfaithful husband what she has seen. "An unwritten rule was that whatever you saw while you were on the trip, it wasn't something that you really discussed or gossiped about, it was just basically whatever you saw you just look the other way, and you just didn't say anything," Beth explained. "It would not be your place to tell another wife that her husband's cheating on her if you knew for sure that's what it was."

Although the wives share the belief that some kind of code work is necessary, they may interpret their moral responsibilities differently. Referring to her elevator incident, Sheila said, "I didn't care anyway. I would never tell another wife that I saw that. I wouldn't just rush back here and say, 'I saw your husband with someone else.' If someone asked me directly if I had seen their husband with somebody, I'd probably have a hard time lying about it and I absolutely wouldn't volunteer that information." Skylar preferred the ignorance-is-bliss approach: "I would not lie for somebody—that's one of the reasons I asked Carter not to tell me anything, because I wasn't getting into that. So it was better for me not to know, and then I could just be with everybody and, whatever's going on, I was out of it. So it might have been harder on him, because he was upset when things would happen, but I was like, 'You know what? I don't want to be a part of that. I don't need to know all of that.'"

To establish a trustworthy reputation among her husband's teammates, a wife should not jump to conclusions, spread gossip or rumors, share clubhouse/road-trip secrets, or talk about what she has seen. "The more you talk, the less people trust you, because it's like everybody's doing it," Olivia said. "For those wives who have told things they've seen, they're like the plague. Nobody wants to be around them." In their travels with the wives, the men soon learn which wives they can trust. The longer a husband is in the MLB world, the more it shrinks, and the more likely his wife is to acquire some type of reputation on the ball club or in the league. Her reputation, whether it's positive or negative, may precede her among the teammates and wives on new ball clubs.

Traveling wives are expected to be inconspicuous, and building a reputation for being "cool" plays in a woman's favor. "I was like one of the guys," Emma said. "If I saw them with a woman, I'd roll my eyes and look at them and they'd laugh or, you know, if they were single, especially if they were single, I would definitely say something or do something. There was one guy on one team that they called the team whore. That's what they would call him, 'He's the team whore.' He was a single guy. He did some crazy stuff, so we always made fun of him. We would point out women for him." It can be advantageous for a wife to be accepted as one of the guys in this way, and it also can be risky. Establishing a reputation as someone who can be trusted also can have serious drawbacks. If unfaithful husbands or single men on the team know that they can depend on a woman's silence, they may try to exploit her silence or take her silence for granted as they engage in their extramarital or sexual activities. By maintaining her silence, she is, again, included as a conspirator in the teammates' extramarital or sexual activities.

Despite the knowledge and consequences of the various parts of the code that apply to unfaithful husbands on the road, it's worth mentioning that if a wife is aware that her husband is engaging in extramarital activities on the road, and if she married the professional athlete rather than the man, she may be more inclined to obey the code and ignore his extramarital activities. Consequently, she may accept it during his career and divorce him when it's over.

If a wife obeys the code, it also may be because she wants to support her husband and protect his standing on the team and because her husband and his teammates enforce it. When teammates enforce it, it becomes a way of controlling the faithful husbands, and when the majority of the husbands enforce it, it becomes a way of controlling their wives. The amount of pressure a faithful husband receives from his teammates is often so great that he feels backed into a corner, and he may resort to some form of verbal abuse, intimidation, or guilt to control his wife. To protect his standing on the team, and possibly his standing in the MLB world, he believes that he must be a "team player" or that he must "take one for the team." He may know which husbands have female partners, are having affairs, or habitually "play around" on the road. He enforces the code because it's in the best interest of his standing on the ball club and his occupational security. "It's important to Glenn to be a team player and to fit into that team," Marsha said. "Sometimes it's more important, I think, than it should be. I mean, sometimes, I have so much respect for some of these ballplayers that will just go against the team and say, 'No.' And Glenn never would. He will not go against his team." As we will discover later, this influence can have serious consequences, and it can play a part in ending a marriage. So the more uncertain his standing—for instance, if he's a struggling rookie, if there are rumors of an imminent trade, or if there is the possibility that he will be sent down to the minor leagues—the more inclined a faithful husband is to be a guardian of the code.

Contending with this part of the code can place a great deal of strain on a couple's relationship. According to their wives, these husbands want to be loyal and protect their teammates' standing on the ball club, but they may secretly despise their extramarital liaisons and consider them to be inferior husbands and fathers. Even though his marriage is important to him, he will most likely feel obligated to comply with the code. If a wife follows the code to protect her husband's interests, she may be angry with him and his teammates because of it. She also may be furious because she wants him to be more concerned about her and their marriage and less concerned with what his teammates think of him if he decides not to cover up for the unfaithful husbands. It seems that the more insecure a husband is about his standing on the team and the state of his career, the more forceful he can be with his wife in his attempts to enforce the code.

The road behavior of these husbands suggests that the issue of monogamy is central, but what seems to make it central isn't sexual behavior itself. Instead, it's the issue of loyalty and control to which sexual behavior is inevitably connected. One byproduct of the team's collective rites that offer the husbands sexual freedom is that the wives are subordinated, controlled, and personally hurt. At some point in her marriage, such a woman has to come to terms with the reality that her husband is also married to his team. Similarly, a faithful husband has to confront his own competing loyalties. Having a wife along on a road trip splits his attention in two directions, and he uses this part of the code to manage this conflict and keep his wife and teammates in their respective places. In so doing, he may exaggerate the differences between them.

The bottom line is that when a husband is on the road with his wife, he puts his team and career first and his wife and marriage second, and he clearly demonstrates where his first loyalty lies. He may actually be afraid to be caught with his wife when his teammates unexpectedly enter a public place he assumed was safe to frequent. Robyn discussed an incident that involved her husband's enforcement of the rule about hotel bars: "Tyler told me the rules: 'You're not going in there.' We got into a big fight," she said. "I was going in there. I didn't care what he said, and he marched me up to the hotel room and he said, 'Okay, you're on the next flight out of here. You're going home.' We got in a big, big argument about it." Understandably, a wife's initial emotional response to this type of code enforcement is confusion and anger. She may direct her anger at him rather than at the team when she disagrees with the code but feels powerless about having to obey it and to somehow manage the situation. From her perspective, he makes a sensitive issue even more stressful. When Tyler's team, for instance, was passing through the couple's hometown during a road trip, Robyn was delighted because she and Tyler would be able to be together. Much to her chagrin, when they arrived at their favorite bar one evening, he told her to stay in the car while he went into the bar to make sure the "coast was clear" before allowing her to enter. Robyn was infuriated, and it was worse for her because it wasn't an isolated incident. Tyler's pattern of code enforcement began early in his career, and it explains why Robyn had never seen a certain straying husband with another woman. "I was protected," she said.

EMMA

Mason's team was on a long road trip toward the end of another pressure-filled season. After Emma and Mason arrived at the hotel where the team was staying, they checked in and went up the back stairs to get to their room. As he opened the door to their room, the elevator doors suddenly opened and two women and one of Mason's married teammates walked out of the elevator. With drinks in their hands, they were singing and dancing down the hall, and as they entered the teammate's room, one of the women turned to Emma and, pressing her fingers together, she said to Emma, "Naughty, naughty."

Emma was insulted and angry. She dropped her purse, put her hands on her hips, and said, "Excuse me, I'm a wife. I'm not a slut like you." Mason quickly grabbed her hard by the arm, and with her long hair flying across her face, he quickly pulled her into the room, slamming the door shut. "I cannot believe you just did that,"

Mason said. "That's the kind of thing that could get me in trouble, and you're not allowed on the road anymore." Emma said, "Did you hear what she said to me? She pointed at me like I'm a slut, like she is. I'm a wife. I'm not a groupie." He said, "I get it, but you can't do that. You just need to keep your mouth shut and just stay in the room." Still angry, and smarting from the heated exchange, she thought to herself, "I'm not a whore like her. I'm a wife."

Code Busters

As Emma discovered, a woman can't always successfully challenge the code on her own. She requires the support of one or more of the men on the team. A wife who has her husband's uncommon support may accompany her husband to the hotel bar to hang out with some of his teammates, but even so she's careful to monitor herself. "I might see another player in there that's married with somebody that doesn't look like his wife. Well, as long as he stays at his table, I stay at my table," Dana explained. "I don't see anything. I don't hear anything. I don't know anything until he pushes that person on me. Now, I'm not going to invite him over to sit down beside me, and I'm not going to chat with his woman."

Stacy recalled how a legendary teammate would sometimes bring her and her friend, another wife, into hotel bars without opposition: "He would tell me, 'You guys come in and have a drink with me,' when we'd get back from a game. I'd say, 'No way, I'm not going in the hotel bar.' And he'd say, 'If those guys are screwing around right in the hotel, then they'll have to take their chances that you're going to be in here because you're coming in and having a drink.' And I sat there the whole time and just looked straight ahead at the counter, feeling very uncomfortable." Because the famous teammate is a star on the team, when he invited Stacy and her female friend into the hotel bar, his teammates were less likely to question their presence. His actions show us how teammates with considerable status can persuade wives to challenge teammate bonding and demonstrate that not all teammates support the code. Stacy was initially uncomfortable as a code buster, yet she came to feel comfortable in this role. "He made me feel more comfortable and I was really proud of him for doing that. It's a story I've told a lot because it made me feel good that he could just tell those guys to shove it, because I was coming in there. At the same time, though, I did feel bad, because I didn't want Dennis to feel the repercussions of it either." Under these circumstances, a woman may define the hotel bar more as a harmless gathering place for teammates and less as a place for them to hook up with interested women, but she will still follow her own self-defined requirements, which are guided by the code, in her use of code work when interacting with her husband's teammates.

In specific situations, a player's wife may refuse to blend in with the immediate surroundings, look the other way, or pretend that she doesn't see an unfaithful husband. When she sees an unfaithful husband with another woman and knows that he sees her too, she may acknowledge him and try to make him feel less uncomfortable, and let him worry about the consequences. So she violates one part of the code by acknowledging that she has seen him, but follows another part of the code by not saying anything to anyone about it, with the possible exception of her husband. When emotional situations occur, such as encountering her best friend's husband with another woman, she may support her friend by expressing her disapproval and possibly attempting to publicly embarrass him. Like Stacy, this wife resents feeling that she should be at fault, and this part of the code angers her.

A code-busting husband can take pressure off of his wife when she travels with his team, and this allows her to freely interact with others in the hotel or in the city at large. Robyn recalled a code-busting incident that involved Tyler. "Well, we did have one player the first year we were here, who I think changed it for the team, because he wanted his wife in the bar with him and Tyler happened to be good friends with him. When his wife went in the hotel bars, it changed it for everybody, and now it's okay. We go in there all the time. I mean, if the rookie guys see that the veteran guys are bringing their wives in, then they figure it's okay."

Code-busting husbands, who otherwise could be instrumental in challenging this part of the code, are decidedly rare. As Robyn and Stacy illustrated through their stories, a teammate's elevated status or friendship with a star player can offset the influence of this part of the code; thus the wives of high-status husbands may enjoy more freedom on the road. The wives of low-status players tend to be the most compliant.

The code also excludes wives from certain road trips, as Emma recalled: "We were told, 'No, you can't go on this road trip,' this is when we're going to have the team party. . . . They were pretty disgusting events. They'd have women show up at the hotel and it would be gross. It would be pretty nasty."

At first glance, code-busting wives may appear to have certain advantages, but there also can be major disadvantages. A wife may find herself in an emotional and moral quandary to which there seems to be no good solution. When she develops friendships with her husband's teammates, she has earned their acceptance, yet these relationships may be conditional in matters affecting her husband's career. If one of his teammates is unfaithful to his wife and she has knowledge of his betrayal, the code tells her that she shouldn't disclose to his wife what she has seen, especially if she and the wife have developed a friendship. She doesn't want to betray her friend by withholding what she knows, particularly if her friend learns through other means that her husband has been unfaithful and that she knew it all along. But she's also—and in most cases, primarily—committed to preserving her husband's standing among his teammates. If his teammates believe they can trust her, both she and her husband avoid any negative consequences that could affect their relationships with his teammates. This unspoken bargain among a traveling wife, her husband, and his teammates—exchanging secrecy for acceptance—can be regarded as a passive conspiracy that puts a substantial emotional burden on the traveling wife.

This was Emma's predicament. She developed friendships with and was accepted by many of his teammates during their extensive travels together. Like Stacy and Dana, she had access to hotel bars, so she was privy to many team secrets. She told me, "When I went into the hotel bar, I would see them with other women, and so I had to watch myself, because I would go back to the season home and have to sit next to the wives in the stands. And the rule was that I couldn't ever say anything. And if I did, I would not be allowed on the road or even in the hotel bar, ever."

Players can find themselves mired in a similar emotional dilemma. Mason's teammates liked and respected Emma and perhaps considered her an honorary member of their brotherhood. Their high regard for her sensitized them to Mason's infidelity on the road, yet none of them informed Emma about his indiscretions. Their conspiracy of silence is another indication of the lengths to which teammates will go to cover for and protect each other. As Emma explained to me later, "One of the guys—my friend's husband who she's still married to—saw Mason go into a room with another woman, and because all the guys on the team knew me and liked me, he got so upset he called [his wife], and he was crying. He was so upset because of how much they thought that my husband loved me, and how I had traveled so much with the team, that when he saw him do this he was just upset."

As an aside, it was only later that Emma realized that her decision to travel with Mason affected his behavior on the road. "I traveled a lot with Mason. He wanted me to," she confided. "And when I look back, I think it was because it was his way of preventing himself from being unfaithful. But I've heard from other women that I'm still friends with that he was unfaithful to me when I wasn't with him. So the times that I didn't travel with him were the times that he was not faithful to me, which is—in hindsight—why he really wanted me to be with him." Emma's story might explain why some husbands encourage their wives to travel with them, and it helps us to understand how difficult it is for some husbands to avoid temptation on the road.

Perpetuating the Code

Many traveling wives talked to me about holding a simmering resentment about following the code of conduct, but said that they didn't express this outwardly in any way to others. They put marital interests above personal interests, and this prioritization prevented them from taking steps to challenge or question the practice. Most teammates know they are expendable and this belief permeates their careers. Likewise, a traveling wife believes that nothing is worth the risk of damaging her husband's career.

Except for keeping the extramarital secrets of straying husbands on the team, the code of conduct doesn't carry over into off-the-road situations. As these wives say, the difference is "like night and day." Off the road, teammates don't normally enforce the code, and wives can comfortably socialize at charity events, team functions, or small informal parties.

Even if a husband wants his wife to travel with him, he may occasionally feel awkward about her presence. When a wife like Stacy travels on every road trip, she's understandably conspicuous, and this may lead her husband's teammates to pressure him to leave her at home.

Generally speaking, the more status a husband has in the team hierarchy, the more privileges his wife enjoys. If a younger veteran wife attempts to cash in on her husband's star status on the ball club when she's off the road, or if she has an "attitude," it's common for an older veteran wife to put her in her place, even if the older woman's husband doesn't command the same status in terms of salary or stardom. But even if an older veteran wife has more power than other wives, and even if she has earned the respect of the wives and teammates (which is difficult because many don't hold the wives in high regard), her power is limited. Organizational management won't always grant her wishes for changes that will benefit the families, and any off-the-road power she possesses is for all practical purposes nonexistent on road trips. Moreover, any pull she may have with organizational management can vanish if the sport organization is sold and new management takes over. Although some wives have more status than other wives, any status they enjoy off the road is essentially irrelevant when they are on the road.

CHAPTER 4

Star Power

JILL

Jill had a deep need to avoid disappointing or failing others. As a full-time homemaker, she did all she could to support her husband Craig, an NFL veteran. Unfortunately, Jill's resolve to support him was sorely tested when he was home during the offseason, when Craig sought to be in control. "He thinks that somebody's controlling him all the time, through football," Jill observed. "He feels that he wants to control somebody." She described Craig as critical, overbearing, and demanding, which she not only found stressful, but personally stifling.

Craig's power in the marriage was evident when he used his career, public visibility, and high income as leverage when the couple was making decisions around marital and family issues that were important to him. "He always says, 'We wouldn't have what we have today if it wasn't for football,'" Jill said. "Or he'll say, 'How many professional football players are there in the United States?' So he's one of the chosen few. He's special. He's important. He uses that on me."

During the NFL season, Jill's willingness to take responsibility for the domestic front freed Craig to focus solely on the game. But when the season was over, he reasserted his influence in the home. "When he's home . . . he's usually in control," Jill said. "Everybody was on their best behavior [to make sure] that there was nothing that would set him off. You had to be walking on eggshells and that was stressful. . . . I can't just go off and do what I want to do. . . . He'll say, 'Where are you going?' And I'll tell him. . . . 'I'm going shopping,' or something. And he'll say, 'You know, you can do this instead of going shopping.'"

Jill could hardly wait until the offseason ended and Craig went back to work, but she felt guilty for thinking that way. As soon as he left for training camp, she felt like an enormous weight had been lifted from her shoulders. Her feeling of reclaimed autonomy and her personal empowerment were exhilarating, and her self-esteem improved with each passing week during the season. "I might complain about not being able to see enough of Craig, but I tell people how wonderful it is not to have him here, because I'm getting a huge break," she told me.

Jill was of the opinion that Craig's personality was quite suitable and expected for the game, but not at home with his family. He undermined Jill's self-esteem and parental authority by indulging their children, and she became the disciplinarian who carried out parental responsibilities that he actively avoided. "I like the kids to be in bed at a certain time," she said. "But a lot of times, he'll let them stay up. But he hasn't been with them all day. So I'm really tired and I want them to go to bed. I just want some peace and quiet. If I try to play with them, when we're all playing here on the floor, they don't let me play."

Jill relied on two main strategies to deal with Craig's controlling behavior: "tuning out" and giving in. When his requests or demands overwhelmed her, she tuned out, denying what was most upsetting or disturbing to her. She did this not only in dealing with Craig's use of power, but in coping with the stressors caused by his career. Marital stability and family functioning were exceptionally important to her, so she decided that it was best to acquiesce to Craig and not challenge him or his authority. "I think it's a way of just not having to hear what's going to come out of them," she confided. "You don't want to hear it, so you just give in."

Later in their marriage, Jill decided that she could no longer suppress her anger, tune out, or give in, and she confronted Craig. For a time, they were able to resolve the issue to her satisfaction, but when Craig's controlling behavior became abusive, and more stress permeated the family household, opportunities to confront him were limited. After he retired from the game, his use of power and control worsened.

As we have seen in the previous chapters, numerous issues related to power and control emerge between partners in the sport marriage. Couples may share an implicit or explicit understanding of their use of power and control,[1] but that doesn't discourage or prevent their attempts to use it to try to achieve some desired outcome. The strategies they use to do this are variously influenced by gender, dependency, family-of-origin history, interpretations of self and identity, the husband's career, and the husband's public visibility.

A person can have power and not be controlling, and others can be controlling but lack power. In the sport marriage—and possibly in other marriages—the use of control can be an attempt to compensate for a sense of powerlessness. Players have little, if any, control over their careers. They do have some measure of control over their bodies, and they understandably feel physically empowered by what they can achieve in athletic competition. But their bodies can let them down, and no athlete is immune to the looming possibility of a career-ending injury, the deterioration of athletic skills, and the unrelenting aging process. Their workaholic approach to their careers may be an attempt to control it, but their efforts may not compensate for gnawing feelings of uncertainty and insecurity that never seem to go away. As Jill noted during the first study, a player may perhaps subconsciously compensate for the lack of control over his career by trying to control what he can or thinks he can control: his wife and his children.

A player's wife may be able to anticipate and even welcome certain situations in her husband's career. All the same, the emotional impact of an unexpected crisis can be difficult for her to cope with. Even if she tries to be optimistic, she may feel powerless and vulnerable due to occupational stressors that inevitably spill over into her home and become marital stressors. These feelings can intensify if her husband limits or completely avoids providing domestic or emotional support, and they are further exacerbated if she's socially and emotionally isolated. Depending on what is important to a woman and how she interprets her experience, isolation can be extremely challenging in this type of marriage. In her efforts to adapt, a wife attempts to control what she can: her domestic life. "As the household manager, I was definitely in control," Alaina said. "A lot of fans and people don't know that, don't know how much control the wives have. I think that's what makes the teams a little better." But how much or how little power and control a wife has can be a complicated issue in her marriage. Women like Alaina and Jill become the controllers in their families because they believe that it's necessary for marital stability and family functioning. Significantly, it's the type of control that husbands shy away from. This empowers a wife, but it also makes her husband dependent on her and thus locks her into fulfilling certain roles and responsibilities.

The efforts the partners make to use what power they have to try to control each other or a particular situation, or to cope with occupational or marital stressors, involve their use of control work.[2] The husbands rely on aspects of their occupational lives to try to control their domestic lives—often through a passive use of power—and the wives rely on aspects of their domestic lives in their attempts to have control in their marriage and family, to cope with what they can't control about their husbands' career, or to respond to their husbands' efforts to control them.

Couples that are capable of negotiating, sharing, and compromising in their use of power and control have a greater chance of achieving compatibility and satisfaction in their relationship, especially when they are tested during the season or during the husband's occupational setbacks, failures, or crises, but these couples still may be challenged due to the career-dominated nature of the marriage and the unpredictable nature of the husband's occupation.

Husbands and Control Work

Like other entertainers, successful professional athletes are celebrated in their displays of athleticism and masculinity. When they are in the flow of the game, they come to life; they are "on." But this public man isn't always the same man a wife gets at home, and as Robyn told me, "I'm jealous of that." Many of the qualities a woman admires in her husband during a game can be the same qualities he leaves at the ballpark, stadium, or arena when the game is over. He may have difficulty in transitioning from his occupational life to family life, and this can be a continual source of disappointment for his wife. During the season, the transition may be difficult for him because he's so heavily invested in the game that it is difficult for him, or he is unwilling, to disengage and devote himself to his family, as Sharon observed: "Walt was

Mr. Up, Mr. Jolly, Mr. Placator," she explained. "It was a real act. What was exhausting is that he lost who he was in the act, and he would come home with the same act. The reality is that we all bought into this act. And when he had a down day, we didn't know what to do."

A husband like Craig (in the opening vignette) will overtly exert domestic control.[3] Many other husbands take a relatively passive approach to their marriage and family, but because of the implicit power they hold as the family's main provider in a highly visible career, their passive control work still gives them the upper hand in the marriage. Although players must be confrontational during a game, this husband's first line of defense at home typically is to avoid any kind of confrontation. Where his marital and family responsibilities at home are concerned, he tends to be "off." He can be emotionally unavailable and passive as he "recharges his batteries" for the next job-related activity. In extreme cases, he may even be a stranger in his own home and to his family. In certain private situations and particular areas of his marriage, he will defer to his wife as an authority figure. This may not be surprising when we consider that these men have learned to respect, or at least not question, authority figures. In their occupational lives, they defer to owners, managers, coaches, trainers, and veteran teammates. In their domestic lives, they may have learned early to defer to an overinvolved parent. As a result, a husband may be conciliatory or give in first during major arguments or when his wife makes an effort to resolve a marital dispute. On the other hand, he may become angry or irritated with her, for instance, when she fails to "know her place" and tries to control him. In particular, her assertiveness in public can make him appear weak and incapable of controlling his wife.

Many women in the first study wanted their husbands to be more involved in domestic responsibilities, such as helping with childcare and participating in decision making, but their husbands were either unwilling to share family responsibilities or their efforts to do so caused more problems than they were worth. Many husbands were unable or unwilling to share or express certain emotions or to effectively cope with everyday life outside their occupational worlds. Discussing this contradiction, Stacy recalled a time when she was watching Dennis pitch in the late innings of a game: "I look at Dennis and see him in front of millions of people at the ballpark, out there on the mound, and he's keeping his composure instead of just throwing the ball into the stands, like I would do. Yet, at the same time, he comes home and I think, 'I want him to be more of a man.'" The women in the second group indicated that this pattern in the sport marriage may be improving. Realistically, however, the nature of the career-dominated marriage limits what is possible for these men in terms of carrying out domestic responsibilities.

When Rhonda thought about marrying Brent, she assumed that she was marrying the man the fans loved, and she was perplexed when she learned about his tendency to avoid his family and marital responsibilities. Yet he still maintained some measure of control over her and their children. "What I saw in Brent back then was what I think . . . people see in him on the field—the fun guy, the great sense of humor, the giving guy [who] would do anything for anybody. . . . And, you know, that's what I truly believed that he was like. You know? And, for a while, the majority of the time he was that way. But then he began giving more of himself on the field, and [he] would have less when he came home." Nicole, who was married to an NFL player, discussed how the private man differed from the public man. "No one knows that he's weak but me, okay? And lets me know right away anything that happens. . . . He gets very defensive. He has to make me go through a whole bunch of changes when he's going to stay mad for two or three days, just to keep his power intact."

If a husband believes that his wife is demanding or critical of him, or that she doesn't really understand him, or that she doesn't offer him support when he needs it most, he may take refuge in and use his occupational world to avoid confronting or resolving the issue. If he's in the middle of a heated argument with his wife, for instance, he may leave their home and go to a game, a sport bar, a trendy eatery, or a sporting/social event where he can trade on his celebrity to receive "pats on the back." His wife finds using appreciation from fans to be one of the more annoying attempts to control situations because it limits, suspends, or terminates any meaningful communication and may result in making resolution difficult or impossible. When he's home, a husband may fall back on his occupational responsibilities in the same way, by saying that he has to leave for practice, a training session, a home game, or a road trip. This passive use of control work illustrates his star power. It can enable him to save face, instill confidence in him, make him feel important, and shield him from criticism or responsibility. Realizing the importance of his career in their marriage, his wife may not have comparable power with which to counter his use of this valuable resource. Alyssa shared her thoughts with me about this common issue in sport marriages:

> In what I would consider a normal marriage, the husband is upset with the wife or whatever, and he may leave home and go grab a beer or go to the liquor store or to the grocery store. By the time he comes home, he's,

you know, apologetic, that's what I'm saying. Whereas, with those guys, if there's an argument or disagreement and they leave the house, by the time they get down to the corner, ten people have told them how wonderful they are, and how great they were in the game, or how awesome they are as athletes, or whatever. So their ego is stroked so much that by the time they come home they've forgotten that the wife was even mad at them. So, it's like they're wondering, "Well, why is she upset?" It's not like, "I need to get home in a hurry and apologize," or anything like that. I don't know if it even occurs to them that it matters, that they ought to go home and apologize. I don't think it even really occurs to them that, I hate to call it an infraction but, you know, that they stepped on your feelings.

Extreme aspects of the spoiled athlete syndrome may account for the nature of a husband's control work and the unusual amount of influence some men have over their wives. For example, he may emphasize the importance of his career to gain or regain power in his marriage. Reminding his wife of the widespread perception of a career in professional sports as a prestigious vehicle for upward mobility, and thus of her own upward mobility, is typical behavior. He may continually emphasize his high income and importance as the family's main provider. Gwen's husband would occasionally say to her, tongue in cheek, "I own you." When Arisa and Nathan argued or when he teased her, he would put his hand in front of her face, gesturing for her to kiss his Super Bowl ring as an act of deference. "Now, he gets a charge out of that, let me tell you," Arisa said. "You know, I'm lying there and I'm getting this ring in my face." Nathan also liked to display his power when he announced family decisions. "He believed that this house was his castle and he was king of the castle," she confided. "When he was here, he'd strut his stuff. He'd get on the landing up there and address us at the bottom of the stairs, and we'd play along with it." Her family found his proclamations humorous because he was announcing decisions the family was already aware of and that Arisa had undoubtedly initiated, planned, and carried out. Nevertheless, these displays were symbolic[4] reminders of his implicit power. These types of declarations also may emerge from his interpretations of masculinity, and they give him a significant advantage over his wife in negotiations that only he benefits from or in his direct use of power.

Even if a player's wife is employed outside of the home during her husband's career, she may be financially dependent on him, and this provides him with more power in the relationship. Rationalizing that she has to comply with his attempts to control her (since no one else will do what is necessary for family functioning), she initially learns to give in to him. Accepting his influence over her reinforces his belief that she won't offer resistance and that she's less likely to challenge his behavior. His control work can become quite effective and can result in a marital pattern that is difficult to reverse.

If a husband has doubts about his athletic abilities, or if he's trying to cope with major occupational stressors, he may try to exert considerable control over the family finances, even if his penny pinching is unjustified. Or he may try to benefit from his wife's support in specific ways. As we learned in chapter 1, Nathan expected Arisa to provide care work when he was recovering from a serious hip injury. Despite initially performing the caregiver role willingly, she became angry when he took advantage of the situation:

> When he injured his hip, I gave him a bell. I think he had that bell half a day and that thing was gone. He rang that damn thing every five minutes. You see, he couldn't get up, and we were all downstairs. Oh, he drove me nuts. He took advantage of it, or he just needed so much attention that I didn't want to hear it anymore. He was seriously, seriously hurt. I mean, I had to literally dress the man. He couldn't do anything. But he didn't need the bell. It was too much.

When providing such care, a wife like Arisa may not only feel angry but perhaps exploited if the husband takes advantage of situations in their relationship.

A husband may exercise his power directly by rewarding his wife or by taking away something she values. He may discourage her attendance on road trips or away games, her volunteer work in the community, her participation in wife-oriented activities, and her enjoyment of his job-related perks. Depending on the circumstances, he may try to maintain control by advising her to limit her interaction with other wives on his team and not to get involved in the "wife stuff." His reasons for offering this advice are varied and may include self-centered reasons that may not always be in the best interest of his wife. If a wife should undermine her husband's use of power, his control work may become more extreme, or he may think that she wants more control and grant it. If he grants it, he probably will limit it to family responsibilities or tasks that he's reluctant to perform.

How a husband uses power and control can contribute to or increase his wife's feelings of anger, resentment, and alienation. Although she may expect more from him, she usually will avoid expressing her feelings because such expressions may anger him. In this case, she acquiesces to his power.

CONTROL DURING THE OFFSEASON

When a player returns home after the long season is finally over, he transitions to the offseason. He may spend time getting reacquainted with and carrying out the roles of an engaged husband and father, and he most assuredly spends much time preparing for the next season. At this point, there may be a transition of power. He may share power with his wife, relinquish it to her, or take it back from her. If he takes it back, he may become more controlling by insisting on doing things his way. Instead of stepping into the roles of loving husband and father, where a different definition of masculinity or mastery may be required, he may be more comfortable exerting the same type of power and control he uses in his occupational world. As Jill's experience illustrates, the spillover effect of his direct use of control work is most vividly expressed in family life during the offseason, when he can be critical, overbearing, and demanding and his wife can be the recipient of his controlling language and actions. "Walking on eggshells" may not be an uncommon family norm for her and their children.

A husband's control work limits a wife's autonomy, with the result that she feels essentially powerless. With a "changing of the guard" after the season is over, the rhythm of home life is disrupted. A wife may find it difficult to relinquish the control she has become accustomed to, as Kaylee discovered:

> I would say that is definitely a struggle. I would head back before the end of the season to let our kids finish out the school year, and you get into a routine and you're doing things, and you've got things rolling, and then your husband comes home. All of a sudden, he thinks things should be done differently, and you think, "Well, I've been doing it this way for, you know, a month, and we've been just fine, and now you come in and want to do things different." So that's always a challenge.

During this transition, a wife also can be demoted not only in her own eyes but also in the eyes of their children. As we will see later, this behavior is consistent with a husband's effort to motherize his wife.

Society's double standard and the invisible power[5] that many men take for granted are evident in the degree of freedom a husband enjoys during the offseason in comparison to his wife. Robyn expressed her feelings about some of Tyler's offseason habits:

> Tyler just leaves and goes out with his friends. It's like he can't go a week without getting away one night to go out with the boys and stay out until

two o'clock in the morning. He has to do that. That bothers me too. He knows that, but he still does it, because I never get a chance to do that. I think I'm jealous. I don't ever get to do that. If he'd say, "I'm going to go do this." It would be fine. I wouldn't care. But he just goes. I've asked him for eleven years to at least let me know what's going on—I don't care. Or he'll go work out, lift weights and stuff, and then go and have something to eat with his friends, and then just stay out all night, and he never calls me. God, I hate that. It just makes feel neglected, and it makes me feel like he doesn't care. You know, something could happen to us and he'd be out boozing it up, and he would never know.

When he's with his wife and children on a consistent basis during the offseason, a husband may try to cajole his wife into catering to him. He may expect his wife to know his habits, anticipate his thoughts, and read his mind. Such efforts to control his wife illustrate his belief that his marriage and family life should revolve around him, and it demonstrates the spoiled athlete syndrome.

A husband may use guilt-inducing behavior to convince his wife to perform or stay in her subordinate role. "He'll say, 'We don't have any bread. I'm going to the store. What else do we need?'" Robyn explained. "And then I feel bad because we don't have any bread, like it's my fault we don't have any bread. Why do I feel guilty?" Robyn said that this control tactic works because she's hard enough on herself—she's a perfectionist who is afraid of failing others—and many other wives had similar things to say. At times, however, it isn't necessary for a husband to rely on guilt-inducing behavior. His career is a source of power that she has no control over, and she doesn't want to be at fault if he has a terrible game. Sheila explained:

> The thing that bugged me the most was if I was mad at Frank about something, if it was his day to pitch I couldn't say a word about it. I had to go the whole day acting just like everything was great, because it would be my fault if he didn't pitch well. . . . I have to keep my mouth shut about stuff, and I would just about explode by the end of the day. I could not wait for him to go to the ballpark, and that's very irritating when you feel like you should be able to have a discussion with your husband about a disagreement and you can't because it's their day to pitch.

Even after the husband retires and stays in his occupational world in a related career or in some other form of employment, this pattern may remain intact in certain areas of the marriage. Sheila described how it continued after Frank retired from his MLB career: "During the years that he was actually home, that he was retired, we talked about stuff when it happened and there was no reason to suppress anything then. But now that he's coaching, I probably wouldn't, when I know it's something that is going to be controversial, like during the playoffs, he's under so much stress then, or if it's been a particularly bad game, or if he's gotten chewed out by the GM that day, or something like that, I'd probably still wait."

Other control tactics a husband might use to influence his wife or keep her in a subordinate role include continual teasing, selective listening, criticizing her habits, and sharing his opinions about her shortcomings as a mother or a wife.

SEXUAL SUBORDINATION

In the process of motherizing his wife, a husband may expect her to take control of the emotional part of their relationship. He may not be as expressive about his emotions as he could be, perhaps believing that expressions of certain emotions could result in vulnerability and thus a loss of control. His wife may learn to accept this attitude during the season because she knows how important his career is to him and she understands his single-minded focus. When this pattern continues in the offseason, however, her subordination to his career may be more defined. His emotional distance is a painful reminder of what is missing in her marriage. Expressions of love become scarce, and lovemaking begins to have more to do with power and control.

Whether or not a husband is a spoiled athlete, in certain situations he may attempt to negate his motherized image of his wife as a nice girl by imagining her as a bad girl. Interacting with her in this way may make her uncomfortable and put her at a power disadvantage. His sexual readiness may have less to do with love and more to do with trying to control her by sexualizing or hypersexualizing her, and this can lead her to believe that he's interested only in sex. Nonetheless, she may believe that it's her wifely duty to fulfill his sexual needs. His control work is evident when he insists on sexual interaction for need fulfillment and little else. This example of the virgin-prostitute syndrome in action reveals the husband's power in the marriage. His interpretations of sex, love, and romance relate to male dominance and thus contribute to female subordination.[6] Sharon confided her feelings about this issue in her marriage:

> You feel like a whore after a while. You just lay down for them and that's shitty. I think a lot of professional sports wives feel like that. It's sex on

demand. It's like demand breast-feeding. Whenever he wants it, you give it because you think, "Oh, god, he might go get it on the road." After you have babies and they go on a ten-day road trip, you're damned sure you've tried to have intercourse before you're ready, and it kills you. But you think, "I just don't want him to get it on the road." So sex is a huge thing.

As discussed in chapter 2, managing her physical appearance is among the numerous pressures the wife of a professional athlete confronts. Driven by reinforcement through mass media, she is defined solely by her contributions to her husband's public image.[7] Fans expect her to be consummately attractive, and they further assume that she will unconditionally "stand by her man."[8] Combined with the accessibility to interested women in the husband's occupational world, these beliefs cause most wives to become acutely aware of how they look. A wife may compare herself to the young female groupies or other women in public life and become self-conscious. These comparisons can make her feel compelled to monitor her weight, work out to stay in shape, make sure her hair and clothes are appropriate and fashionable, and so forth. These efforts can be tremendously taxing and, of course, they don't always guarantee the results a woman wants, which can affect her self-esteem. Her husband's attitude toward her body or his preference for the virgin-prostitute syndrome can further complicate her feelings about herself and her sexuality. Her husband may encourage her belief that she must compete with other women, but this isn't straightforward or easy. She also is conscious of maintaining the public image of the good girl and not becoming too desirable to other men, and if she tries to look too sexually appealing, she becomes defined as the bad girl. As illustrated by Rhonda's hotel room experience, this good-girl/bad-girl role switch can become too much for the husband to handle.

As part of the motherization process, a husband may emphasize the female rivalry to keep his wife in the good-girl role and out of the bad-girl role. This may be an effective control tactic because she tends to view other women as threats to her marriage, and he is aware of this. Expressing the "sexism of sizism,"[9] a husband might compare her out-of-shape body to the readily available, physically attractive women he encounters in the course of his occupational life. Comparisons with other women emphasize the idea that he may be attracted more to these women and less to her, and their presence in his occupational world raises the possibility that these attractions could result in some form of infidelity. As a result, she may blame herself if her husband strays.

Many wives go to extraordinary lengths to keep their bodies in shape before and after giving birth, as Amanda discussed: "That's a whole new problem, too, when you think that once you've had a baby—I've said to myself, 'Even though I'm back in shape, he will see other women and . . . he would just be comparing her body to mine and not think, 'She's just had a baby.'"

One might assume that a wife's physical attractiveness would be to her advantage[10] because it could help her in her attempts to be in control or deal with her husband's efforts to control her. He knows, however, that she's aware of the many opportunities he has to meet interested women and this intensifies her fear of his unfaithfulness.[11] He may exploit this fear.[12] Her effort to be in control is less effective because she has less power, so she may hesitate to withhold sex or otherwise disrupt their sexual relationship.[13] By refusing to control him in this way, she may provide him with more power because he can control her without directly expressing his power.

AMANDA

Amanda lived in a quiet neighborhood adorned by lovely tree-lined streets. Behind this veneer of middle-class perfection, however, all was not well in Amanda's home. Her workaholic father was often absent from family life, and when he was home, he was physically and emotionally abusive to her and her mother and siblings. His angry outbursts, overly critical nature, "bad moods," and use of power were fixtures in her childhood. What Amanda wanted most of all but didn't receive was approval, believing that from approval came love.

Even as a child, Amanda wanted to look pretty. She believed it was the way to receive approval from her father, who had labeled her the "pretty one" in the family. As a young teenager, she became obsessed with being thin. She began dieting, constantly exercising, misusing laxatives, and eating in secret, which finally led to a habit of binging and purging. "See, the thing is, for me to start out one size and think I was going to get smaller, and get larger instead, my whole self-esteem was ruined," she confided. "So I just kept trying. I just thought, 'Well, I just got to keep dieting. That's just the way my life's going to be: dieting, dieting, dieting.'"

Amanda was convinced that she was overweight, even though she was quite the opposite. She believed that there was little in her life that she could control, but what she could control was her body and thus her physical appearance. By controlling her body, she thought she would be able to fulfill her deep need to be perfect and gain others' approval. This pattern continued when she attended college, where she met Casey, a star quarterback on the football team. Ironically, Amanda chose a man who was just as critical of her as an adult as her father was in her childhood. Early in their dating relationship, Casey made it clear to her that he had a strong dislike for overweight women and that he would never be in a relationship with an overweight woman, so Amanda knew that any weight gain was out of the question. Throughout their dating relationship, she tried not to eat in his presence. Amanda's sense of self was dependent on how she believed her body appeared to others. Casey seemed to envision her as a kind of relational decoration in public life, and she strove to fulfill that expectation. As their relationship continued to develop and as his controlling nature became evident, her perception of her body became more exaggerated. In public, she would display to others (and prove to herself) how much control she had by refusing offers of food, but later she would gorge herself in private. When she finally let her guard down and discussed her eating disorder with Casey, he didn't respond in the supportive way she had hoped he would. Instead, he was critical and insensitive to her feelings.

After the NFL drafted Casey, he relocated to play for his new NFL team, and Amanda's eating disorder intensified. She was aware of the sexual availability of other women in the NFL world and believed that she had to compete with them to sustain Casey's interest in her. She quoted Casey as saying, "Other people on the team [don't] have to have attractive wives. I have to have an attractive wife." He told her that he had decided not to marry his high school sweetheart because she wasn't "pretty enough for the NFL."

Casey took advantage of Amanda's insecurities about her body image. His efforts to control her included asking questions about her weight, her eating habits, and her exercise schedule. He used insinuations, jibes, teasing, and direct interactions such as periodically checking to see if she was gaining weight.

Amanda routinely asked Casey to store his preferred foods in the garage to reduce her temptation to eat them, so he kept granola bars in the trunk of his car. After Casey was asleep one night, Amanda thought, "I really want one of those granola bars." Because she didn't want Casey to know what she was doing, she went to the garage in the middle of the night and tripped the security alarm. Casey understood then why food was disappearing, and he confronted Amanda. He habitually shared stories with others about her eating habits, and he later shared this story with friends in her presence, which completely humiliated her. His attitude and actions only served to add to her insecurity about her body image and increase the self-imposed pressure to be thin and attractive.

Later in Amanda's marriage, she was able to move beyond her eating disorder, but the emotional scars remained as an undercurrent to her ongoing relationship with Casey.

Wives and Control Work

Similar to the way a player compensates for his career instability by trying to use domestic control during the offseason, his wife may rely on it to alleviate her fear of the unknown. Her primary objective is making her husband's career family-free so he can concentrate on his game, succeed in his career, and keep her family safe and stable. "I felt like I had to be in control," Skylar said. "I was more in charge of finances and the more responsible, bigger decisions, and he just played ball. In order for things to move smoothly, things had to go by my system—otherwise, it was chaotic."

A wife doesn't always define control as something she needs. Instead, because of her personality, it's something that she "inherits," as Alaina discovered: "If control means being able to make decisions, well, I made those decisions with my husband being aware. I just didn't make decisions without him knowing. But I just didn't do things haphazardly. I was more of the facilitator, the worker bee. I always kept him informed."

A wife's ability to wield power in the home can be a necessity in the marriage, and it can embody various qualities that attract these men. Alaina emphasized some of the qualities she believed wives should possess and professional athletes value in a marital partner:

> They may date other types of girls just for their looks or whatever. . . . But if it's a player who's very serious about his career, he's going to look for certain qualities in a wife who's going to be a helpmate, who's going to be supportive, who's going to conduct business and make decisions,

and be a household manager—a good mom, because he's not going to be around. She's got to be in charge and she's got to be trusted. She's got to be in a position to handle finances. So he's going to want an intelligent woman who can help him—that's what he's looking for.

Kaylee agreed:

> I know that that's definitely a lot of what my husband was attracted to in me—that I was strong and I was supportive of him, and that he didn't have to worry when he was on the road that I was going to be calling him, crying because I couldn't keep things together at home. You know, there's been many times that we've talked about certain situations and, you know, what if this had happened, and he just said, "That wouldn't have happened. I wouldn't have married you if you were like that. I needed somebody that was strong."

Alaina discussed the importance of a woman's inner strength:

> You can't be whining and crying to him about every little thing. You better not, if you want to keep his sanity and your sanity. You got to be able to be tough. Manage things and don't freak out. I feel sorry for the rookie wives who come from sheltered situations and live a sheltered life, and then they come into this high-pressure-cooker situation, and you have to make decisions and be strong and be able to handle a lot of things—women and controversy and instability, all kinds of things. You'd just crack up under that pressure.

> I think baseball wives have a big fault of taking care of too many things for their husbands. And that's why these husbands get into trouble with all kinds of things like addictions, and drugs, and alcohol. They don't feel like they're needed. They feel like they're inept. . . . The wives pamper them, wake them late, keep the kids quiet in the house because Daddy's sleeping, postpone trips because of Daddy, and induce babies because of Daddy. It's not normal. What you want to do, what you want to strive for, is to create a normal lifestyle within an abnormal lifestyle.
>
> —KALYN

As alluded to earlier, a wife may appear to be in control in certain areas of her marriage, but a power imbalance that favors her husband still exists because it isn't always the type of control she prefers. Realistically, if her control is seasonal, then whatever power she has is severely limited and is basically an illusion of control. To compensate for this power imbalance, she may attempt to increase her power by emphasizing her domestic mastery or her knowledge of, her ability at, and her involvement in family functioning, and this can increase his dependence on her.

A wife may rely on emotional influence as a form of control work, suppressing certain emotions or expressing others to influence him. "If you look at power as control, I controlled my feelings," Marsha confided. "I think probably I controlled the situation more than he did. I controlled it so that he just could have that life, and perform. I held my feelings back at times and tried to make everything possible for him." Efforts at control can include expressions of love and affection, displays of anger, or the "silent treatment."

One of a wife's greatest fears is that she will have no control over what happens to her marriage and family. Having no control can induce feelings of insecurity, powerlessness, or vulnerability, all of which she wants to avoid. Robyn told me, "Everything upset me and made me panic. I mean, I actually made myself sick to my stomach. I used to have to take Valium because I was a nervous wreck all the time about things I had no control over." Such fear may originate in a woman's childhood, at a time in her young life when she has no control in a family plagued with troubles, crises, and addictions. She learns to compensate by relying on domestic control, which may help her minimize psychological or emotional distress.[14] "I had to be more controlling and I didn't like that," Robyn recalled. "But I don't see a way to get out of it because otherwise our lives wouldn't function. That's the only sense of power we can have, because everything else in our lives is out of our hands." She believed that she had to do it all or that only she could perform family responsibilities in the right way, which was "my way."

A man who has become the spoiled athlete may become overly dependent on a strong woman and others in his life to carry out tasks on his behalf, as Emma observed:

> They definitely marry women who can take care of everything and leave it to them. They're looked up to, people come to them for things, they want things from them, they expect them to be that person, but they really rely heavily on their wife to take care of matters for them, and they hire people to take care of things for them. So I think there's a lot of push and

pull in that situation for them, and I think that's why they really end up, by the end of their career sometimes, having lost everything because they don't take responsibility for things in their life, and they don't know how to do a lot, and people take advantage of that. So, I know in our home, I did take care of everything, and I did manage everything, and he just sat back and let me, but at the same time he wanted to be the boss. . . . His father made decisions and I think there was some confusion there with him, because he wanted to be the person who made the decisions. But I think he found out he didn't know how to do that, which I think leads to all his confusion in life and why he just has not been successful since baseball.

A strong woman may be most attracted to a partner who won't contest her need for and use of domestic control. From her partner's point of view, everything is "taken care of," including him.

Whether family activities are anticipated or unexpected, a wife in the sport family takes sole responsibility for planning and scheduling them, and this sometimes results in having more control than she wants or needs. A wife may or may not want control, but the reality is that things had to be taken care of, and because there is no one else, she takes control. "I didn't want to plan the whole vacation, or I didn't want to make all the plans for the holidays," Kathleen said. "But if he was around, I don't think he'd be able to do it, and it wouldn't be fair, because he's not as good at that, so I liked it. I guess I wouldn't have to have it, but it wouldn't have worked out so well if I didn't." Even in these situations, a wife will be careful to stay within the boundaries of her control and try to avoid nagging her husband or being too "pushy."

Taking on the organizer role in the family can have certain repercussions when a woman uses it as a way of coping with stressors.[15] She may, for example, rely on "futurizing," planning for every possible contingency or outcome in the future. Imagining certain gains and benefits, she tries to avoid mistakes and pitfalls, even though the effort is an impossible attempt to control the uncontrollable. Futurizing can result in additional stress, burnout, depression, or a sense of futility and may lead to physical ailments. It can become habit forming, and it may become difficult for her to change after her husband retires from his career.

A wife also may rely on various forms of denial or manipulation in her effort to deal with her husband's controlling behavior, or she may confront or challenge him. Using manipulation is a fairly common control tactic a wife will use to try to change her husband's mind or influence his behavior.

"I need to have some subtle ways to approach him so he doesn't really know what I'm doing," Robyn said. "I don't know what else to do. So I need the subtle sneak attack to get him to do things." Early in her marriage, Robyn thought Tyler's power was unquestionable, and she was reluctant to oppose or disagree with him. She didn't want to be the target of his harsh language or seek his permission or justify things to him. She didn't want him to be angry with or critical of her. As their relationship developed and she became stronger and more confident, she would confront him with resolve and less fear of rebuke, and she wouldn't back down. Rhonda tried to put Brent's workaholic pursuit of his career in perspective by reminding him of the value of their feeling for each other and their marriage. "I've noticed over the last few years that I've changed a lot," she confided. "I don't say, 'Hey, you did really good today—four for four. That's awesome.' Because they get it every single place they go. So, I feel, well, I'm tired of this. I'm not going to nudge this guy another step up on his little pedestal."

NORMALIZING CONTROL

As we're learning, a wife's childhood experiences appear to play some part in her interpretation and understanding of power and control, both in her use of and response to it. The wives' relationships with their parent(s) during childhood and their observations of parental power and control in family interactions were influential in determining their need to use power and control in their adult relationships.

BETH

From the time Beth was very young, her father was a heavy drinker and often came home from work in "bad moods." She and her three sisters dreaded those occasions when he came home from work and argued with their angry and disapproving mother. When fights inevitably occurred between her parents, Beth and her sisters retreated to their basement bedrooms. The basement was their sanctuary, and Beth and her sisters thought of it as their "fairyland." It was a safe place where they could escape from their quarreling parents into an imaginary world of make-believe. Unfortunately, escaping to fairyland wasn't always feasible. After picking up his daughters from school, her father often dragged them along on the pretense that he had to run some errands in their small town. Instead, he made a beeline for the corner bar and drank the hours away before eventually passing out. During these benders, the sisters had to remain in the car, neglected for hours. Eventually, it was up to them to figure out how to get their father to take them home. Beth tearfully recalled these painful memories: "Sometimes the only way we'd ever get him out—because I think he honestly forgot us—is somebody finally had to go to the bathroom or something, or we'd just really get tired, or we were hungry, and it was time to go. We needed to go home and it was dark, and one of us would get gutsy and stick a head in the doorway and say, 'Dad,' or catch somebody we knew going in."

> I come from a totally dysfunctional background. My father was an alcoholic. So it turns out, Walt is an alcoholic and didn't stop drinking until a year and a half ago. Well, sixteen years of marriage, I thought everybody drinks too much. You know, I thought that was normal. So, if you come out of dysfunction, you're just going to land right there. This lifestyle is totally dysfunctional. It's perfect.
>
> —SHARON

Beth tried to get on her father's good side and not be the target of his anger when he was intoxicated, and this developed into a lifelong habit of trying to please other people. "I think you please whoever your parent is, thinking that maybe if you're good then they won't drink, right?" she said. But she refused to support his behavior by covering for him, overlooking it, or lying to her mother about his drinking habits, and so she often became the target of his anger and criticism. She didn't measure up to his expectations of his favorite daughter.

Escaping to the basement not only provided Beth with a sanctuary from the upstairs world of her parents, but it seemed to provide her with some measure of control in family situations in which she had no control. During her marriage to Cliff, there were many times when she wanted to retreat to the "basement" in her mind because she had no control over his career and, try as she might, there was no more she could do to advance his career. During her arguments with Cliff, the imaginary basement provided her with a sense of self-empowerment and domestic control. She confided, "You know to this day, like when I go down there, it just has this different kind of feeling. . . . If I didn't want to be around anybody, then that was the place that I went to. You know? When we fight, that's how I feel. Like, 'Oh, I just wish I had somewhere to go right now.'"

As a child, Beth essentially became the family's housekeeper. She made a great effort to keep the kitchen spotless and looked to her mother for the praise she felt she deserved. When her sisters failed to keep the kitchen clean, Beth's control was threatened because it minimized her mother's praise. As an adult, Beth still had a need to keep the kitchen spotless, especially during stressful situations in Cliff's career.

Beth's mother was the controller in her family, but she didn't have any control over her husband's addiction. From observing this lack of control when her mother seemed to need it most, Beth realized how powerless and insecure she felt when she didn't have control and how much more secure she was when she felt like she had control in situations that mattered to her. As a child, she could do nothing about her father's heavy drinking or her mother's angry tirades. But she could escape to the basement and the kitchen, and these became her defined areas of domestic control. As an MLB wife, she believed that having control meant having power in her marriage and that she could avoid making the mistakes her parents made by not repeating the unhealthy aspects of her childhood. She also believed that having power and control in her marriage would put her in a better position to support Cliff and his career and to cope with his setbacks.

Like Beth, several wives in the first study talked about becoming aware of power and control by learning to accept responsibility at an early age in their families of origin. Kalyn recalled, "I was the oldest of eight, and my parents didn't have much, and I had a lot of responsibility. I got mad at that. I was left to be home all the time, working, and cooking, and stuff. I didn't have much." Arisa was on her own as a teenager after her father passed away and her mother was employed outside their home. "I've had to take control a lot," she said. This childhood pattern may carry over into adulthood and influence the choices she makes in her marriage.

It was common for the wives in the first study to describe their mothers as controlling and their fathers as passive, weak, ineffectual, and routinely absent from family life.[16] Jessica talked about how she observed this family pattern repeated in her relationship with Andrew: "I was brought up to be this way and he was brought up to be the other way. So with his background and my background . . . he wanted a mommy. So he got one. My mother, she got out the chair and whip, and my father ran around like a lion roaring, but doing exactly what she said. That's where I learned how to do it. . . . It's scary how it repeats."

This repeating pattern became apparent early in Jessica's marriage. One night, she and Andrew were having a long argument in the well-lighted living room of their modest condominium. As she was shouting and gesturing with her hands in the air, she happened to look over at the sliding-glass door and saw her reflection. She immediately stopped in midsentence and quickly lowered her hands, suddenly reminded of her mother shouting at her father during one of their many intense quarrels. Dumbfounded, she yelled to no one in particular, "Oh, my god, I married my father! Oh, my god, I am my mother!"

Much of what an adult daughter learns about power and control is derived from observing her parents. Mia's father died when she was a child and her mother controlled the family. "It comes from not having a dad when I was growing up, and just having a mom," she said. "We had to look out for each other. My mother raised very strong women, not by choice but by circumstances, and I think that was just the way we were. All of the girls at home are like that. As a matter of fact, my sister's husband always says, 'You guys always want to be the man of the house.'" Because of his occupation, Rhonda's father was seldom home, which left her mother in charge, and then her parents separated when she was a young child. Jill's father abandoned her family when Jill was twelve years old. Her working mother was emotionally indifferent and told Jill to leave home when she was eighteen years old. Alyssa's stepfather was also absent from family life much of the time. He worked nights and gambled on Friday nights and the weekends. His absences and his reserved nature when he was part of family life led her to regard him as an outsider to the family. "He was there, but then not there," she said. She described her mother as overprotective and the "basic caretaker."

A controlling mother may have influenced a wife's need to feel in control, but the same result can occur when this pattern is reversed: when the mother is passive and the father is controlling. Marsha explained, "He always told me

I could do whatever I wanted, but I'd have to work hard at it, that life wasn't easy. My dad was very controlling, very strong, very hard-working in what he did. So that's why, it has to come from him. So that's just how I've been with school, and with work, and with all that I've always had to be in control of."

Unlike Jessica and Andrew, when Marsha married Glenn, she married a man who was distinctly different from her father. "I married someone so opposite from my dad," she said. "Because I was so much like him, I realized I could never have lived with someone like him. And Glenn comes from a family that's totally opposite. His dad is very passive. His mother is a controller. I mean, she is—I've never known a woman to have so much control in a marriage.... He was able to deal with me because he grew up with a very strong woman."

Sandy's father was overly controlling, and she preferred to marry a man who was more like her mother. "Sometimes I wish he had a little more of an aggressive quality," she confided. "But it's nice to be able to say to him something's gone wrong without getting yelled at, which is what my dad would do and my mother would say, 'Oh, don't worry about it. We'll make everything better.' And that's what he does and I need that. I wish I could be like her."

In summary, early childhood experiences can play an important part in a wife's need to be in control and in her response to the controlling behavior of others. If her mother was the dominant parent, she's more likely to be influenced by her mother in her decisions about and preferences for power and control. She also may be attracted to a man she thinks she can control. If she lacked a strong father figure in childhood, she still may marry a man who is remarkably like him, but whom she considers to be a newer and perhaps more improved version of him. Unfortunately, her hope for this kind of man can backfire. Her husband may be passive in and absent from family life, and she may become too domineering, just like her mother. She may discover that she married her father, complete with the flaws that she always wanted to avoid in the man she married. Her need to control domestic life may make her husband uncomfortable with or exclude him from family life, or she might try to include him more in family life when he has little, if any, interest. Initially, he may be attracted to a strong and independent woman, perhaps because she reminds him of the qualities he values in his overinvolved mother. As his way of giving her control in the relationship, her husband may motherize her and she may accept this role, but then he may neglect or pay little attention to domestic life and become a stranger in or outsider to his family.

CONTEMPLATING AN EMOTIONAL DICHOTOMY

A wife's perception of control can be a complex process that involves a plethora of contradictory emotions. To have control is related to her feeling of power, and her need to feel personally empowered is a response to her emotions. She sees herself as someone who is giving and supportive of those she loves and cares for. Although she can be insecure, selfish, or greedy, thinking only of herself and fulfilling her own needs or wishes, she most likely thinks that her needs and wishes will be fulfilled by making decisions that include the needs and wishes of others. She wants to be needed, praised, recognized, loved, or approved of for her ability to manage her family and support her husband and his career, yet she also may believe that she's unworthy of validation for what she does accomplish. No matter how deserving she is, any amount of validation may never be enough. She is convinced that her work is never done. She constantly reminds herself, "If I can do better, if I do the right thing, or if I succeed, then everything will be fine. I will be needed. I will be loved." Her need for love and approval may be so great that she normalizes being controlled and lets others use her as a way of gaining love. She has difficulty putting her own needs and wishes first, and this inability to separate herself from others can create a dilemma for her. She may try to define herself as her own person with her own identity, but because she has internalized a "we" partnership with her husband, establishing personal autonomy may be difficult or nearly impossible to achieve. Her sense of self has merged with the roles that favor her husband, his career, and their mar-

> Well, the last thing you want is to be married to someone who is going to cry every time you get traded or panic if you lose two games in a row. I mean, I just saw my job as to keep things even at home. A lot of stuff happened I never even told him about, because I handled it and it was not a big deal. There's no point in calling him every night and telling him every single thing that went wrong in the day. He doesn't care. It's not that he doesn't care, he doesn't want to hear about it, because I think for them to be successful, you just have to do the thing.
> —SHEILA

riage, and her sense of self is validated primarily by her domestic mastery, her gender work, or her husband's career success, much of which is expressed in her idea of teamwork.

Paradoxically, a wife's feeling of being in control can enhance her self-esteem. When she accomplishes her desired goals or effectively copes with a stressful or crisis situation,[17] she may feel competent, autonomous, and personally empowered. She measures the effectiveness of her ability to exert power or control by the results, which may be immediate or gradual. She feels important and capable because she has demonstrated to herself and to others her ability to master challenging marital or family situations, typically without meaningful support. Her illusion of control may be sufficient in itself to cope with problematic situations, even if they are extreme.

This woman may define a stressful situation as controllable, when in reality she has little, if any, control. Understandably, it can be intensely difficult for a woman to minimize her feeling of control or to relinquish control when it validates her sense of self. When she confronts a particular situation, she may try to minimize or avoid her doubts or faults, and she may not admit to herself that she has no control because to do so would magnify her feelings of insecurity, instability, or incompetence. Despite the lack of recognition, her domestic mastery or her sense of control becomes an intrinsic and essential part of her sense of self. "It makes me feel important," Kathleen said.

Relinquishing control can be difficult for a wife who believes that she's best qualified to be in control. Stacy admitted, "I feel like I'm better being in control than he is." A wife also can feel frustrated when her husband challenges her control. "It takes control to give in, too, because I think you have to control yourself, to bite your tongue, to give in and say, 'Okay, all right, we'll do it your way.' I think it's harder to give in than to fight," Kathleen said. In public situations that include his wife, a husband may attempt to maintain and protect his public image by trying to appear as if he's "in charge." In these emotionally complex situations, which may include his fans, he may express passivity to convey the impression to those present that he's in control in his marriage. In turn, his wife may interpret this passivity as potentially damaging to his masculine image, so she may attempt to subtly encourage him to be more outgoing or assertive. In response, he relies on face-saving behavior because he fears her controlling support may make him appear weak or less masculine than other professional athletes or other men. To maintain the appearance of having control in his marriage in public situations, he may, as Nora reminds us, try to control her by ignoring her or pretending that she isn't present, and then subsequently criticizing her in private. Once she's corrected, she "knows better" than to assert her control in public situations. Stacy shared an example from her many public experiences: "I allow him to look more in control in front of people because I don't want them to think that I'm the one running the show. So I take a backseat to him when we're out in the baseball world, on the road, and things like that. I try to remember not to say, 'Well, I made the reservations here or there.' I let people think that he did."

Many wives described themselves as somewhere toward the high end of a scale of perfectionism. "If I weren't in control things would be in shambles," Rhonda insisted. "I'm not a perfectionist, but I lean that way. But certain things, they've just got to happen the way I want them to happen." This need to be in control may be related to her insecurities, her lack of confidence, or her identity/self issues or needs. Jessica explained, "I'm a perfectionist and that's scary, because you can never achieve your standards. You tend to set your standards so high that you cannot achieve them."

When a wife needs approval from herself or from others, she might attempt to validate her ability to be in control by demonstrating domestic competency or seeking validation from her husband by fishing for compliments from him. "Well, take when I clean the house," Sandy said. "'Adam, how's the house look? Doesn't it look great?' Or I'll say, 'Isn't this a great meal I cooked?' You know? I always need assurance. I like to hear that. Not all the time. I don't expect it all the time. But I want him to notice stuff I do. I'm always looking for Dad's approval."

When an MLB player leaves for spring training before the start of a new season, his wife's domestic control is reinstated, and her feeling of independence can be a strong contrast to her husband's stifling use of power and control during the offseason. But if she loves her husband, or if she's emotionally dependent on him, she may experience a confusing mix of emotions when he exits from family life. As a veteran wife, Robyn had learned to expect and accept Tyler's frequent and extended absences from home. In contrast to Tyler, who regained much of his independence when he returned to family life in the offseason, Robyn relinquished her personal autonomy and domestic control. Consequently, the couple tended to get on each other's nerves and create a tension-filled household during the offseason. Even though she loved him, by the time Tyler was ready to report for spring training in February, Robyn was ready for him to leave. She felt guilty because she wanted him to go, but sad because she knew she would miss him. As a way of dealing with his departure and letting go, she would express her suppressed feelings and initiate a fight with him before he left:

We already drive each other nuts when it gets down to February first. I want him to leave so bad I can hardly stand it. Just get out of here. And then I get all stressed out because he's going to leave and I really don't want him to. I want him to just go "click" and be gone. I don't want him piddling around and saying, "Well, I think I'll leave this or that day." It's the same thing when they leave for a road trip. I hate it. So it stresses me out. So we get into a big fight. I want to go with him and I can't.

Skylar responded in much the same way when Carter had to leave her to travel. She was angry and resentful because she was left alone to care for their family:

It's interesting, the biggest fights and arguments . . . were right before he left to go on the road. It's taken me four or five years now to have him go out of town and not realize that I'm being combative and argumentative with him before he leaves. I finally realized that's because I didn't want him to leave. It sounds stupid, getting in a fight with somebody just makes them want to leave, but I think it's just all that pent-up anxiety of they're leaving. I've got to handle everything. I've got to do everything myself, and feeling resentful and angry before he would leave, I would almost try to make him feel bad for leaving and heap some of that on him.

For Skylar, it wasn't so much that getting angry at Carter made it easier for him to leave her and their family, or for her to let him leave. Instead, she began to understand the looming reality of being on her own again, with all the responsibility for family functioning on her shoulders. Departures also are stressful for a wife because she has no control in these occupationally driven situations and because she may be emotionally dependent on her husband.

Because a player's wife is so invested in her husband's occupation, she may attempt to control his approach to it by trying to influence the way he manages career-related issues like special diets, pregame habits, game performances, occupational decisions, public appearances, contract negotiations, labor negotiations, team politics, geographical moves, and so forth. When she crosses a boundary, she justifies it on the basis of her belief that it's in the best interest of their relationship, their family, or his career. She may find it difficult to avoid nagging or pestering him, or tactfully slipping him a "honey do" list, and this can lead to marital distress. "Every time I let him take control, I'm . . . disappointed, and I have to stay on him all the time," Jessica confided. "Do this, do that . . . but there's a fine line. You have to do it gently, and sometimes you don't feel like doing it gently. So you just flat-out rag on them, and they hate you and you hate them, and you hate yourself."

Even though exerting domestic control can be an effective way for a woman to cope with stress and perform necessary roles, it can adversely impact her marriage. She may minimize or discourage intimacy or compatibility with her husband, intentionally or unintentionally. It isn't unusual for a wife to reach a point where her need to be in control is so intense that she "smothers" her husband and her children. Paradoxically, her need to be in control may be so deep that she becomes controlled by her own insecurities, anxieties, or dependencies, and her husband can more easily control her through his assumptions about her role.

If a wife is uncomfortable in the dominant role in her marriage, she may resent her husband for placing her in this role. When enacting marital and family roles, she's expected to place the cultural resources of matriarchy in the service of patriarchy, with the result that she may feel overwhelmed or powerless. The extent to which she feels this way can involve her dependencies. In her effort to replace feelings of powerlessness and vulnerability with feelings of competence and self-empowerment, she compensates by trying to "do it all" and "fix things." But she also may be overly dependent on her husband's financial success or celebrity, and he may develop an unhealthy dependence on her, so she finds it challenging to change. Her sense of responsibility can isolate and discourage her from turning to others for support. She may embrace a "supermom"[18] role over other domestic roles. Different versions of "cocooning," when she overfocuses on domestic life at the expense of other areas of life, also can evolve and become normalized. "I took a lot of the brunt of the homemaking and family, taking care of the family and the home on my own, and I would get very tired of it and I would get aggravated with it, and I would get overwhelmed with it, and I pretty much kept my mouth shut about it," Susan said during the second study. "I played the martyr a little bit, you know, 'Oh, I can do this myself and I don't need anybody's help.' I definitely played Superwoman for many years."

Later in her marriage, or after her husband retires, a wife may have become so accustomed to having power and control that she finds it difficult to compromise or to relinquish control. "Actually, the problems with that didn't come until he stopped playing," Keira said. "Where he wanted that control and it's not that I didn't want to relinquish that control, I was just so used to having it." If this control pattern is not somehow addressed during the husband's career, it can become so deeply embedded in the relationship that it may be too difficult to change after he retires. Why would changing this pattern be so challenging for couples? It may be because the wife has, in some way during his career, played a large part in creating a pattern that Stacy described as a

"Frankenstein monster": her husband expects her to remain in control, and he expects to continue to be the recipient of her control and remain passive about sharing control. Offering her point of view, Sharon said, "That's why there's not divorce during the career. It's this control thing, it would cause too much chaos. . . . To me, it seems like . . . most of the divorces would come after, through retirement stages, when you see each other as human beings and in a different light."

Most couples in the sport marriage are reluctant to address power and control issues, and it's only after his career is over that they feel the need to address them. When a husband retires, they must re-evaluate and adjust if they are concerned about their relationship. In the meantime, some wives try to avoid maximizing their use of power and control because they will eventually, as Sharon expressed it, "de-ball" the husband, which is to effectively "de-husband" him.

CHAPTER 5

The In-Laws

GWEN

Osten's family was preparing to attend a banquet in honor of his altruistic contributions in the city where his NBA team was located. Celia, Osten's mother, was spending the day in Gwen's home preparing for the banquet, which was her habit on game days. She and Gwen would then go to the game together. As evening approached, Celia set up an ironing board in the living room in the presence of Gwen, Osten, and their guests. With Osten's tacit approval, she ironed the shirt and slacks she had picked out for Osten, meanwhile instructing Gwen about how to be a "real" wife to her son. Despite feeling offended, humiliated, and angry, Gwen said nothing. With much difficulty, she smiled and tried to appear unruffled. It wasn't the first time Celia had performed this type of ironing ritual in the presence of others.

At the banquet later that evening, Celia and Gwen sat together. Gwen knew just how important it was for Celia to share the spotlight with Osten, and as the ceremony led up to the formal presentation, she could sense Celia's excitement. Osten was awarded a large, heavy plaque. In his acceptance speech, he concluded by saying, "If I don't recognize this person, she's going to be mad at me," and Gwen thought, "Oh, he's getting ready to introduce his mom, because if he doesn't, her feelings are going to be hurt." Instead, much to Gwen's surprise, he introduced his wife to the audience. As she stood up to acknowledge the applause, Gwen noticed that Celia was visibly disappointed, so she quickly sat down.

Later, as friends were admiring the plaque, Celia noticed that Gwen's name was inscribed on the plaque along with Osten's, and she expressed irritation that her own name wasn't included. Osten had given the plaque to Gwen, but she had grown tired of carrying it. She noticed that Celia had her eye on it and knew how much it meant to her, so she asked her if she wanted to carry it. Celia beamed as she gratefully accepted it, and they left with a group of friends to celebrate at a nearby restaurant. She didn't part with it for the rest of the evening, and Gwen never saw the plaque again.

The sport marriage comes with a distinctive set of complexities, circumstances, and tensions that make establishing and managing in-law relationships challenging while the player is active in his career. Most wives in the second group reported close and supportive relationships with their mothers-in-law.[1] A significant number of wives in the first study, however, described awkward, distant, and sometimes outright antagonistic relationships that caused significant stress.[2] In these cases, the women observed that the seeds of this tension seemed to be sown during a player's early experiences in organized youth sport programs.

Given what we've learned so far about the nature of control in the sport marriage and passivity the wives ascribed to their husbands, it isn't surprising that a player may tend toward passivity or even submissiveness in complying with his mother's wishes. This relational dynamic can become the basis for a mother-son bond that marginalizes the player's wife in a relationship triangle. This bond can result from the son's learned dependency on his mother and her hope to cash in on it when he becomes a professional athlete.

When her son is single, an overinvolved mother may not be threatened by his relationships with other women, believing that she will always be the most important woman in his life. He may date several women without committing to them or establishing meaningful relationships with them, instead keeping his mother central in his life. When he marries, his mother may feel threatened and become more possessive or controlling as she tries to assert her rights to maintain a close relationship with her son and substantially involve herself in his career.

Previous research[3] suggests that in Western culture, when the traditional middle-class stay-at-home mother has limited opportunities to meaningfully interact with others outside her family, her children can become the basis for her self-affirmation. As her children grow older, she may seek validation by vicariously experiencing whatever success they achieve. Scholars also have suggested that mothers can spousify their sons[4]—essentially expecting the offspring to fulfill certain roles more appropriate to a father or other parental figure—and this clearly was the case in many of these sport families.[5] Among the women in the first study, the general consensus was that if a player's mother spousified her son during his participation in organized youth sport programs and later in the context of his occupational success, she will likely view his wife as a threat. This may be specifically true for mothers who view a career in professional sport as a vehicle for upward mobility, financial security, and the fulfillment of their idea of the American Dream. Some of the wives described their mothers-in-law as disappointed in their husbands for various reasons, such as the inability to achieve the desired financial success or to establish a lucrative career. In these cases, the mother may regard her son as an improved version of her husband. The son becomes a social replacement for the husband, and if the son becomes extraordinarily successful, he becomes the means for satisfying his mother's hopes, goals, or dreams. "Cliff's a lot like his dad," Beth confided. "But he also has enhanced what his father wasn't. So that's why she wants to be around him so much. She's trying to enjoy what she missed out on because of what her husband didn't accomplish, or he hasn't made the money that Cliff has." Sandy described this pattern in her husband's family: "Adam's father could care less about anything," she said, recounting her first visit with Adam's parents. "I noticed that doting, and I'm thinking, 'If I was a husband, I'd be really pissed off.' I'd say, 'Look, he's your son. I'm your husband. . . . He doesn't come home that often but give me a little attention, too.' But that's what it is. So it's like they're seeing their husbands—the son is a replacement. It's like they get hurt: Poor me, I've done all this.'" Sandy noticed that her mother-in-law took great pride in her son's career and viewed it as public validation of her lifelong sacrifice.

Much of this isn't lost on the father or son. The tendency for a mother to substitute her husband for her son as the object of her interest and support can affect the father-son relationship, and such favoritism can contribute to tension or conflict between these men. Gwen explained what she observed in Osten's family:

I think there may have been some competition for the attention of the mother. She paid so much attention to Osten. I mean, it's easy to see that. But his father had no spine. All he had to do was stand up to his wife and he could've controlled his family. But Osten would always tell anyone, "Well, my mom raised me. My dad was never home." And I think he resented that because his father was never home with him. So maybe that's how she got all the pull in the family.

Because a mother-in-law may be seeking what she thinks is missing in her own life, the spousified son may be valued more for what he achieves and less for who he is. If so, as a professional athlete he may be expected to be his mother's financial caretaker or financial partner. Many players' fathers limited their involvement in family life and took a subordinate role in their marriages and families. In these families, the wives described their fathers-in-law as passive and were disappointed in them. These fathers-in-law didn't offer support or suggest any kind of father-in-law/daughter-in-law relationship that might counterbalance the inherent power in the mother-son relationship.

Not all players' parents want to share in their son's career. Emma told me that Mason's father was rarely around. "His father went to one game, versus other parents that are very involved, come to Opening Day, participate in the career. They felt like he needed to get a real job. . . . So they really never thought what he did was important, never cared that he was a major league baseball player, which I think really hurt him, hurt his feelings, didn't make him feel that it was an achievement that was worth acknowledging." Emma described Mason's mother as emotionally distant: "He always wanted her to acknowledge him, and so I felt like that was a lot of the reasons why he was constantly looking for that, even outside of our marriage, while he was married to me." As Emma's insight implies, Mason's search for what may have been lacking in his relationship with his parents continued throughout his adult life, and this ultimately affected his marital relationship.

If the son isn't spousified and a relatively harmonious relationship between the in-laws exists, his wife may take the initiative and reach out to her husband's family or encourage him to support his mother. "When Logan wanted to do things for his family, I never stopped him," Alaina said. "I actually wanted to be even more generous and he was like, 'No, you doing that, you crazy?' I said, 'We should give her an allowance.' He was like, 'I'm going to find out what she needs and then I'm going to do that.' So, of course, we bought cars and renovated homes, and all that. So we were very good and generous to our family, and I encouraged that."

In the rest of this chapter, we will focus on the type of daughter-in-law/mother-in-law relationships that were troublesome to the wives, where the mother spousified the son to some extent.

Building Daughter-in-Law/Mother-in-Law Relationships

Paula met her future mother-in-law Doris for the first time at a holiday gathering at Doris's home. From Paula's perspective, the meeting didn't turn out well. In their brief conversations, Doris made continual references to the couple's four-year age difference and strongly implied that Paula had beguiled and taken advantage of her naïve son. After this initial encounter, Paula tried to be pleasant and deferential to Doris. Still, nothing she said or did seemed to please her future mother-in-law.

Like Paula, most of the wives were anxious to make a good first impression with their mothers-in-law. Several told me, however, that they were caught off guard and confused in the beginning. A player's mother may greet an unsuspecting prospective daughter-in-law with friendliness, but she can soon become aware of her future mother-in-law's indifference toward or disapproval of her.

Like Doris, a future mother-in-law may implicitly question or challenge her prospective daughter-in-law's motives for marrying. She may imply that the younger woman used seduction to steal her son from her, took advantage of his naïveté, or married him only for his substantial income or status as an accomplished athlete. She typically doesn't make these insinuations in her son's presence, and she frames them as innocuous comments or jokes while delivering them with an undercurrent that warns the future

> Well, it's like they say, you don't really ask for this power. But you're expected to take it on, or this control, and then it snowballs, and then before you know it you're doing everything. And they're doing their little career, and then they're coming home and popping their beer tabs, and that's it. . . . You know, it's all being done for them. It's like it's by design, almost. It's the mothers. It's all these mothers that have raised these guys.
>
> —ARISA

wife to watch her step. Matching wits with his mother on these occasions, a prospective daughter-in-law quickly learns to suppress her irritation, smile warmly, and rely on sociable conversations and a deferential attitude as she tries to gain approval and maintain some measure of control over his family's perception of her. She may make comments suggesting that the son is important to her and that she's looking forward to their marriage. Or she may emphasize that he loves her or that he will be a terrific husband and father.

Sandy discussed how she initially became aware of the special place her mother-in-law had in Adam's life the first time the couple had dinner with his parents:

> His mother made dinner and we're all sitting at the table, and she serves dinner and she said, "Adam, do you like dinner? Is everything okay?" The husband's sitting there and I'm thinking to myself, "Why aren't you asking your husband this? Why don't you ask everybody?" But she said, "Adam, is everything okay? Can I get you anything?" It was like husband and wife and it nauseated me, because she catered to him the whole time as a husband. She'd go up to him and hug him in front of me like, "Ah ha, he's mine."

Through these and similar interactions, such as hugs and other tie-signs,[6] a prospective wife becomes aware of how her future mother-in-law's overinvolvement in her son's life may affect her marriage. She begins to understand how her future mother-in-law regards her, and it's not an altogether enviable position. "She controls everyone," Gwen said. "I knew it. I was aware of it from the beginning. But I didn't know it was that strong." In light of these initial encounters, we can see why a prospective wife may become bewildered, disappointed, or upset. She realizes that she's at a distinct power disadvantage and isn't sure what to make of it.

Before or early in her marriage, a wife learns that excessive discussion about or any kind of criticism directed toward her future husband's family, and especially his mother, is unwanted, often inappropriate, and sometimes taboo. She learns that her husband may become "touchy" whenever his parents or other family members become the topic of conversation, and that he's decidedly sensitive when his mother is discussed. When Beth began to have problems in her early attempts to get Cliff's family to accept her, she became increasingly frustrated and turned to him for support. She wasn't prepared for his reaction, which she thought was defensive. Trying to make sense of this, she said, "You have to know that you're hitting a sensitive nerve when you're talking about his family, about his mom or dad, everyone. But I had to talk to him because I didn't know what to do with the frustration I had because I didn't know them. I don't know why they do the things they do. That was probably my biggest adjustment." Even when a prospective wife anticipates some adjustment to his family, she may soon become aware of underlying family issues and may feel unprepared to confront them.

Once the prospective daughter-in-law has had a few interactions with her future mother-in-law, she quickly learns to "know her place" in her husband's family, just as she's learning to know her place in her marriage and her husband's career. Knowing her place early in her relationship with her mother-in-law can involve some level of competition between the women, which, as we will learn, can accelerate into a spirited female rivalry. Gwen described some of her early encounters, which were filled with much frustration:

> It was so subtle. I knew what was going on. He didn't know what was going on, but she knew that I knew what was going on. So she wouldn't overstep her bounds, because from the beginning when they first met me, I was so outspoken that I think she knew that if she overstepped, I would say something to Osten. She didn't want that wedge in between her, and him, and me. So she did everything she possibly could to try to make me think otherwise. But I'm no dummy.

Sandy's reaction was similar: "I thought, 'I'll beat her at her own game without me looking bad.' You know? Because at the beginning it was a power play. It was like, 'Who's going to get more attention? Me or the mom?'"

When Lewis was establishing his MLB career, Lewis and Olivia were living together before they married, and this arrangement angered his mother Rita. Olivia conjectured that this was because Rita had less influence and was losing control over her son. Recalling one certain occasion, Olivia discussed how she stood up to Rita:

> She would tell me, "When's Lewis coming home?" I said, "Oh, he'll be back here on such and such a day." She would tell me, "No, when is he coming home?" I said, "Oh, but he lives here. Mama, he lives here. This is his home, here with me." She would tell me, "Well, you know what I mean when I say home—home, because his room's here." I said, "That's not his room and that's not his home. He lives here and his room is upstairs with me." But see, she can't accept that. That's why she doesn't like me, because I took her baby away.

When a mother is the dominant parent in the sport family, she probably becomes the family gatekeeper,[7] testing outsiders and guarding her family's boundaries and her son. She may test her daughter-in-law's worthiness to be a part of the family and her capacity for control, to see if she might be a threat to her or her family. Discussing this family pattern several months after their marriage, an annoyed Paula said, "His family automatically judged me the moment they met me. The moment they heard about me, they figured it was somebody chasing after Jason for his fame and fortune. And they let me know that in roundabout ways and let Jason know that." Sandy encountered similar, unanticipated issues with Adam's mother:

> Just when they were ready to reap those benefits, I come into the picture. But I got around that by buying more things for Adam. Well, I did have more money than him at the time; I'd been working all those years. So it was real hard for them to find something wrong with me, and it killed them because they liked me. But they didn't like me because I took their son, and their only son, and it really bugged them—the mother, not so much his father.

In most instances, the mother-in-law's gatekeeping serves to protect the privacy of the family or to keep outsiders out of the family. As Paula became more familiar with Doris's boundaries, she realized that Doris could be influential in encouraging Jason's brothers and sisters-in-law to protect him from people she feared would take advantage of him. But Paula felt excluded by a conspiracy of silence when the family tried to keep certain secrets. She wasn't alone in experiencing this exclusion, yet it emphasized her outsider status within her husband's family.

A mother-in-law's boundary work can be difficult to challenge, let alone change. Despite years of marriage, a wife who has proven that she married for the right reasons may find that she may always be viewed as a subordinate outsider to the family.

Mother-Son Bond

As we are beginning to see, when a husband maintains an unusually strong attachment and loyalty to his mother, it can become a durable bond. This bond consists of a presumably unspoken agreement between the mother and son in which the son prioritizes the needs of his mother over the needs of his wife, and it can adversely affect a marriage. When a husband fails to support his wife when disagreements arise and to challenge his mother when necessary, his wife may become disappointed and irritated, and she may even believe that he's betraying her. When he doesn't intervene on her behalf, she may be initially confused, but she eventually becomes upset as she realizes that his passivity undermines any power or control she may have in managing her mother-in-law's intrusions into her marital and family life. "It's funny, because if it was something he really didn't want her to do, and it was for his benefit, he could easily tell her," Gwen said. "But if it was something that I didn't want, or we both really didn't want, but he didn't feel comfortable saying it to her, he didn't say anything. He just let it go. That would piss me off."

> The sons don't want to make waves, and this would be Cliff. So it might bother him to hell about certain things, but he just doesn't say anything, and it just stays like that and it's so ridiculous.
> —BETH

A husband who sides with his mother rather than his wife contributes to a power imbalance not only between his wife and mother but in his marital relationship. Seemingly trivial family and marital issues can become the basis for power politics, and clashing agendas may cause jealousy or, as suggested earlier, foster open rivalry between the women. A wife may come to believe that she's in direct competition with her mother-in-law for her husband's love.

It may not be enough for a husband to be fully aware of his mother's dominance or her need to be in control. Confronting his mother on behalf of his wife may be so unnerving that he may think twice about it. He may believe that challenging his mother is somehow questioning their relationship. Beth discussed this aspect of Cliff's relationship with Martha, his mother: "Unfortunately, the way he deals with it, he doesn't want anybody's feelings hurt. So he's not always up front with his own mom and it bothers him. You have to realize that your mom's not perfect, or there's things that bug me about his mom. It's hard to accept that. So then it bothers him, which he only takes internally and stews on it, and that doesn't help either."

If a husband is reluctant to challenge this parental power, a wife may eventually decide to take it upon herself to try to change her mother-in-law's behavior. Without her husband's support, however, she finds herself in an impossible situation. His passivity results in his complicity in his mother's use of power when, for example, he allows her to control him or to continue spoiling him, and this may carry over into his marriage.

SKYLAR

One of the reasons Carter's parents retired early was so they could devote their time to his MLB career. Skylar described this decision as "really weird," and it happened early in Carter's career and their marriage. Carter was in the minor leagues at the time. He and Skylar married shortly before his first spring training, and Skylar was excited to stay with him while he trained for the upcoming season. Carter's parents lived near the couple's offseason residence, and they made it clear that they wanted to be an integral part of the couple's life. Carter's mother often helped Skylar with laundry, and the four of them frequently dined together. Skylar, who was in her early twenties, soon felt overwhelmed with the way her in-laws insinuated themselves into her life, but she had no idea how to handle it. "I didn't know then about boundaries and separating from parents, and really respecting boundaries, and telling them it's not okay," she told me during the second study. If she did try to set a boundary, her in-laws would counter it by explaining how important Carter's career was to them. "They wanted to be able to follow him around and see him play everywhere—that was their goal," Skylar said. "So part of it was that every time I would speak up, it was like I'm taking away their dream. They live for this, they don't have any other friends, they just love being at the ballpark."

In her attempt to make sense of this situation, Skylar chastised herself for being selfish and less understanding than she should be. But she also felt justified because Carter was consistently at the ballpark in the early afternoon and didn't return home until late in the evening, so the newly married couple had limited time together, and she resented it. One of the things that made it difficult for her to speak up was that she and Carter struggled to live on his minor league salary and they had become financially dependent on his parents.

After the season began, Carter was struggling on the mound. Hoping to support him, Skylar offered to join him during an upcoming road trip. He refused her offer, worrying that she would be a distraction and he didn't want to lose his job. Skylar understood Carter's concern and reluctantly agreed, but was dismayed when she learned that his parents had made arrangements to go on the road trip. "I wasn't able to go, which was really hard, because he wouldn't really tell them no, but then he would tell me no," Skylar said. "I'm older now and, as I reflect back, he was probably really honest with me, but he couldn't tell them no."

Skylar's efforts to accommodate her in-laws early in their marriage made it exceedingly difficult to be a new wife, to find her way in Carter's occupational world, and—because she had to share so much of her life with her in-laws—to make new friends. It was "really suffocating," she said.

Surviving Subordination

A player's wife ordinarily tries to maintain as much control as she can for as long as she can, but she soon realizes that she must somehow respond to her mother-in-law's use of power through subordination work.[8] Her subordination work, which she believes is in the best interest of her marriage, includes acts of deference and accommodation in her interactions with her mother-in-law. She is convinced that subordination work is necessary to preserve her marriage without alienating her husband or his mother or impairing his career. She tries to avoid upsetting her husband and his mother by expressing feelings only in ways that work to her advantage, and she actively manages her marginalization from his family by negotiating her power position in relationship to her husband and his mother. She's convinced that her control work and subordination work are necessary to establish and defend her areas of control (such as her home), so she tries to be polite, friendly, and agreeable. She knows that situations involving her mother-in-law can become emotionally complex, and she places a high value on keeping the peace, so she learns to avoid ruffling any feathers and to sidestep any direct confrontation. Unwanted conflict with a mother-in-law is less likely to occur when a wife doesn't challenge her mother-in-law's dominance, authority, or her bond with her son. "It seems to me that in order for me to get on their 'good' side, I have to fall all over myself to be good to Jason, and I have to do millions of favors for the family," Paula said. "I have to be exceptionally sweet to Doris, and I don't want to do it." Using the same approach, Sandy explained, "I'm just real nice to her. I don't want to give her any reason to dislike me, especially in front of everybody, because sooner or later it pays off."

Subordination work in no way implies that players' wives are passive or weak. Quite the contrary, trying to control uncontrollable situations calls for guile, patience, and resilience. Not only is this tiresome for these women, but there is no assurance that it will provide the hoped-for result. If these women were fully subordinated, they wouldn't struggle; they would just accept the inequality. But because of what they have at stake in their marriages, they believe that they have limited choices in supporting their husbands and responding to their mothers-in-law's control work, and so they are confronted with a vexing dilemma. A wife is deeply aware of her need to avoid jeopardizing her relationship with her mother-in-law, which may affect her relationship with her husband. But she also is concerned about compromising her own sense of self and her marital and family priorities. The more she works to establish her identity as an empowered woman and a "good wife/mother," the more she feels compelled to accept her subordination as she tries to ensure the stability of her marriage and family. She lives with the struggle because she wants to keep her family intact and to be viewed as a woman who loves her husband and supports his career, but the struggle can cause her considerable confusion and anger. She knows that she's strong and capable, and she believes that her husband and his mother should recognize and acknowledge her exhaustive efforts to "hold it all together." She feels trapped by her choices: the more she loves her husband, the more trapped she is, and she doesn't see another possibility, especially early in the marriage. Her husband and his mother know she will accommodate them because of what she has at stake, so there is no reason for them to change. As a result, various control issues emerge and lead to power struggles with her mother-in-law.

In-Law Relationships in Private Life

Although a mother-in-law in the sport family capably enforces boundaries in caring for her family, when the daughter-in-law tries to enforce the boundaries of her marriage, she predictably fails. Perhaps because these mothers-in-law feel ignored, or because they feel excluded when their daughters-in-law disregard their uninvited guidance, they insinuate themselves into the son's marriage in several ways. Many of their intrusions follow patterns that are not that unusual in many other families, yet the son's all-consuming occupation and high-profile status, and the long-lasting bond between the mother and son, add layers of intrusiveness that may be unique to these types of marriages. As Olivia told me, "She'd like to come between us if she could."

According to the wives in both studies, advice-offering mothers-in-law are common in their marriages, and their advice may not always be welcome. As

Callie explained, "She liked to give him advice when it wasn't always needed, and he was a grown man at that point and making decisions on his own, but—and she is still like this—she likes to give advice whether you want her to or not, and there were times when it would frustrate me." In Skylar's case, both in-laws liked to offer advice, and she, like many other wives, relied on some form of subordination work when this happened. "They're very opinionated . . . like, big-time advice givers—just constantly having opinions about things. I felt very obligated to just listen to everything they had to say. I didn't want to upset the apple cart, because I don't want Carter to choose between me and them. And then what if he doesn't choose me? That's even worse. So you just always were on edge."

Beginning in the first year of Gwen and Osten's marriage, Celia developed a habit of dropping in to visit the newlyweds on a regular basis—unannounced and uninvited—and outstaying her welcome. Gwen eventually became really annoyed with these regular visits. Whatever control Gwen had in her home was compromised, and she was emotionally trapped between Osten and Celia as she attempted to gain control of the situation. Gwen alternately tried to ignore, appease, and discourage Celia while simultaneously trying to avoid antagonizing, irritating, or alienating Osten. When Celia and her husband (who may have been reluctant but was nevertheless passively compliant) visited the couple, Gwen didn't prepare meals for them or do anything to encourage them to stay. She purposely didn't include them in the couple's plans or activities, or she explained that they had plans and wouldn't be home. "I wouldn't play this little good-hostess type thing," she said. But Celia ignored these and other attempts to dissuade her interference in the couple's lives. Gwen was upset with Celia and gradually became more frustrated with Osten when she tried to enlist his support in dealing with his mother. He didn't discourage the constant visits and denied that they were creating problems. He continually made reference to the way

> See, this is another thing I noticed. This makes me so mad. She asks my opinion and then when I give her an answer, she does just the opposite. It happens a lot. You should have seen me at dinner. I was so mad. I was just, oh, you could feel the tension at the table. But I can't blow up. She doesn't think she's doing anything wrong.
> —PAULA

his mother treated him as a measure of how Gwen should treat him. "His mom was constantly telling him, she doesn't know that I know, that I didn't treat him right," Gwen said. "I'm like, 'How am I supposed to treat you? Wait on you hand and foot like she does your dad and you? I'm not your maid. If you want a maid, hire one.'"

Gwen's case points to the extra strain a mother-in-law can put on a sport marriage. When the mother-in-law lives close to the couple, she often spends too much time in their home. She's typically critical of household functioning and may attempt to discourage or prevent her son from carrying out various tasks in his home.[9] She may attempt to make his wife feel incompetent or self-conscious about her ability to perform household tasks or to be what her mother-in-law considers a "good wife" to her son. In turn, a wife may try to prevent these types of intrusions by attempting to reinforce her own home as an area of her control. When Celia constantly questioned Gwen's homemaking abilities, Gwen attempted to set a boundary by emphasizing her preference for her own mother's domestic skills:

> It wasn't anything of a shock because I knew, "Oh, she's going to try to tell me how to do everything in this house." But see, as soon as she would say it, I was like, "Well, I don't like that. My mom did it like this and this is how I do it." I mean, I could tell it would piss her off. But see, at the same time, it gave me pleasure, because it was like, "I know I'm getting ready to push buttons, because I'm not going to do what you want me to do and watch me watch you try to hold it in."

Unfortunately, these types of boundary work are not normally successful, and a wife can begin to feel trapped in her own home. Sheila explained how her mother-in-law often relied on relatively passive forms of control work, which made boundary work impossible without risking a direct confrontation. "If I would cook something, she would go back and do it again, you know, 'Well, let me make you one.' Or 'Let me make his steak. This is how he likes his.' Just little subtle things."

As Gwen had feared, Celia's visits progressed to the point where her in-laws almost moved in. Gwen's friends joked and gossiped about the couple's inability to do anything about the situation. Suppressing her anger and tactfully faking a lack of concern, Gwen tried to manage what she regarded as Celia's attempts to challenge her right to control her own home. Unfortunately, her efforts became increasingly difficult and emotionally draining. Just when Gwen was ready to express her anger at Celia for her constant intrusions, Celia would back off and withdraw from the household, revealing that Celia knew just how far she could push Gwen and how much she could get away with. Celia's habit of dropping in continued during the first few years of Gwen's marriage, making no distinction between the season and offseason, until she finally understood that Gwen would no longer allow impromptu visits.

Brent's mother Colleen had always moved into Rhonda's family's seasonal residence during the MLB season to help with her young grandchildren and the household labor while Rhonda worked outside the home. Even though Rhonda knew that Colleen could be controlling, she appreciated her support during the stressful seasons, so she initially thought of the situation as mutually beneficial. But the arrangement gradually created dissension and additional conflict in the household. What irritated Rhonda most was Brent's acceptance of the way his mother treated him. For example, Rhonda expected him to carry out certain domestic responsibilities, such as packing his own travel gear for road trips. When Colleen packed his travel gear for him, Rhonda was upset. "She caters to him," she said in exasperation. "The other night, before he went on the road trip, she goes in there and starts packing his suitcase and I just about came unglued. I've not packed his suitcase in nine years. I refuse to pack his suitcase. He's a big boy. He can pack it himself. I just about went nuts, because she undoes a lot of the things that I've tried to do. It's a killer."

A small number of couples in the first study agreed that for financial or occupational reasons it was in their best interest to temporarily live with the husband's parents or mother. These arrangements, however, can be exceptionally stressful for a player's wife. Unlike other wives who have greater power over their mothers-in-law,[10] a wife in this situation lacks the power needed to adequately challenge her mother-in-law's dominance or resist her attempts to control her. Her mother-in-law can use her home and her relationship with her son as leverage. The situation can be awkward for the wife and can escalate any existing conflict, especially if the relationship began on a rocky note or has become increasingly stressful.

PAULA

The MLB lockout in 1990 led Paula and Jason to experience such serious financial difficulties that they decided to accept Doris's invitation to move temporarily into her home. Anticipating the move, Paula had serious misgivings. "It just kills me to watch her wait on him hand and foot. I hate that," she said.

After they moved in, Paula's worst fears were realized when she began to sense that Doris wanted to control everything that went on in her home, including her. "She's not right out controlling like, 'You guys do this, and do this, and do this.' She never says that. It's always under-the-table stuff. That's why it's pissing me off so much." To Paula, it felt like a game of cat and mouse, and it angered her. "It seems to me that she's testing me to see if I'll break—to see if I'll do what she wants me to do or how she would like it to be," she said.

Paula was able to manage her irritation by trying to pretend that everything was fine, but it became more and more difficult as time passed. Discussing the emotional strain and alienation she was experiencing, she told me, "I get a feeling of weakness and helplessness." Jason's occupational situation forced the couple to stay longer than they wanted to, and the tension in the house was so thick that Paula finally decided to try to do something to minimize it. Her boundary work was unsuccessful because Doris ignored her, minimized her concerns, and continued to indulge Jason. "Like this morning she brought him the newspaper in bed!" Paula said, pointing out that this "baby treatment" was not limited to Jason, but included Paula. "She treats me like a baby, too," she said with irritation.

Exasperated and clearly at her wit's end, Paula decided to ask Jason to intervene on her behalf. Jason was well aware of his mother's behavior and knew how hard things had been for Paula, but he was initially reluctant to comply with her request. The second time Paula asked for his support, she gave him an ultimatum: it was either her or his mother—if he chose not to speak to his mother, she would move out of the home. One evening, Jason reluctantly talked to his mother as Paula eavesdropped from an adjacent room, and she interpreted his attempt to support her as feeble and ineffective. She managed to suppress her anger toward Doris and buried her disappointment in Jason, trying to remain optimistic that things would eventually improve. Her dilemma was resolved only when the lockout finally ended, Jason signed a new contract with an interested team, and Paula and Jason moved out of Doris's home.

Living in her mother-in-law's household where her power may be intentionally or indirectly expressed, a wife soon learns that her personal autonomy is threatened. She must adjust to, contend with, or resist her mother-in-law's attempts to control the people and situations in the home. In the wife's effort to gain control in what is seemingly an uncontrollable arrangement, she will slip into a subordinate role and make a sincere effort to better manage confrontation or conflict through subordination work. She learns to suppress the "wrong" emotions and express the "right" emotions as she tries to avoid disagreements with her mother-in-law. Like Paula, she manages a pleasing, friendly attitude and attempts to be deferential when she greets, compliments, or offers to lend a hand in interactions with her mother-in-law. She learns that having the right attitude can put her in a more favorable power position and help her avoid any criticism from her mother-in-law and her husband, or ostracism from his family. Beth, who lived with her mother-in-law Martha for a time because of occupational changes and financial constraints, explained how she dealt with the situation: "Sometimes, if I'm upset, I just ignore her. I just go into another room and just ignore her. Sometimes, I skirt around it and hope that she gets the point—while my teeth are grinding—because I'm not sure if I would end up alienating her by really expressing how I feel." But, as Paula and Beth learned, subordination work takes strength and resolve and can come with an emotional cost to the wife.

Interestingly, according to the wives in the first study, separation by long geographical distances doesn't seem to minimize or deter a determined mother-in-law's intrusions into her son's marriage or to minimize or prevent conflict with his wife. A wife may still find it necessary to use control work or boundary work with her mother-in-law over long distances, which can be challenging. Some mothers exclude their daughters-in-law by relying on communication methods with their sons that can marginalize a wife. Adam's mother, for example, sent correspondence meant only for him and his children to his workplace rather than his residence and included critical remarks about Sandy that were not meant for her to read. She also sent birthday and holiday gifts to him and his children, but only token gifts or none at all to Sandy, offering apologetic excuses or no explanation for the oversight. Lacking control over these long-distance situations and finding it difficult to manage her anger, Sandy referred to these incidents as "control tricks" and viewed them as efforts to maintain a power advantage. To avoid offending Adam's mother, she pretended that her feelings were not hurt. Try as she might, she wasn't able to sustain this pretense, so she attempted to persuade Adam to intervene and support her. In this situation, she used a passive-aggressive form of control work by trying to appear naïve, concerned, and confused by his mother's actions:

I had it manipulated so that I made her look bad without cutting on her. You mention it once, and then when his mother would call, I'd say, "Oh, your mom called. You really should call her." You know, say something like "Why don't you give her a call?" I'd always mention that or, "It's your mom's birthday. How about if I go buy something?" I would always buy it. When she would do things, I'd say, "Oh, isn't that nice, she gave all these people Christmas gifts." But I got shit on Christmas and I'd never say, "Look, she never did anything for me." I'd say, "Isn't that really nice. I really like this trinket she gave me." Pretty soon he'd start saying, "She's not nice, Sandy." I mean, make her look good, and it started pissing him off.

Sandy learned the hard way that when she resorted to criticism, it didn't have the outcome she had hoped for. She told me:

> She did something that really pissed me off. She wrote a letter saying something about me, or something like that, and I said, "Well, fuck her. I'm sick of that bitch." He went off on me. "How dare you call my mother that," and this and that. I sat back and I thought, "You know, really, Sandy, this is ridiculous. You have to rise above this. You're smarter than this woman. Is this a matter of me just wanting to see how I can beat my husband down like she does to him? To get him to the point where he'll just look at me?" I knew there was a side of her that was doing it to get at me and to get at him.

In the end, almost all of Sandy's efforts to establish control or set boundaries were fruitless and, like Gwen and Paula, her attempt to develop an alliance with Adam failed. But where their mothers-in-law are concerned, wives still believe these efforts are necessary because, as Gwen reflected, "If you give an inch, she takes a yard."

Olivia felt fortunate that she was able to keep some measure of geographical and emotional distance between her and Rita, who resided in a different state. But when Rita learned that Lewis had been traded to an MLB team in his hometown and was going to relocate his family, she insisted that they move in with her. She told Olivia that she had already renovated the basement in her house to accommodate the family. Although Olivia wasn't surprised at Rita's presumption, it upset her. Trying to keep her composure and avoid any emotional outburst, she exuded cordiality while directly challenging Rita's plans. Even though she was angry, she diplomatically declined the invitation in a phone conversation, explaining that she had already planned to purchase a house for her family. In response, Rita attempted to enlist her son's cooperation by calling him to complain. She told him that if he wasn't going to accept her offer and if he had enough money to buy another house, the least he could do was to reimburse her for the basement renovation.

In-Law Relationships in Public Life

As we discovered in chapter 2, women married to professional athletes try to keep their personal and public lives separate, and most tolerate but are not always comfortable performing the role of player's wife in public life. In strong contrast, wives in the first study said that a mother-in-law may gladly perform the public roles that rightfully belong to her daughter-in-law. She may enjoy the spotlight that her daughter-in-law would rather avoid.

Like Celia, a mother-in-law may try to share aspects of her son's occupational life and take great delight in it. She may even become so preoccupied with his career that she makes it the center of her life. Emphasizing this point about Martha, Beth observed, "She gets excited and that's great. She really loves the fact that her son plays baseball. It gives her something to talk about. It gives a lot of meaning to her life. I mean, what better to brag about than your son playing baseball, right? But it also, I think, puts her a little bit in the limelight, too, because I think mothers look at it like, 'Well, he wouldn't be there if it wasn't for me.'"

An overinvolved mother-in-law's eagerness to be connected in some way to her son's career may be embedded in her belief that she's entitled to benefit in some way from the fruits of his career because she alone unselfishly sacrificed for him when he participated in organized youth sport programs. This is especially the case if she has spousified him, with their shared goal of occupational success serving as the continued basis for their bond. She follows his career with great devotion, expressing joy at his triumphs, taking an avid interest in the nuances of his career, showing deep concern with his occupational setbacks, and boasting with pride about his athletic skills, celebrity, or high income. She regularly attends his games, gossips with the wives, stays informed about the latest rumors regarding the people and activities on his team, attends wife-only functions or team events, basks in his spotlight, enjoys being interviewed by members of the media, anticipates expensive gifts from him, or expects financial support from him. Describing Rita in this context, Olivia said, "She comes to the games. I mean, she's okay at the games. But you know what she wants to do? She wants to know who everybody is, and she wants you to introduce her to everybody. She's always excited. She says, 'Well, who's that? Well, tell me this, who's that? How'd you meet her? How long they play baseball? They millionaires? Well, what kind of money they make?' That's her, that's probably why there's such a thing as a mother-in-law syndrome." She compared Rita's attempts to include herself in aspects of her son's occupational life to that of a female groupie, referring to her as a "mother-in-law groupie" (see chapter 6).

A mother-in-law's continual attempts to include herself in her son's occupational life tends to be intensely stressful for her daughter-in-law, but as long as her public behavior doesn't impair her son's reputation, she can expect his approval, and a wife will have little recourse but to accept the displays of parental power. But if a mother-in-law fails to practice game etiquette, intentionally or not, it's the wife not her mother-in-law who is embarrassed or placed in an awkward position. A wife's ability to maintain her own composure can be sorely tested when her mother-in-law accompanies her to various public events and doesn't adhere to the unwritten rules. Beth shared with me an embarrassing incident involving Martha during a particular game:

> I was thinking of a time when she said, "Oh, can you believe they're taking Cliff out to put so and so's husband in?" His wife was, like, two seats over from me. So I, like, slid under the seat. I looked at her and said, "Well, why should you be surprised? They're throwing a lefty and he's a right-handed hitter, and he's really good. So what?" You know, like that, because she said, "Oh, he went zero for three, anyway." Inside I was dying like, "Oh, my god, I hope his wife hears everything I had to say, and that she doesn't take it the wrong way, and maybe she didn't hear it at all." I was terribly embarrassed and turning red from inside out. I wanted to hit my mother-in-law. I mean, I wanted to level that lady. That's how upset I was about the whole thing. I was so furious. I wanted to just look at his wife and say, "I am sorry for what my mother-in-law just said." See, the thing is, if she didn't hear it then—I mean, you never know what's going to be heard. So that's why I had to think really fast when she said that.

As illustrated in Beth's story, in a public situation like this, a wife may be so deeply embarrassed that her efforts to repair or salvage the situation or save face by trying to "smooth things over" may not be enough,[11] and all she can do is suppress her feelings and avoid any emotional outburst that might embarrass, offend, or anger her mother-in-law.

These types of situations can test the limits of the wife's subordination work and also her ability to properly manage her emotions in public. Beth discussed some of her concerns about Martha's behavior at the games:

You don't know who's going to be there and something you might say, they might take completely out of context and blow it out of proportion. Which is true, I mean, it could happen to anybody. One time at a game . . . she leaned over like, "So how are things between so and so?" You're like, "Who's sitting behind me?" I mean, she can rock the boat for both of us. It's just the fact when she makes a comment about a player and say his wife is there, then she takes it personally, which then reflects off of me because this is my mother-in-law. You may not like that wife and your husband may not like that husband, but you play on the same team and you have to get along, right? That's just stuff that you keep to yourself. You had to really be careful what you wanted to tell her because who knew what she was going to discuss with her best friend who came to the game with her.

Likewise, should a player's mother intentionally or unintentionally disclose personal or occupational secrets when she, for instance, indiscreetly participates in gossip, contributes to rumors, or shares sensitive information, it's the player's wife who may be blamed or experience other unpleasant outcomes. Even her husband may believe it's his wife who is at fault and that she should keep his mother "in line." This wife, then, repeatedly finds herself firmly wedged between a rock and a hard place. Even though she has no power or resources to gain control when her mother-in-law breaks the unwritten rules, she risks losing face with her mother-in-law, her husband, his family, the other wives, and possibly the sport organization. It's even worse if media outlets exploit a humiliating incident.

A mother's public behavior and disclosures can affect her son's reputation among his teammates or his sport organization, but he still may be unwilling to confront or correct her. Beth discussed this perplexing issue. "The only thing that ever really bothers me about her is when she wants to be a part of baseball. And she'll even want to know about the gossip end of what's going on with the wives and things like that I won't tell her, and Cliff is glad that I tell him, because then he has to remind her. He says, 'I'm glad you told me because I need to remind my mom to keep her mouth shut when she's in the stands.'" Even though a husband like Cliff may say to his wife that he will remind his mother about appropriate public behavior and the consequences of improper disclosures, he may not want to upset his mother or hurt her feelings. Instead, because a wife like Beth regularly accompanies his mother in most public situations involving his occupation, he expects his wife to keep her in line. His wife may believe it's his responsibility to discuss his mother's public behavior with her, but when he fails to do so, it becomes her responsibility.

GWEN

From the time Osten was a young, promising basketball player, Celia had been his most avid supporter. When her son finally reached the NBA, each home game became a major event in her life. She didn't report for work on game days, staying instead in Gwen and Osten's home for the entire day. She took great care with how she dressed, applied her makeup, and accessorized, trying to achieve the "look" of an NBA wife before leaving with Gwen to go to the game. Gwen observed, "It's funny, because all the wives, they're like, 'Oh, is Osten's mom coming tonight?' I'm like, 'Yeah.' They're like, 'Oh, I wonder what she's going to have on.' . . . I think she thrived off of that, because she would be like, 'I don't know what I'm wearing tonight.' I'm like, 'You're lying because you brought it from home.'"

Osten's father was a good intercollegiate football player, but he never made it to the NFL. When Osten made it to the NBA, Celia was finally able to step into a role for which she had been preparing for many years. Gwen said, "Osten's mother was a surrogate wife. I mean, if you ask anyone, if you go to one of our games, everyone would tell you she was there. If we had three games a week, she was there three times a week. She knew the statistics better than anyone on the team. It was her grandstand appearance. It was her stage show." She felt a need to share her son's celebrity, and this was evident in her attitude toward others. "I don't think they really knew what to think of her, because if she didn't think you were someone, she treated you real shitty," Gwen confided. "And that's what embarrassed me. I didn't want her around me. I didn't want anyone to associate her with me."

Celia barely concealed her effort to embrace the role of NBA player's wife. Discussing Celia's tendency to do this, Gwen described an incident involving Celia at the first home game of the new NBA season. "So during the game, when they saw her jumping up, they said, 'Oh that must be Osten's wife.' I could hear them talking because they're behind me, and I'm cracking up because I was like, 'I'm not saying anything. She won't be here all the time.' But she was here most of the time. She loved it because the first thing she said to Osten was, 'Oh, guess what? They thought that I was your wife.'"

Role Reversal

In these sport families, it's fairly common for an exchange of parental and marital roles to occur, and an extreme aspect of the daughter-in-law/mother-in-law relationship is a daughter-in-law/mother-in-law role reversal.[12] This role reversal can take place over short or long geographical distances, and it's supported through the mother-son bond. A wife accepts the role of mother in private life and, as a separate process, her mother-in-law takes the role of player's wife in public life by actively including herself in different aspects of her son's occupational life. This role exchange may reflect the mother's desire for fans to define her as a player's wife. She may be reluctant to step out of this public role. A mother-in-law may actively seek to continue the "we" partnership she established when her son was a young athlete. When she performs the public roles that are more appropriate to her daughter-in-law, it suggests that she has a need to vicariously experience her son's achievements as a professional athlete, in much the same way she identified with his success as a young athlete, but on a much larger scale and for much higher stakes.

When a mother-in-law oversteps boundaries and takes or borrows her daughter-in-law's role in public life, a wife may feel threatened. It leads her to think that her mother-in-law is "out of control," as Callie observed. She worries that she, the wife, will be the target of criticism because of her mother-in-law's inappropriate public behavior. She also worries that she will be displaced in her relationships with others, including the wives on his team, the members of his family, and perhaps her husband. Interestingly, the mother-in-law doesn't view her behavior as inappropriate. Making this point about Celia, Gwen said, "She wanted people to know, 'Hey, he's here because of me.' I mean, she wanted you to know that. She always made announcements to people: 'Look at me.'"

The husband's mother's effort to spousify him in this role reversal can further subordinate a wife and provide his mother with additional power to disrupt the marital relationship. When her son condones this role reversal through his tacit approval, a wife has little choice but to accept it. She will always be challenged to defer to his mother because she doesn't have enough power to defy or minimize her mother-in-law's influence. When combined with his mother's power, a husband's power can be a factor in the role reversal. His mother's need to perform certain public and domestic roles can contribute to the motherization of his wife. Despite her resistance toward playing the role of mother to him, she may relent when trying to cope with the occupational stressors in her husband's career. This role reversal can be the basis for or expose power struggles between the women. Discussing Doris's tendency to control and displace her from certain domestic situations, Paula said, "She just won't give him up. She won't give her baby up."

Playing to Win

Female subordination has long been recognized in relation to male dominance in patriarchal cultures, yet the sport marriage also unveils a form of female subordination: an intergenerational inequality in which older women dominate younger women. Although this process of subordination might outwardly look like a strictly female rivalry, it's cemented through the mother-son bond. Given what we've learned so far about the sport marriage, one might assume that the professional athlete holds the crucial power position in this triangle. But if the mother has spousified her son, the relationship can also include some form of male subordination, which the son responds to with his own subordination work with his mother, and as we have seen, he can be emotionally wedged between the two most important women in his life as they compete for his compliance, loyalty, or support. He may feel pressured to choose sides, which may include selective passivity or an unwillingness to support his wife when a family disagreement arises. He will most often acquiesce to his mother, and this leaves his wife in third place. (The wives in the first study also reported that this normalized pattern of passivity was apparent among their fathers-in-law and their own fathers, and thus may suggest a recurring intergenerational marital/family pattern among the men in these families.)

For everyone involved, power struggles are motivated by a desire to "win" and are interpreted differently according to the meanings

> Don't get me wrong, I love my husband, I really do, but if I really knew what his mother was like, I don't know if I would've married him.
> —GWEN

they assign to a given outcome. In the husband's effort to win, he seeks occupational prestige (which translates into power), which he believes is partially possible because of his wife's investment in their marriage and his career and because of his mother's investment in her relationship with him. Both the overinvolved mother-in-law and daughter-in-law experience vicarious achievement. Each seeks validation of their relational investment through the son's/husband's occupational success and fame, and thus share this perception of winning. In the wife's effort to win, she competes for her husband's loyalty and love and for the stability of her marriage and family.[13] She believes she can achieve this by preserving the relationship with her husband and protecting her marriage from her mother-in-law's intrusions. Similarly, the mother-in-law seems to further define winning as validation of her maternal nurturing and support and her identity and power within her family, which she can achieve by preserving the relationship with her son and subordinating her daughter-in-law or excluding her altogether from her family.

Calling a Truce

In rare instances, a husband may confront his mother. "There were times where she would just keep pushing and he would say, 'Hey that's enough,' and she would stop," Callie said. During the second study, Sheila fondly recalled when Frank stood up to his mother when she was talking about Sheila:

> He was still playing when I really saw a turning point. We were actually visiting them and his dad got sick and had to be in the hospital. So he spent the night with her in case something should happen during the night, and she took the opportunity to start pointing out all my faults. And he stopped it. He told her, "Don't force me to choose." And ever since then—I think until he actually stood up to her and made it clear that we're married and it's going to stay that way—I think she accepted us being married and she's been great ever since.

According to almost all of the wives, however, it is rare for a husband to set these kinds of boundaries with his mother.

Even though most husbands wouldn't confront their mothers on behalf of their wives, some husbands did support their wives when they were having a difficult time with their mothers-in-law. "Douglas told me that nobody had ever been good enough in her eyes for him. So he told me, 'You just keep doing what you're doing. I got your back,'" Alyssa said.

The second study reveals that some mother-in-law/daughter-in-law relationships can change in ways a wife may not anticipate. This improvement seems to be connected to two significant transitions in the lives of the couples and their in-laws: the end of the husband's career and the arrival of grandchildren. "It's better, much better than it was," Paula said during the second study. "I think she is closer to me than her own daughter. In the beginning of our marriage, my husband was playing baseball, and his family was very suspicious of me. I think it began to change after baseball, but then after our first daughter was born was when it really started to get a lot better, because my mother-in-law was really close to my daughter." Alyssa, like Paula, saw a shift in the relationship over the years: "It's definitely changed," she said. "At first it was difficult, because I felt like she didn't think that I was the one for her son. But as time went on, she became one of my biggest allies. Even now that her son and I are estranged, every time I talk to her, every time I see her, she repeatedly tells me how much she misses me. So, yeah, it definitely improved." Besides the passage of time, the end of the husband's career made a difference in how the women related. Beth referred to both factors in discussing how her relationship with her mother-in-law changed: "I would say probably that by the time his career was pretty much over and he was transitioning into a different kind of a role in baseball, I think that helped. We also moved closer to where they were. So that also was a little less of a strain, because we saw them more often and, for her, that was really important."

CHAPTER 6

A World of Groupies

LISA

After a long, grueling NFL season was finally over, Lisa and Raymond decided to go on a much-anticipated vacation cruise with friends. One evening during the cruise they attended the formal captain's ball, and after they were seated a young woman, whom Lisa clearly regarded as a groupie, approached Raymond. Ignoring Lisa, she told Raymond, who was one of the more famous and respected players in the NFL at the time, that she was a big fan. Without an invitation, she promptly sat down on his lap and wiggled around flirtatiously. Lisa was furious that a complete stranger would behave in such a way right in front of her, and she demanded an explanation for her behavior. The woman explained that she only wanted to have her picture taken with Raymond. Raymond did not discourage the attention; instead, he smiled and spoke to the woman in a friendly way. Lisa tried to suppress her anger and manage her composure, but the woman continued to move around on Raymond's lap and he chatted amiably with her while ignoring his wife. Unable to restrain herself, Lisa suddenly stood up and pushed the young woman off his lap, dumping her unceremoniously onto the floor. The woman stared up at Lisa with a look of stunned surprise, then stood up and straightened her dress as she defended her behavior, insisting that she only wanted a photo with Raymond. Lisa loudly chastised the woman in front of startled onlookers. Raymond attempted to placate Lisa, but she reprimanded him for disrespecting her by not discouraging the woman's advances, telling him that the woman was nothing but a "loose goose."

Early in her marriage, Lisa managed to follow the unwritten rules when she had to deal with female groupies, but she found it increasing difficult, partly because she found the groupies' behavior difficult to manage emotionally. Perhaps more important to her, however, was that Raymond failed to support her or understand her feelings. He allowed and often encouraged even the most aggressive advances toward him. His passivity and relative indifference angered Lisa, and it predictably put her in awkward and embarrassing situations. Throughout his lengthy NFL career, she was never able to enlist his cooperation or gain his support in trying to deal with groupies. His refusal to see her point of view was resolute, and this contributed to ongoing tension between the marital partners.

Lisa's story points to a common experience that players' wives know only too well. As the wives in both studies shared their stories about women and men from all walks of life who are avidly interested in and continually orbit their husbands (and, by association, the wives themselves), I became aware of a complex social world of groupies[1] that overlaps and intersects the occupational worlds of professional sport and the social world of players' wives.

The wives explained to me that certain characteristics, behaviors, activities, motives, and roles differentiate female fans from female groupies. Female groupies may be die-hard fans of a particular team, the players, or sports, but they are not necessarily so. They may be viewed as an extreme version of female fandom. They are by far the most visible and recognizable, and, according to the wives, they tend to represent the greatest threat to the sport marriage. They may not always have sexual conquest as their primary goal, but the wives viewed them this way and were decidedly ungenerous in their assessment of women they identified as groupies. These young women have always been common in the larger entertainment landscape, most visibly in the occupational worlds of movie stars, television stars, rock stars,[2] country stars, and hip-hop stars, but they also are present in other male-dominated occupational worlds, such as law enforcement and space travel.[3]

Sport leagues and organizations are keenly aware of the presence of groupies. "The NBA actually preps their college players going into training camps,"

Nora said. "At the time my ex-husband was going into the NBA, they actually did a little course on groupies and what to expect of them, and how to navigate that. So they're basically being told by the NBA that there are groupies, and don't make a fool of the team that you're on."

Becoming aware of the wide range of groupies is also a significant part of a wife's marital experiences, and responding to them can require her to rely on certain measures, such as boundary work in public life, to try to protect her marriage and family. For certain wives, female groupies symbolize the fear that their husbands will be unfaithful. Because the activities of female groupies can and do result in extramarital relationships with players, and because the players don't always discourage the attention that can lead to these relationships, this fear is understandable.

Groupie Roster

The wives in the first study described an eclectic spectrum of social types and subtypes,[4] which I have categorized as groupie types[5] and named using the wives' vocabulary. Identifying these loosely defined yet distinct types isn't meant to stereotype or dehumanize individuals but to help us understand the interest people have in male professional athletes and their wives. As the typology suggests, certain groupies may defy categorization because groupie identities, roles, characteristics, behaviors, activities, and motives are not always dissimilar. When types overlap and intersect with each other or one individual embodies more than one groupie type, either simultaneously or serially, I call the process groupieism. Individuals practicing groupieism may adopt a chameleon-like personality, accentuate a strategic physical appearance, or convey a particular mannerism to try to keep their activities secret and avoid being identified as a groupie, which can result in stigmatization,

> Some of them are obsessive. How many people would travel all over the world just to follow these players around? . . . I don't like the old groupies. I don't like the young groupies. I don't like the women groupies. I don't like the high-class groupies. I don't like the low-class groupies. I don't like the fag groupies. I don't like none of them. You can be a fan, but don't be a groupie.
>
> —OLIVIA

ostracism, or reprimand. Groupieism can serve the purpose of gaining or sustaining access to the players or their wives, thus maximizing the chances that the individual will achieve the goal of involvement in the players' and wives' social worlds.

The evolving nature of the social world of groupies includes two notable subworlds: visible groupies and invisible groupies. All groupies, regardless of type, have one thing in common: they want something from the player, the wife, or both. For many groupies, both single and married players are fair game, according to the wives in the studies.

VISIBLE GROUPIES

The range of groupies who are the most noticeable to insiders and outsiders inhabit the subworld of visible groupies, and these types include *married-couple groupies, family groupies, male groupies, young female groupies, seasonal groupies*, and *camp groupies*. These individuals are clearly captivated by and try to include themselves in the players' lives, and some try to make players the center of their lives. The first three types don't normally pose a threat to the sport marriage.

Married-couple groupies tend to be middle-aged or older, although young married-couple groupies exist. The couple is usually financially secure, well-established, and well-connected in the team's hometown. These couples try to become socially or personally involved in the lives of the players and their families, and they often succeed. They are season ticket holders, and they relish rubbing shoulders and being seen with the player and his teammates in public life. In an effort to ingratiate themselves and develop a friendship, the couple will share business information, civic information, life/business experiences, and team gossip with players' wives. They may expect to be invited to important team functions and take great delight in it when they are. It signifies their acceptance among the players and their wives and enhances their status within their own peer group. In turn, they invite players and their wives to dinners in their home, to social or civic

> To me, a groupie, all you're saying is, "Screw me, screw me, and leave me." . . . I don't know. I don't get it. I don't get it. It's just that they're disgusting. . . . They're a threat to the sanctity of your marriage.
> —EMMA

events, and to large, extravagant, socially exclusive parties. They may offer free memberships to private clubs. Introducing the players and their wives to the nuances of their community's life are acts of reciprocity and an effort to be included in the occupational worlds of professional sport. In this way, they can meet and befriend other players, thus establishing and maintaining a social network of players and their wives.

The wife of this couple often sits with one or more players' wives at games. She may socialize with the wives and play with or supervise children if a wife has to leave her seat during a game. When she or her husband invites a wife to gala events, the wife may be flattered and impressed, but she may also understand that it isn't her as a person but her status as a player's wife that these couples are interested in. "It's like, 'You're really a nice person, but if he wasn't who he was, you'd have nothing to do with us.' That's what I keep thinking," Gwen said. Realizing that it's a tradeoff, a wife may feel indebted to the couple and value their social contacts or business advice, and this can make it difficult to refuse invitations and requests and contribute to her stress. Like Gwen, she may have unpleasant reactions if she suspects a groupie's motives or believes that she and her husband are being exploited. "We have absolutely nothing in common with them when you really come down to it, nothing except basketball," Gwen said. "That's all they ever talk about and then they throw in, 'Well, I know this person that could probably get you a great deal on blah, blah, blah.' It's always like that. And then I think, eventually, 'They want something.'" Some wives, however, develop close friendships with these couples.

Although younger married-couple groupies are less common and perhaps less well-known, they can be just as enterprising as their older counterparts in their attempts to establish relationships with the players and their wives. Susan shared with me an incident that illustrates how extreme some young couples can be in their pursuit of NBA players: Susan's friend, Mandy, and her husband Carl, who was on the same NBA team as Susan's husband, were on an ocean cruise. A young married couple who had struggled with the husband's infertility approached Carl and asked him in earnest to father their child by whatever means necessary. They were on the cruise for this specific purpose. They explained that they had spent a great deal of time thinking and considering whom to ask, and they had decided on him. Carl was caught completely off guard and was unsure what to make of such a proposition, so he laughed. The couple, deeply embarrassed, left the ship.

Family groupies are members of a husband's family who are anxious to share in the advantages afforded by his career. These family members believe that because they made sacrifices for the player, or because he's so well paid, he can afford to be generous with one of the family. Expectations include the various perks and benefits of being related to a professional athlete, including free tickets to games and invitations or access to social events, team functions, and other related occupational situations. In certain public situations, family members can be an embarrassment to a wife and, in this case, it's she and not her husband who must cope with their antics and manipulations in private and public life while trying not to irritate or anger her husband. One of the most conspicuous family members is typically the player's mother.

Male groupies vary in age, sexual orientation, occupation, and social class. The wives in the first study described three subtypes of male groupies: *businessman groupie, working-class male groupie,* and *gay male groupie.* If older, the businessman groupie may be financially successful, socially prominent, and possibly an important civic leader. He may befriend a player with the primary goal of transacting a business deal or developing a business partnership. He enjoys basking in the spotlight with players because such an association can benefit his contacts, reputation, or image in the community. He may behave like a giddy adolescent fan in public situations, shedding his brusque and businesslike veneer in the players' presence. Typically, in such public situations, he will openly ignore the wife and others who may be present and give his full attention only to her husband.

Like the married-couple groupies, male groupies may try to gain access to the player and his wife—and eventually the team—in various, creative ways. Lisa explained how a physician used her and Raymond as a steppingstone to meet and gain the acceptance of his teammates: "He asked Raymond if he could tape the birth of my baby. Raymond said, 'Heck no.' But when I had my baby, he came to the hospital to see me. He wanted to videotape my baby. He just really latched on. He bought my baby all kinds of clothes. I mean, it isn't like he was a personal friend. Raymond would invite him to the dinners after the games sometimes. He just hooked right in and then he got know all the players, and everyone started having him around." Lisa's story shows how these men try to gain access by ingratiating themselves in ways that achieve the best possible result. Once accepted by the wife and her husband, they may try to use the couple as a way of gaining access to other players on the team. This is also a pervasive pattern among other groupie types.

Working-class male groupies may behave in ways that are similar to female groupies. They are anxious to meet the players, get their autographs, get their pictures taken with them, and tell others that they interacted with them. They can be pushy in their attempts to greet, meet, and speak with the players in public situations. As Tracee discovered, "They'll trample the young kids to get to the players."

Several wives insisted that there are as many gay male groupies as female groupies who were interested in their husbands. These men are usually season ticket holders who follow with great interest the careers and achievements of the favorite players. They try to communicate with the players by various means, such as phone calls or correspondence. Player's wives don't really view gay males as a threat to their marriages or as a source of stress, but these men can be a source of stress for a husband, especially if he has masculinity issues or a need to preserve heteronormativity, or if he feels pressure to emphasize heterosexuality in a team culture that values, expects, and reinforces hegemonic masculinity.

The three types of visible groupies that do pose a threat to the sport marriage are the young female groupies, seasonal groupies, and camp groupies.

Young female groupies are generally in their late teens to mid-twenties and are easily the most recognizable and ubiquitous of all groupies. These women are commonly seen in any situation or setting where there is a likelihood of encountering the players. "We call them jersey chasers," Callie said. "Some of them are super smart and conniving, and some of them are just there and want to be seen." From the perspective of insiders in the occupational worlds of professional sport, these young women are accorded low status; they are sexually objectified[6] by most male insiders. The devaluing attitude underlying the use of language to describe these young women is evident in the way the players define female groupies. A case in point: when an MLB player is mired in a batting slump, he and his teammates understandably want to end it as soon as possible. A common practice is for the teammate in the slump to approach the least attractive woman he can find (often with help from his teammates), usually a young female groupie who is perceived as an "easy score." The teammates call these women "slump busters," which is evidence of the shared belief or superstition that there is greater redemption in "scoring" with a woman they regard as unattractive because they have lowered their standard of feminine beauty. The lower the standard, the greater the sacrifice, and the greater the likelihood of ending the slump. It may take more than one slump buster to end the slump. Sexual conquest with an attractive woman isn't considered sufficient to end a slump.

A young female groupie displays a conventionally constructed and accepted, yet exaggerated, form of femininity. Her sexually suggestive appearance[7] tends to set her apart from typical female fans and most other women and is intended to attract the players' attention and gain their approval.[8]

Emphasizing femininity[9] and using displays of femininity as tactical ways of doing femininity,[10] she is easily spotted at games and other sporting events because she exudes a self-presentational tendency to be scantily dressed or overdressed[11] and to use flirtatious body language. Her personal front includes attire that ranges from the trendiest fashions to what the wives described as "sleazy" styles of dress, such as tight-fitting or short skirts, skin-tight or ripped jeans, plunging necklines, high-heeled pumps, bikini tops, skimpy swimsuits, and fashion fitness outfits.[12] Heavy makeup and a trendy hairstyle will often complete the look. "They dress like they're ready for it," Marsha said. Beth described one young woman's physical appearance:

> This girl was at one of the ball games waiting for the players, and the new thing was that jeans are ripped out and holey. Well, hers had a rip right here in the rear. She had no underwear on. Now, she might have had a G-string on for all I know, but you wouldn't have seen it. But, anyway, that was sleazy to me, just pure sleaze. So it's just the way they dress: low-cut tops, breasts hanging out. But this girl knew her jeans were that way. I mean, she walked around in front of everybody, standing out in front, waiting for the players to come out after the game was over.

Young female groupies openly compete with other young women for the opportunity to interact with the players, and they may resort to physical confrontations with other young groupies. The wives are well aware of this competition. "You'll see them fight over players," Lisa said. "We have seen women pull their clothes off one another, and we have watched the players stand there and watch them fight. And then the particular player they're fighting over comes out, meets his fiancée, and walks to his car and looks at them. And they're on the ground, wrestling and tussling, with their bras or pants pulled off."

During MLB games, many of these young women won't hesitate to engage in breast flashing[13] to attract the gaze of relief pitchers and others in the bullpen. After a game, other young women will position themselves near the gate of the players' parking lot and try to follow a player to his residence. "I just ran into two of them at the ballpark," Olivia said. "They're real pretty women and definitely have money. They ride around and follow the players home, certain ones that they're after. They know people in high places, so they throw their weight around and get where they want to go. But they are groupies. They followed a player home twice. His wife was pregnant, but she comes out to cuss them out."

The NBA, MLB, and NFL wives in the first study and second group described three subtypes of young female groupies: *hotel groupies*, *bar groupies*, and *nightclub groupies*. They share the goal of interacting with the players, but routinely engage in specific behaviors and activities in distinct settings to achieve their objectives. Hotel groupies prefer to hang out in the hotels where NBA and MLB players reside on road trips or in the hotels where NFL players stay for home and away games. Typically, they loiter in the hotel lobby with the hope of attracting the players' attention through their physical appearance, body language, and location, and they may directly approach the players. "They would just stand right by the elevator, and then a lot of the guys would just point to who they wanted to join them up in their room, and that would happen," Susan said. Alyssa also easily recognized the objectives of these women: "Usually they're more loosely dressed and they carry themselves like a hooker. They'll stare a lot, or sometimes they're bold enough to just come over and introduce themselves. So it's easy to spot them."

After the players reach their hotel rooms, it isn't uncommon for more than one type of groupie to try to contact the players with the hope of hooking up. Emma shared with me an incident in which two young women tried to meet Mason in the hotel: "One time we were in the city, and there was a knock on the door. I opened it up and there were two girls. They said, 'Oh, I must have the wrong room.' And I said, 'Well, either you do, or on this trip you do.' And they walked away. And my husband said, 'Oh, my god, I can't believe you said that.' And I said, 'I can't believe they knocked on this door.'"

As we learned in chapter 3, hotel bars are favorite gathering places for MLB players on the road, but a bar groupie doesn't limit herself to these bars. She also will frequent bars adjacent to or in the airports where MLB or NFL teams depart from and arrive back to the city where the team is located, standing or sitting at the bar while waiting for the players to arrive. After observing the behavior of these young women on several occasions, Alyssa explained, "If a player comes through the door, they all start adjusting their posture. I mean, it's real easy to see. There's definitely eye contact, and they follow them around the room with their eyes or, if the player is on the side of the room, they get up and try to get closer to him. They'll also stand at the bar, because the players hang at the bar, and the girls know this, so they'll also sit at the bar."

The nightclub groupie likes to frequent the noisy and energetic nightclubs that are popular hangouts in the city where the players' team is located, or in other cities during spring training, road trips, or away games. She also has high hopes of meeting or hooking up with the players in what are often frenetic settings. Although the strategies she uses to attract the players' attention are similar to those of hotel and bar groupies, she typically emphasizes strategies that are more specific to nightclubs, such as dancing with great enthusiasm. "If you're in a club, they might, you know, start dancing—just gyrating provocatively," Keira said. "But you know that they're doing it because they want the athletes to see them. Like that's going to make them run over and sweep them off their feet."

In their attempts to gain access, young female groupies may try other direct forms of communication with the players. A typical practice is to pass a greeting card or scrap of paper that includes a hastily scribbled phone number to players at the stadium, ballpark, or arena before, during (when seated near the bullpen), or after a game. In the past, when the players received mail through the post office, they jokingly referred to this type of communication as puss mail, because it included a woman's contact information in addition to personal information such as body measurements and direct offers of availability. It often included pictures of these young women in various stages of undress. The wives in the second group noted that young women today are more likely to make contact through the internet or social media. Any young female groupie's effort to do this might encompass sexting,[14] which often includes digital images (e.g., selfies) revealing herself in provocative poses and explicit body positions.[15] Keira emphasized how social media now provides easier access to the players. "Now you're seeing where the groupies reach out to the guys in social media, then the guys are liking their pictures, and even hooking up with people, random people you're meeting on social media just because they saw you at a game or they liked the way you look." In these situations, the female self is sexually objectified and self-sexualized.[16] These and other attempts to attract the players' attention are intended to appeal to male sexual desire.[17]

Seasonal groupies are typically young women in their twenties, but they also may be much older women. Many wives unflatteringly refer to them as "seasonal bitches." These women usually engage in personal or sexual relationships with one player at a time in a particular sport during the season, although they may extend their scope of sexual activities to a player in a different sport. Some work their way sequentially through the seasons, moving, for instance, from an NFL player to an NBA player to an MLB player, or they may engage in these relationships simultaneously.

Similarly, camp groupies can be any age. These women reside near an MLB team's spring training facilities or an NFL team's training camp facilities. Although they tend to hang out near the players' entrance, they also frequent sport restaurants or the players' favorite nightspots in the city where the team's training facilities are located. A camp groupie may set her sights on star players or talented rookies who have the potential to become star players, but not always. If she has a relationship with one or more players, the relationship(s) will most likely end when spring training or training camp is over, although she may resume her relationship with a particular player if he is still with the team the following year. She normally doesn't travel or relocate to continue her relationship with a player during the season, but she may try to maintain some kind of correspondence with him.

Although a camp groupie has only short-term access to the players, some wives regard her as the one of the worst types because she has greater access to the players. She takes advantage of the only time during the year when all the players on one or more teams are together for a fairly lengthy period of time and many of the married players don't have their families with them.

Many players savor the flattery and attentive reassurance visible groupies are more than happy to provide. The wives maintain that their husbands enjoy the female adoration in particular because it positively contributes to their public image and self-esteem. They also believe that the existence of female groupies wouldn't be so pervasive if the players didn't condone their presence, encourage their sexual availability, or create a demand for them. Olivia shared her frustration with me about this challenging issue: "You know what ticks me off more than anything else? I could sit here and blame that girl until I'm blue in the face, but she cannot do what she does unless the men let her. . . . If they'd stop giving them an inch, they wouldn't take a mile. Just stop it in its tracks. Walk away. . . . You can stop them from being the way they are if everybody did it."

According to the wives in the first study, there appear to be inconsistencies in how sport organizations handle the presence of groupies. They may "look the other way" or they may initiate strict security measures. Security measures, for example, include secluding NFL players at the hotels during the season as a deterrent to ambitious or determined female groupies. "On away games, or even at home games, they stayed in the hotel the night before, and it was high security. Nobody could get in there, not even to their hallway," Callie said. Despite security measures, groupies seem to be able to circumvent such measures, and the wives are aware of this.

INVISIBLE GROUPIES

Publicly available knowledge about sport groupies is generally limited to the young female groupies who are the center of media attention. Explicit media accounts about their intimate relationships with certain players can become public knowledge, and social media contributes to this public awareness. But other female groupies are largely invisible to the public and are not easily identified unless one is an insider to an occupational world. In some cases, they are not even visible to insiders. Their social invisibility can work to their advantage in their attempts to include the players in their lives because their interactions, relationships, and activities are not publicly recognized or performed. They don't fit the typical young female groupie image and are initially invisible even to the players' wives. These types include *grandma groupies, wife groupies, organizational groupies*, and *team groupies*. The wives do gradually learn, however, that invisible groupies also are fixtures in their husbands' occupational world, and they can become another source of stress.

Grandma groupies tend to be older women (about fifty to sixty-five years of age). Their primary motive is to get as close as possible to the players and become "regulars" in their occupational world. This woman may even attempt to make the players and their occupational world the center of her life. She may be a member of the team's official or unofficial "backers" or informal booster club. She may frequent ballpark and stadium parking lots before or after games, appear at team functions, and attend civic events to meet and interact with the players and their families. She may presume to have a friendship with the player or his wife, which can grate on the nerves of some wives. Like many other groupies, she usually knows the players' statistics, follows their exploits during the season, and stays informed about and enthusiastically supports the team's activities. Even though her physical appearance and demeanor may appear to be innocuous,[18] she can be quite resourceful in her progressive attempts to become personally involved with the players and their families.

> You know there's groupies out there trying to get your husband all the time and be where you are, but you're aware. It makes you uncomfortable, it makes you distressed and feel a little unstable and anxious. But, then, you have to just say to yourself, "I'm the wife." So I can't worry myself with somebody who's just a groupie trying to get what I got. You just can't allow yourself to worry about that and relinquish your power.
>
> —ALAINA

Beth provides us with some idea about grandma groupies: "I think they probably were booster club members," she said, recalling her experiences with two older women. "They would give Cliff flowers and cards, and they had lots of pictures taken with him. I'd be waiting for him after the game and I might wave to them if they were looking at me. But, for the most part, they would corner him as he's coming out and bend his ear."

A grandma groupie may be single or married, but most often is single. She may have assumed the role of groupie as a younger woman, or she may be or have been a married-couple groupie or transitioned from some other type of groupie. The wives consider these women a nuisance rather than a threat, even though in certain public situations a grandma groupie is just as enterprising in her advances toward the players as is a young female groupie. She will, for example, greet the players at the stadium or ballpark before or after the games, or as they disembark from a plane when they return from a road trip or an away game. She may give players flowers or homemade cakes. Even if the wives are present, her greetings may include hugs, kisses on the lips, and even sexualized touching, such as fondling or grabbing a player's buttocks, which can occur directly in front of the wife. Gwen was totally surprised when she first encountered this behavior: "A lot of older women had approached Osten. We're both looking at each other and I'm like, 'What was that?' And then I'll give her the look, instead of him. He'll look at me like, 'I can't believe this old lady did that.' And I'll look at her like, 'What are you doing?'" This woman may believe that her age will excuse these actions and that she can interact in this manner without reprisal because she knows that the wives are reluctant to create a public scene by chastising her or expressing their disapproval in other ways. Although their public behavior may seem innocent, it may make it difficult for the wives to be pleasant and respectful to these women in public situations. Gwen further expressed her irritation about these groupies: "There's this group of older women that are doing very well. And you think, 'Don't they have anything better to do?' It's like, 'Why are you around here? All these men are married, or taken, and you're older.' It's like they're out of place. You know what the young ones are looking for, but with the older ones, this looks weird. They'll come up, regardless of what you're doing and say, 'Oh, hi,' and push you out of the way, and just cuddle between you and your husband. The younger groupies aren't going to do that unless they're absolutely bold."

The invisible groupies who do pose a threat to the sport marriage include wife groupies, organizational groupies, and team groupies.

Wife groupies look for ways to meet the players' wives so they can socialize and be seen with them. Although they have the ultimate goal of gaining access to single or married players, another goal can include becoming friends with a wife. Nora remembered how these women approached her: "They look at me or sit next to me, or know me but don't tell me what their intention of getting to know me is. They just want to get to know me, because they want to get to him. But, sometimes, you can sense that that's where they're going."

The wives in the first study described three subtypes of these groupies: *vicarious wives*, *pseudo wives*, and *pseudo friends*. Each subtype has a particular way of gaining access to the wives. Some may follow a progression of involvement that begins as a vicarious wife (the least threatening), progresses to a pseudo wife, and ultimately becomes a pseudo friend (the most threatening).

The vicarious wife has season tickets and her seat is located near the players' wives' section at the games. She doesn't pretend to be or try to create the impression that she's a player's wife,[19] and she knows she will never be. Nevertheless, she enjoys being seen with the wives and attempts to meet and interact with them before, during, or after the games. Any contact she has with them tends to be superficial, but it's a thrill she values and looks forward to. Marsha described one such woman, who might also be regarded as a grandma groupie: "There's one woman, she's got to be in her fifties, and she comes up in low-cut dresses and I'm thinking, 'Oh, give me a break.' I don't know what her purpose is. She looks like some showgirl from the twenties. I mean, the woman should give it up. Anyway, she's nice enough. She has little gin and tonics or whatever they have at the games. But I think it's just a thrill for her to be able to sit next to the wives."

The pseudo wife has successfully gained access to an inner circle of wives on the team. She seems to have a deep need to make the women an important part of her life. She tries to emulate them through her actions and physical appearance and seeks acceptance so that she can become personally involved in the husband's occupational world, his family, or perhaps his everyday life. Many of the wives refer to her as a "wannabe wife." She also may be a married-couple groupie. She sits with the wives in their section during the games and gladly does favors for them. When invited, she enjoys attending team functions. The wives are comfortable confiding in her because she avoids being pushy. After she has managed to establish trusted friendships with one or more of the wives, she tries to manipulate and use the friendship to her advantage. Isabella, for example, came into contact with Gwen and Osten through her job as a talented interior designer. She helped others on

Osten's team design, decorate, and furnish the interiors of their luxurious homes. Over time, as a "friend" of one of the wives, Isabella was so successful in including herself in an inner circle of wives that Gwen initially assumed she was a player's wife.

The pseudo friend's ultimate goal is to become involved in a close relationship with one or more players, regardless of the players' marital status, which is why the wives believe that she's the most threatening wife groupie. Like the pseudo wife, she initially meets the players and their wives through her job or a friend of a friend, sits with the wives during games, and eagerly attends team functions. She deliberately conceals her real motive, gradually developing a friendship with one of the player's wives and earning her trust. Using the wife as leverage, she successfully establishes and sustains access to one or more inner circles of wives and uses her acceptance to gain access to the players' occupational world.

Organizational groupies are relatively young women who are employed by sport organizations to enact specific occupational roles in various offices. Administrative and support staff members such as receptionists, administrative assistants, office managers, and interns may moonlight as organizational groupies. Whatever her guise or motive may be, this woman often tries to conceal her activities or interactions with certain individuals within the sport organization. She will take the same steps if she's employed by another sport organization and is interested in the players who play for another team. Her employment allows her to be a part of the familiar surroundings associated with the players' workplace and, depending on her job, she may have access to and direct contact with the players and their families and to players or coaches with other teams. A wife knows this woman as an employee first and initially interacts with her on this basis without total awareness of her activities and motives.

This woman's objectives are consistent with those valued by young female groupies, but she relies on identity work to mask her groupie identity and carefully manage her employee identity. She avoids any demeanor, personal front, or physical appearance that could be remotely associated with young female groupies and relies on impression management in her attempts to seem "normal" and to avoid discovery that might result in stigmatization or other consequences. At the same time, she secretly[20] suggests her sexual interest and availability to the players and coaches. The wives will undoubtedly learn to know her real motives through the sharing of team secrets or when certain indiscretions become public knowledge. Some front office workers, ushers, cheerleaders, and interns might be regarded as organizational groupies.

NFL and NBA cheerleaders represent sport organizations when they perform at the games. They are considered ambassadors of goodwill in the sport organization's city, and they make special appearances as organizational representatives. Even though many sport organizations may have policies that prohibit intimate relationships between employees and the players, such relationships can happen anyway. Among the wives, it's common knowledge that the single players, especially the rookies, discreetly date the cheerleaders. Many wives have a low opinion of cheerleaders and regard them as nothing more than opportunistic groupies. Marsha didn't mince words in describing these women: "They're a bunch of groupies, sleaze bag groupies. They want to get into bed with anyone they can. That's my view of them." When Nora was a cheerleader in college, she became aware of this negative image and quit the squad to avoid any stigma that could affect her fiancé and his potential NBA career.

Of course, not all cheerleaders are groupies, but most NFL wives believe that many are and that a cheerleader's real aspiration is to marry an NFL player in an attempt to improve her financial situation and elevate her lifestyle. During the first study, Lisa reported that after one of the players married a cheerleader on the same team, the wives kept their distance from her. "They kicked her off the squad, so she married him," she said. "Then she knew how the wives always treated the cheerleaders, so she never had anything to do with the wives. . . . As soon as he retired, she left him."

Gwen learned that Lillian and Henley, both front office employees with her husband's NBA team, were having sexual relationships with some of his teammates as well as players on other NBA teams. They teamed up to "go after" certain NBA players, competing with each other for the men while remaining friends. As a way of earning Gwen's trust and confidence, Henley offered to share personal information with Gwen about others in the sport organization (which Gwen had not asked for and wouldn't listen to). Later, Gwen was surprised at how naïve she had been not to suspect Henley's motives, and she wished she would have been more aware of her behavior in their first few encounters. Organizational groupies may run the risk of losing their jobs if their activities are discovered.

Team groupies are typically young females who have somehow gained access to the players, wives, or sport organizations. This woman initiates and engages in serial or simultaneous sexual activities with more than one player on the same team and, in some cases, with players on other teams in the same occupational world, regardless of their marital status. Apparently, her determination to be sexually involved in various relationships can be so great that nothing will stand in her way, and it can have serious consequences. In one case, for example, a woman had sexual relationships with at least five different players on the same NFL team. She became pregnant, and the five men were tested to determine who the father was. When results were made known and one of the teammates was identified as the biological father, neither parent took the revelation seriously. After the baby was born, the woman brought the child with her to visit the biological father at training camp and, according to Lisa, she "would go over and sleep with one of the other players in a room, and when she got through with him she'd go back over to the other room and get her baby. . . . That's why you don't trust groupies."

This woman may begin her association with the players as a seasonal groupie, a pseudo friend, or an organizational groupie. For instance, according to Gwen, Rachel was a seasonal groupie but became a team groupie with her husband's team. "Rachel has gone through, you name it, guys in football, baseball, all of it," Gwen said. "But, I mean, it's like this one player knows all this and he's still with her, and everyone is like, 'What is it? What is it? You know about her don't you?' But he's so nice and it was like she just moved in on him." However clandestine their activities or relationships may be, these women may not always be able to conceal their intentions, as Alaina pointed out: "Oh, yeah, you can see through them if they're dating several players, especially on the same team or the same league. That's not a person you really want to get to know. You just stay away from them. They don't have the same values that you have. They're just trying to get a player." Like the pseudo wife, pseudo friend, or organizational groupie, this woman may try to establish friendships with the wives or use her job as a way of gaining access to the players. Whether or not she achieves her goals, pregnancy can be an important concern for this woman because it can minimize or limit her groupie activities, prevent her from participating in groupie life, or possibly end her groupie life. Olivia shared her views of these women: "They can't continue to be a groupie with a baby. They may get pregnant, and they make you pay for it, and then make you feel like you owe them something. But most groupies are groupies to the point where they don't know who the father is anyway, and the man that they were with knows that. The first thing they'll say is, 'Yeah, right, prove it.' Most women won't have them because they don't know who the daddy is."

Setting Boundaries with Groupies

However innocuous female groupies may seem to be as they attempt to impress a player with their knowledge about his performances, career, team, and the game, they clearly have ulterior motives for greeting or interacting with players in public life.[21] Sometimes, as a last resort, players' wives use boundary work in public situations to attempt to discourage female groupies from approaching or interacting with their husbands or to exclude them from the marital relationship. The husband occasionally participates in boundary work, but he rarely initiates it.

Two factors in the husbands' occupational world may serve as impediments to effective boundary work in public life. First, the wife voluntarily imposes limits to her own public behavior by trying to follow the unwritten rulebook, which includes a "chapter" on responding to female groupies. An unwritten rule, for instance, is that a wife shouldn't chastise or embarrass her husband in public situations for failing to discourage a female groupie's inappropriate advances toward him. Discussing her husband's reluctance to be more assertive when interacting with a female groupie, Stacy said, "Normally, I'll say something or do something: 'What do you think you're doing?' It's normally addressed to the woman, not to my husband. Later, it might be addressed to him when he says, 'I can't believe you did that.' And then I'll say, 'Well, I can't believe you didn't take charge.'" The rule is that a wife shouldn't create a scene with a female groupie (or any other woman) because it might make people think that she can't manage her emotions and it will make her appear jealous, possessive, or mean-spirited, which can result in making her, her husband, and his team "look bad." If this catches the attention of social media or other media outlets, it may prove to be genuinely awkward. She will try to express only emotions she defines as publicly appropriate and wait for a better time and place to privately express frustration, irritation, or anger to her husband. Unfortunately, finding the right time and

> [My daughter] and I were in the car behind Keith. . . . As we were slowing down to get through the gate . . . two women . . . in T-shirts and tight jeans, opened the door and jumped in his car! They wanted him to autograph their T-shirts across their chests!
> —DONNA

place is rare because of other unwritten rules, such as those meant to protect a husband's psychological and emotional state so he can focus on his game. As we learned from Lisa's story at the top of the chapter, a wife may follow the rules only until she reaches a breaking point.

Second, a wife's responses are constrained by her husband's passive demeanor in his interactions with female groupies. Like Raymond, a player is typically reluctant to discourage female interest in him, and he may even encourage it. A wife is essentially on her own in finding a way to live with the presence of female groupies in her husband's occupational world, and this can be challenging for her. She may, for example, feel guilty if she complains about them, refuse to admit that they annoy her, have difficulty dealing with them, or have to confront the reality that they are a problematic issue in her marriage.

A wife's boundary work ordinarily begins with her effort to avoid including herself in a public situation involving female groupies or to escape detection by avoiding female groupies in public situations. When their presence can't be avoided, a wife like Tracee first tries to ignore them: "They're like a pesky fly that just won't go away. You keep shooing them. You don't want them there. You don't want to be rude. Sometimes, you have to be outright rude by almost ignoring them or saying, 'Hi,' and go on with your conversation, and make them feel like they're outsiders." Beth recalled a public situation involving an infatuated groupie: "I've also been in a situation where the groupie got blatantly upset—you could tell that she was so infatuated with Cliff that she got visibly upset—when she knew that her presence didn't affect me as we were all standing communicating in a group. I wasn't going to be baited into that."

A wife also will try to avoid any behavior that could be embarrassing or misunderstood, although that may not always be possible for her. If she finds herself near groupies, she may avoid eye contact or other forms of nonverbal communication, or she may give groupies "the look" in an effort to avoid direct confrontation and still convey disapproval. "When someone comes up to Dennis asking questions or saying 'Oh, you're just so wonderful,' a lot of times it'll just be the look I give the person," Stacy explained. "I just look at them like, 'Oh, you're so embarrassing.' . . . It's funny, because I used to look at older wives when I was just starting out in the game and think, 'How can they do that? How come they don't get more upset?'" As Stacy discovered, when a wife is offended or humiliated by a groupie's actions or is somehow caught off-guard, she will suppress her feelings and rely on her wife face as she tries to be tactful, polite, and pleasant and show that she isn't annoyed or possessive.

If a wife's attempts to avoid female groupies are ineffective, she may decide to limit or discontinue her public appearances altogether, and this may involve some aspect of denial. In the most extreme cases, she may minimize their existence or avoid thinking about the implications of certain events related to her husband's interaction with them. To illustrate: toward the end of an NFL season, Jill and Craig attended his team's annual charity fashion show in a ballroom at a hotel in the city where his team was located. At the conclusion of the event, Jill noticed that two female organizational employees were giving Craig more intimate attention than she thought was appropriate, and their behavior embarrassed her, in part because her husband seemed to casually encourage it. Jill assumed that others would be observing her reaction to Craig's behavior, which made her feel more uncomfortable and self-conscious. She dealt with this situation in much the same way she dealt with similar stressful situations in her marriage: she blocked it out of her mind and pretended not to notice what was happening. She was able to maintain her composure during the incident, but she later experienced a great deal of difficulty suppressing her feelings. Craig assured her that his association with the women was well within the context of their roles in the sport organization. Nevertheless, she still had difficulty managing her irritation with him for allowing it to occur. She also continued to feel shame about what others must be thinking about what happened.

Like Craig, most husbands are routinely friendly and easygoing in public situations involving fans and groupies, but when they are approachable, female groupies can misinterpret their affability or respectful demeanor as encouragement for their unwanted advances. "I think my husband's just a super nice, friendly guy," Callie said. "He loves people in general and he's social, so that can come across as flirting." The belief underlying the unwritten rules is that certain groupie interactions could lead to situations that could tarnish his reputation and his team's public image, particularly if these public encounters become unpleasant or they become the focus of publicity or social media attention. "I know he doesn't think he's leading them on," Marsha said. "But, to me, I think maybe he's leading them on by even just talking to them." A wife might think that because her husband is a genuinely "nice guy," she should give him the benefit of the doubt and trust him. This can complicate her emotional response, however, because a wise woman knows that even the strongest man can give in to temptation under the right circumstances.

Marsha, Nora, and Lisa held the unshakeable belief that their husbands were "just being nice," but this belief later backfired (see chapter 7).

Most of the women in the first study believed that female groupie interest in their husbands would be minimized or negated if only their husbands would discourage them by taking the initiative and politely enforcing boundaries of appropriate interaction in public situations. "He's the one who puts himself in that situation," Rhonda insisted. "He could very easily say, 'I'm not into this. See you later.'" In rare cases, a husband might use a tie-sign to signal his devotion to her, such as holding her hand, drawing her toward him, putting an arm around her waist, whispering in her ear, or maintaining eye contact only with her in the presence of interested female groupies. Through these actions or others like them, he announces that she's his chosen partner, thus defining how female groupies should interact with him. Actions like these can reassure a wife, but, in reality, his boundary work isn't normally effective in discouraging persistent women. Most will pointedly ignore his attempts to discourage their interest in him because they know full well that most players' wives won't publicly confront them.

If a husband is unable or unwilling to discourage female groupie advances and a wife's efforts to avoid or ignore the behavior fails, she may take it upon herself to try to establish and enforce appropriate interactions in public situations using boundary work. Her first line of defense is to try to keep female groupies away from her husband while still honoring the unwritten rules. She may use tie-signs to convey to onlookers that she's confident about their relationship. If that isn't possible, she may tactfully pressure her husband to politely but firmly attempt to discourage female groupies from approaching, interacting, or speaking with him. Her approach will vary depending on the severity of the intrusion, including how intimate women become in their advances, or how hostile, belligerent, or offensive they are. Olivia described one of her less extreme strategies: "I like to make them feel stupid. I like to try to lower them when I talk to them. I guess that's what I do, because I will say things to them like, 'Why are you doing this?' 'What are you getting out of this?'" If the behavior is particularly objectionable, she may feel compelled to break the unwritten rules and engage in some form of confrontational behavior.

If, like Lisa, a wife resorts to physical interaction or strong verbal rebuke, it's probably because she's embarrassed by or encounters a spiteful groupie, or a groupie's behavior seems particularly outrageous, or she herself becomes a target. Susan described an incident when she resorted to direct action: After Bill's team had qualified for the first round of the NBA playoffs, Susan and Bill arrived at the hotel. As they walked through the lobby and around the corner to the elevator, Susan noticed a group of young women standing around. As the couple walked by the group, one of the women walked up to Bill and said, "Oh, Bill, you can do better than her. You can have me!" Susan immediately lost her temper. She told me later, "I almost took her out right there. I wanted to tear her eyes out." Instead, she turned around and walked back to the women, who were joking and laughing about the remark. She stopped, stood her ground, and stared at them until she had their attention. When the woman who had spoken realized that Susan had not only heard what she said to Bill but that Susan was fuming, she was visibly shaken. Susan didn't speak to her; she just stared at her until she believed that the woman was properly embarrassed in front of her friends. Susan understood that female interest in her husband was the price of fame and one of the consequences of public life, but in this public incident she believed that the insensitive and disrespectful comments were meant for her, albeit indirectly, and was offended. After staring down the woman, she felt justified in breaking the unwritten rules about direct confrontation when she saw that the woman was contrite. Nora recalled incidents in which she believed that she had to forcefully discourage overly enthusiastic groupies: "It has varied from pushing a groupie off of him, you know, or when someone cut into us while we're dancing and pushed me out of the way, so I pushed back."

As these stories illustrate, in certain public situations involving female groupies, it may no longer be possible for a wife to suppress her anger, and she may disregard the unwritten rulebook. "It's like this rage takes over and you don't know what you're doing," Stacy confided. Depending on the circumstances, if a wife loses control, her husband may lose his patience with her and chastise her publicly. If he doesn't, he may be the target of criticism or ridicule by his teammates or others in the sport organization, who might think he isn't "man enough." Incidents like these are comparable to road-trip situations; teammates share the expectation that a husband should be able to control his wife. His inability to control her in these public situations can compromise his standing among his teammates or the sport organization and raise questions about his loyalty.

The wives in the first study told me that their husbands offered various reasons for their failure to discourage female groupie interest, and they were often defensive about their inability to limit their interactions with them. A husband may say to his wife that a woman only wanted to compliment him or ask for his autograph or get a picture with him, and he didn't want to hurt her feelings or be rude. He may say that he didn't know that a woman was actually a groupie, or that groupies are relatively harmless and dealing with them is part of the job.

On the other hand, a woman might appreciate the way her husband was gracious and generous in his interactions with certain women, such as women who are rude. Donna described how her husband often interacted with two grandma groupies who were staunch supporters of his NFL team:

> They're a couple of little old ladies that hang out in the parking lot. Keith calls them the "hug sisters" because they hug him all the time. It drives him crazy, but he's so sweet. He goes up and hugs them and tells them how happy he is to see them. One of them gave us a present, a little plaque, and just little things. I feel really bad if they're wasting their money on something I'm going to throw away. They go home and that's all they talk about to their friends and their relatives, and their [team name] friends. So let them have it.

If a husband is serious about discouraging female groupie interest in him, he will introduce his wife after he greets them. He also may use references to his wife, and this strategy can serve two purposes: he communicates his unavailability and, if he informs his wife about such advances, it can strengthen his marriage. Skylar discussed one such incident: "There was someone that worked for a team that Carter was on, and she actually had a reputation for getting with players, and came to him with some kind of an emotional issue. He talked with her outside of the clubhouse for thirty minutes to try to figure out what was going on, and then he referred her to me, 'Well, I think that my wife could really help you.' And she backed away. I don't think she had any intention of talking to me." If a husband makes an effort to inform his wife about these kinds of encounters with female groupies, it can serve to minimize the wife's stress. "If there was something weird, he would always call me or if he got a letter he would show me the letter, and I didn't have that as an issue," Skylar said.

All rules aside, on rare occasions when other attempts have failed, a wife may confront her husband in public. Alyssa remembered an incident involving her husband and a young female groupie:

> We were at a party and we were standing near the bar, and she was just pouring all this attention on him. It got to the point where he turned his back and he was in this conversation with her, and then she invited him to go to the dance floor. At that point, I had just had it. I just stopped him in his tracks, because I called his name, and he turned around and

> I said, "Come here." And I told him, "If you go out to the dance floor with that woman, that's it."

Douglas was upset with Alyssa because he thought she overreacted, and Alyssa was angry with Douglas because he didn't discourage the young women's obvious interest in him or resist her advances. "It was like he didn't understand what I was upset about, and I felt like I was just totally disrespected. He could have said, 'Excuse me, but I'm with my wife this evening.'" Douglas later apologized to Alyssa.

Stacy discussed her frustration with Dennis's passivity in similar public situations. "A lot of times she'll be a real tramp, real ugly, not even someone that you'd sit back and say, 'Boy, I'm really threatened.' I mean it could be just a horrible-looking person. But at the same time, your pride is hurt because you feel like he's letting her get away with this in front of me. I wish he'd just take care of it." When a wife believes that she has to take the initiative in dealing with female groupies in public life as a way of pressuring her husband to show her the respect she feels entitled to, she can end up feeling humiliated on top of her worries about what his actions might mean about their marriage. As we saw in Skylar and Carter's case, if the quality of communication in their marriage is good, some couples find it beneficial to confide in each other about different situations involving female groupies. These couples may use humor as way of diffusing the seriousness and stress of unwanted female groupie presence in public situations. Susan recalled a situation that sheds light on the quality of communication she and Bill valued in their relationship:

> I can remember on one team somebody had a birthday and somebody sent a stripper to practice. She showed up right after practice in the gym and Bill came home and he told me about it, and I said, "What did you do?" And he said, "Well, as soon as I realized what she was doing—it took me a second, because she just came in and she was singing or dancing and everybody was clapping and singing happy birthday, and I didn't really think anything and then I realized what she was doing—and I got the heck out of there." I think communication and being open and, you know, I wasn't stupid. I could see the women around, and if they're brazen enough to walk up to him when I'm standing right next to him, imagine what they're like when the wife's not standing right there. I was under no grand illusion that those things weren't out there and taking place.

Some female groupies can be so obsessive about their interest in the players that it leads to invasions into the couple's personal lives. Skylar recalled her initial confusion about one woman's unusual behavior: "A mom with two kids, [who had] written him like tons and tons of letters, viewed him as a stepfather to the kids. He met them once on the road and took a picture with him and her kids, and then something's not right with her. So she sends letter after letter, like for Father's Day, and it's weird. It's just strange." When Paula's husband played in the minor leagues, one of his teammates became the object of a young female groupie's attention. He received letters from her that presumed they had a relationship, and the couple was quite concerned when the woman suddenly appeared at spring training. She left after he confronted her, but she continued writing letters and calling him. Obsessive groupies like these can become frightening in their devoted interest in a player because it can lead to stalking or actual interference in the couple's life. Alyssa was aware of a young woman who initially made several players on Douglas's NFL team the targets of her obsession. Finally focusing on one particular player, she wrote letters declaring her love for him. He tried to inform her that he wasn't interested in having a relationship and she should leave him alone, but she wasn't dissuaded, and her pursuit continued over a long time. At one point, she was observed loitering in front of his home. After she threatened to kill him and his wife, law enforcement became involved. According to Alyssa, a jealous or angry stalker may even target a wife or female partner, although that situation is less common.

With or without their husbands' help, wives find ways of contending with female groupies. Emma and Olivia tried not to let female groupies intimidate them, and instead put faith in their marital status as a way of coping with groupies. Emma insisted that if a groupie approached her, she would stand firm: "I would never have walked away," she said. "I would never have cowered. I would have stood there and waited to see what she had to say, or hear what she had to say. I have a place. My place was in that stadium, in my seat, next to my husband. You're not going to stop me."

Even if a wife is able to convince her husband to discourage female groupie interest in him, which is unusual, his public interactions with them still can adversely affect the marriage. The topic of groupies, largely female groupies, is a sensitive issue between marital partners and in professional sport in general, especially when it involves any possibility of infidelity or scandal. Many wives are reluctant to admit to others—or even to themselves—that female groupies annoy them or that they have difficulty dealing with women who have designs on their husbands. They may even feel guilty if they complain about groupies, or they may reproach themselves for their inability to cope with this aspect of their husband's career. Consequently, even though the existence of female groupies is common knowledge, the women may avoid any mention of it to other wives on the team or avoid seeking support from others, which can further isolate them and increase tension or strain in the marriage.

Most of the wives expressed contempt toward some groupie types, particularly those who had a sexual interest in the players, but they were much more willing to forgive or at least understand the players' sexual interest in these groupies. The players themselves legitimize and normalize their sexual interest and sexual desire, largely because of the value they place on hegemonic masculinity in male-bonding processes and male interactions. The presence of female groupies is therefore a reflection of male hegemony, and it is evidence of the subordinate status women occupy in male-dominated occupational worlds.

Because of the persistent fear that their husbands will take advantage of the continual presence of female groupies in their occupational worlds and of the opportunities to engage in extramarital relationships of any nature and for any length of time, almost all the wives regarded female groupies as a major source of stress in their marriages. In view of the existence of the institutionalized brotherhood and culture of infidelity, and because groupies of all types are inextricably linked to and coexist in the players' occupational worlds, the wives' concerns that their husbands will be unfaithful are not completely unfounded. When combined with the numerous other stressors that impact the sport marriage, the pervasiveness of groupies is even more troubling and has the potential to end a marriage.

CHAPTER 7

A Closer Look at the Culture of Infidelity

TANYA

Tanya was in her early twenties when she met Ryan, a talented wide receiver in the prime of his NFL career. Ryan was good-looking and personable, and fans idolized him. The couple's respective fathers had a history of extramarital relationships, and a similar family pattern began to emerge during the couple's two-year courtship. Even when they were engaged, Ryan continued to date other women. Tanya was aware of Ryan's unfaithfulness, but, as a result of her childhood experiences, she normalized his behavior and survived on the hope that he would "settle down" after they were married. He didn't.

Early in their relationship, Tanya came to view Ryan as her personal project and wanted to change him. "That's what's appealing to us," she said, referring to herself and other players' wives. Her propensity for fixing and enabling made it easy for Ryan to motherize her, and Tanya accepted the mother role because it seemed to validate her efforts to support his success. "I used to do everything," she said. "I've got five arms—lay it on me, Ryan. Let me show you what I can do for you." Ryan, on the other hand, avoided his marital responsibilities and hung out with his male friends almost every night and weekend, meeting with extramarital partners at his favorite nightclub. Even after they conceived a child together, Ryan continued his pattern of infidelity. Tanya knew about his affairs and was extremely upset about how he was acting, but because she didn't want to dissolve their marriage, she decided that she just needed to find a way to accept the situation. At a deeper emotional level, she was challenged by conflicting needs. By performing an enabling role, she fulfilled Ryan's need for domestic and esteem support, which, in turn, made her feel loved and valued—a human need that wasn't adequately fulfilled in her painful childhood.[1]

For a brief period, Tanya tried to deconstruct the role she had initially agreed to. One evening, she publicly confronted Ryan in a nightclub. "I think you forgot who I am," she told him. "I'm that same girl that can put on that short skirt—the same as those girls out there." This anger-filled attempt wasn't successful. Ryan continued his affairs and, in fact, became less discreet as time went on. "He was taking women to the games and the postgame dinner parties, and stuff like that, in front of all the friends and people who knew that he was married and I was pregnant," Tanya recalled. "They met him outside of our doors. They would call him at my house."

As a way to come to terms with her failing marriage, Tanya sought therapy, first alone and then with Ryan. Tanya didn't know who Ryan's extramarital partners were or how many there were, so when Ryan disclosed in therapy the extent of his infidelity—he was involved with several different women during the first few months of their marriage—she was stunned. He was initially repentant and said he felt guilty, but he didn't change his behavior. The couple agreed to a trial separation and Tanya, several months pregnant, moved to another residence. Meanwhile, one of Ryan's extramarital partners moved in and lived with him in the couple's home. After only fourteen months of marriage, Tanya initiated divorce proceedings.

The couple later reconciled, with the understanding that Ryan would be faithful to Tanya and work on their relationship, even though their history gave Tanya little reason to hope that things would be any different in the future. In the end, the marriage couldn't be saved. Through her experiences in therapy, Tanya had learned how she had compromised her own sense of self and emotional well-being. "I wanted to be the best wife I could for Ryan," she said. "I never even thought about what's the best wife for Tanya to be, to Tanya."

Despite the passage of time, the second study confirmed that the culture of infidelity is still alive and well in the occupational worlds of professional sport. Whether a professional athlete is single or married, he may use his prestige and power to interact with interested women. As he develops in his career, he may become more aware of women who wouldn't have noticed him before he became a professional athlete, and he may acquire qualities that increase the temptation for him to exploit opportunities that are not typically available to other men. His extramarital interests may lead to multiple sexual encounters over a lengthy time period or to a lasting emotional attachment. Whatever form the infidelity takes, acting on these temptations can seriously jeopardize his marriage and his career. Some players' wives, particularly if they married the professional athlete and not the man, also may engage in extramarital affairs, but this did not emerge as a significant marital issue in my research, so this chapter focuses solely on male infidelity.

Most wives fear that their husbands may be sexually and perhaps emotionally unfaithful, and their fears are understandable. The culture adds layers of tension and conflict between partners and creates significant distress for the wives. Susan discovered just how widespread the infidelity was among the NBA players she knew during Bill's career and after he left the game. "I was shocked back in the day at how prevalent it was," she told me. "I mean, I was shocked at the people I knew that I would never in a million years [suspect of cheating]. I found out in later years, well, yeah, they all did. They all pretty much had a woman in every city. I was stunned. Really? That person? That guy? With that family? Yeah, very, very prevalent." Emma echoed Susan's observations: "I just can't think of any man that could actually, honest to god, say, 'I was faithful to my wife the whole time I played.'"

The women I interviewed discussed some of the realities that can help us understand why so many players stray from their marital vows. "I think there's a sense of power," Nora said. "I think there's almost like an addiction to attention. There's an entitlement . . . you can do what you want to do and get away with it. You have all the control, because you have all the money and you have all the fame, and no one's going anywhere because no one's going to tell you what you're doing is wrong." Skylar explained it another way: "You have unattractive baseball players who in regular life would not meet a twenty-year-old girl who would want to have sex with him and jump in their bed. But they make a ton of money . . . so I think you have much more of an opportunity."

Access to the internet, social media, and smartphones can make it easier today for husbands to engage in some form of online infidelity, an emotional attachment, or a sexual relationship. "Someone who texts you or sends you emails or pictures, and that in itself becomes a relationship, and then it becomes infidelity," Emma insisted.

As discussed in chapter 6, it might be assumed that seemingly "nice" husbands wouldn't be unfaithful to their wives, but Nora learned that this isn't always true. "I was very aware of indiscretions. But, you know, I also believed that my husband at the time didn't partake in that," she said. "There are some good boys, so I thought he was one of the good boys, and he surrounded himself with some of the good boys. But that wasn't the case. When I found out about the indiscretions, I felt powerless." Many wives strongly believe that even the most devoted husband can be tempted to be unfaithful. "I think they can't help themselves," Emma said. "So, infidelity, to me, is something that any woman should be cautious of." Some of the women observed that a husband who is morally weak or easily susceptible to temptation may be more likely to be unfaithful regardless of his level of fame. Also, if the marriage is in trouble, he may be more inclined to seek another relationship outside of his marriage. "I would say it's more common than in regular marriages, just because of the men that often become professional athletes," Kaylee said.

Emma reported that "sex talk" was common in the MLB world during Mason's career and that the marital relationship was not exempt from public discussions:

> Talking about sex was very free in that world. . . . Men talked about it. The girls talked about it. It was just a given that you would talk about sex freely anywhere, anytime, about you and your husband, at all times. And your husband would talk to you about other people on the team and their sex life. . . . One time we were staying at a friend's house on the team, and it was more of a road trip and she said, "Well, you guys, you can go in the guest room, because I know you haven't seen each other for a while and haven't had sex since you've seen each other." So my husband said, "Okay, thanks." Then they said, "Well, we might as well have sex, too." And I'm thinking, "Oh, my god, I can't believe I'm living in this world and that it's okay to talk like this." I remember another time in another city, I met my friends in the city we played in and they were visiting, and I was with a few of the other girls on the team, and then another girl came down about an hour later and we were like, "Gee, what took you so long?" and she was like, "Well, you know so-and-so, he has to have sex before a game or he's not going to do well, so that's why I'm late." And I was even then thinking, "I don't even know these girls and they're freely discussing having sex in front of me, and how that's just

this world, this lifestyle. It's all about sex. You don't even have to know the person, and you can sit there and talk about your sex lives in front of somebody you don't even know."

Emma's observations reflect a laxity toward sexual behavior in this male-dominated culture and perhaps some peer pressure among the wives to perform their "wifely duty" when their husbands have been absent from home for long periods. As we have learned, the implicit understanding is that he may "get it on the road" otherwise.

We've also learned that the fiercely protective brotherhood of teammates can implicitly or explicitly encourage husbands to participate in extramarital activities. The men may mistakenly assume that others will help to cover their tracks and protect their marriage or public image, which may or may not be the case. It isn't uncommon for the wives to be put in the position of feeling responsible for protecting the men's sexual privileges. Discussing a buddy-system arrangement involving Mason and his teammate, Emma recalled an uncomfortable situation:

> My husband said, "Hey, we're going to go out after the game with so-and-so." And I said, "Okay." And then he showed up with a woman, and he was married. So we went out to eat something and afterwards I said to my husband, "Don't you ever do that again. I know his wife. I sit next to her at the games. I know their children. I don't ever want you to put me in that position again. It makes me feel cheap." . . . But the whole time I was there, I had to be nice to this girl, and I felt like I was being steak-knifed—and I was. . . . So I just was sick about it. I thought, if his wife ever found out, what would she feel about me? It was just awful. It was horrible.

When a husband has sexual liaisons with interested women, or when he shares his sexual exploits with his teammates, he may not always be discreet about his extramarital opinions or activities, and his affair(s) can become common knowledge among teammates and within the sport organization. When brotherhood secrets leak out or organizational privacy is violated and wives become aware of sensitive information about the activities and habits of the husbands' teammates, it will test their patience and become an unwanted burden. As Courtney observed in the first study, "Every year there's somebody, and I usually find out about it whether I want to or not." Skylar confided that affairs can affect almost everyone on the team. "There were a lot of groupies, but I think it would be harder to figure out a mistress," she said. "But we dealt with that. I mean, there was a couple teams—one in the minor leagues and then for sure one in the big leagues—that was just really awkward because someone got caught, and it was so hard on the wife and all of your personal business kind of aired, because everybody knew. It was just very hard. Plus, you also had flight attendants, too."

A husband's affair can be stressful for a team because of what is at stake, exceptionally so when media scrutiny becomes intense. If the unfaithful husband is the star player or the team is ranking high in postseason play, things become even more nerve-racking. Awkward situations can cause teams and wives to be drawn into a conspiracy of silence to protect their shared interests and priorities. During the first study, for example, an extramarital partner was accidently seated next to the wife of an unfaithful husband at an NFL game, and the wives and others knew it. Although neither the wife nor the extramarital partner was aware of the other's identity, the husband's worries about whether his wife would discover the affair ruined his performance. Lisa also told me, "There's been situations in football where a wife will be sitting in the stands with her three children in one section, and the girlfriend, pregnant, will be sitting in the other section watching the husband. If the other wives know, I don't know why she doesn't."

Finding interested women becomes easier for players when the team is winning. A winning season will increase a husband's public visibility, especially if his team wins prestigious championships, such as the Super Bowl or World Series, or if he's singled out as a hero because he scored a touchdown to win the Super Bowl or hit a home run to win the World Series. "It only becomes more scary, too, when they're winning because that means more groupies," Amanda insisted. "It's like, who wants to wait in the lobby of a hotel for a team that's six and ten? And who wants to wait when they go to the playoffs? It becomes a whole new deal."

Patterns of Infidelity

According to what the wives told me, a husband's extramarital relationships usually tend to follow at least one of three basic patterns. In a one-time encounter, he has an impulsive liaison with a female stranger or an acquaintance. This woman may or may not be a groupie. In a short-term affair, he has a temporary relationship with one female partner, or a series of encounters with different female partners he meets on road trips or away games, in the city where he resides with his family or in the team's hometown. In a long-term affair, he commits to an ongoing relationship with a significant female partner (or more than one partner) outside of his marriage. A short-term affair may become a long-term affair if, for example, the husband continues to meet the female partner on road trips or away games in the city where he resides with his family or in the team's hometown.

Contrary to commonly held views, the wives in the first study believed that the long-term affair rather than the one-time encounter is a more prevalent pattern. In this type of affair, a husband may place more emphasis on emotional fulfillment than sexual fulfillment. Although most affairs are cloaked in secrecy,[2] a husband's long-term affair is perhaps one of the best-known "secrets" among teammates and perhaps among members of the sport organization and other close insiders in his occupational world.

> I've talked to baseball wives, and I've heard a lot . . . of them say that as long as he takes care of home, they don't care. I even know of wives that find plane tickets in the glove compartment that prove their husband has flown somebody to their home while the wife's out visiting her family. They'll fly a girl to their home while she's away. She won't stay in their home, but she'll stay in their hometown . . . things like that.
> —LISA

The wives described three basic patterns in a long-term affair. In the first, a player has extramarital relationships with several different women in different cities. "There could be five girls in town, and each time you come in it could be a different one, or it could be one of them this time and two of them next time," Gwen explained. In the second, different women travel along with a player or travel to meet him when he's on the road or living at his seasonal or permanent residence. In the third, a player is involved with only one extramarital partner on a long-term basis, and many describe her as a "mistress." This woman is undoubtedly single and may or may not have children, and she lives in the city where the husband keeps his permanent or seasonal residence. She may travel with him or meet him wherever his team is playing.

Some women may become involved with players because of what they stand to gain in liaisons with materially successful men, as Lisa pointed out: "These women want them for one thing. They're intrigued with what these guys do. And a lot of them get into it with those kinds of guys because they know they have big contracts and they think maybe they can help them out. They're really materialistic relationships."

Many short- and long-term affairs occur during the season. Seasonal affairs may include a husband having a relationship with a woman who is also in a relationship with a teammate, with or without the husband's knowledge. In another risky variation, a wife may have a relationship with her husband's single or married teammate, which also can create a heartbreaking situation if the affair is discovered.

Any type of affair—most notably the short- and long-term affairs—can create numerous issues not only for the marriage, the extramarital partner, and the unfaithful husband, but for those who know about the relationship. Seasonal affairs are especially difficult to conceal from the wives, teammates, and sport organizations, and they can cause difficulties for all involved, even more so if the husband's partner doesn't wish to end the affair.[3] The extramarital partner may be extremely reluctant to accept the husband's decision to end their relationship just because the season is over and he wants to return home to his family, and the unwanted and widespread media attention that would result if the affair were discovered gives her a certain amount of leverage in pressuring him to continue.

Managing Suspicion

For reasons that should be obvious by now, trust is a significant issue in the sport marriage. A few of the wives told me that it was tremendously difficult to trust their husbands. Some wives said they wanted to trust him. Other wives said they completely trusted him. "I've said that many times: maybe I'm stupid for believing in what he's doing, but I just trust him," Donna said. Most women in the sport marriage manage their suspicions about other women through the use of suspicion work,[4] even if they say they trust their husbands to be faithful. A wife's use of suspicion

> I have my suspicions every time he goes away. Every time. But I haven't found anything. I haven't gotten a clue.
> —JILL

work allows her to cope with the anxiety or fear that her husband is being unfaithful to his marital vows, and it involves two motivating factors: the need to discover evidence of infidelity and the fear of discovering such evidence.

When a wife doesn't trust her husband, she typically searches for evidence of his infidelity. She continually seeks to prove her mistrust by searching for fan mail, notes, letters, phone numbers scribbled on pieces of paper, voice-mail messages, email messages, or text messages from other women. She won't trust him even if she doesn't find any evidence of other women in her husband's life; she believes that it's only a matter of time until she does. If she does discover something, her lack of trust in him is justified and, depending on her reasons for suspicion work, she may or may not confront him with the evidence. Interestingly, wives who say they do trust their husbands also use this strategy to quiet any doubts. In the first study, Alyssa said she trusted Douglas when he played in the NFL, but she still periodically sat in her car in the parking lots of clubs and bars where she knew he was hanging out with his teammates on certain nights, watching to see if he left with a woman.

If a wife who trusts her husband doesn't find anything, her trust in him is confirmed and her mind is eased, at least temporarily. If she finds something, she may ask him to explain the evidence. Olivia struggled with this:

> I used to hate going on road trips, especially if he was in the room already, and then I'd get to the room when he's at the game or something. And then I'd have to go in there and it's like, "Okay, what am I going to find? Who left messages? And all this here stuff. Here we go again." And then I have to be one of those, "Do I believe him or don't I?" Because people call their rooms and leave little messages. And then I find a phone number written down. You know, what do I do with these little pads they write on? I can see the indentations and take the little pencil, and it's like, "Okay, who were you calling?" And see what the number is and call it.

A wife who wants to trust her husband but is afraid of discovering something that would destroy her carefully protected belief in him, decides to or tries not to search for evidence. We can think of this as the ignorance-is-bliss approach. "He would have some big explaining to do if I ever found a girl's phone number," Sheila said. "But I haven't had any shred of evidence, not that I go around looking for it." Not searching for evidence might seem to be a validation of a wife's trust in her husband; still, she normally remains deeply concerned and she may accidentally make discoveries that implicate him.

KELLITA

Kellita began to wonder if her marriage to Donald, a durable NFL veteran, was in trouble while she was pregnant with her fourth child.

Donald typically was introverted and remote during the season, and she was used to his solitary behavior, but during those months he had become even more withdrawn. Although she was concerned and wanted to get to the bottom of things, she didn't want to initiate any serious discussions until the season was over because she knew how important it was for him to focus on his game.

After giving birth, she primarily concentrated on her new daughter and three young children, but she also did what was expected of her as an NFL wife. Donald's primary concern was his demanding career, and his job-related commitments left little time in his schedule for Kellita and their children. As he became increasingly absent from family life, often for unexplained reasons, she became worried and felt neglected. She was reluctant to ask him what he was doing because of what he might tell her.

During this period, Kellita blamed herself rather than Donald for his absences. Because she failed to ask him to curtail his activities, she convinced herself that she shared responsibility for their estrangement. As Donald became even more withdrawn during the offseason, she began to suspect that he was having an affair, but she didn't want to nurture this suspicion. She desperately wanted to trust him, and she took comfort in the fact that she had no proof that he cheated on her. One day, while reviewing the family's phone bills, she noticed an excessive and escalating frequency of calls to one particular number. She also noted that the timing of the calls often followed their arguments. As she pieced things together, everything pointed to a developing relationship that was significant and meaningful to Donald, and she could no longer give Donald the benefit of the doubt.

Armed with evidence from the phone bills, Kellita confronted Donald, hoping he would reassure her of his faithfulness. Instead, he told her it was just a friendship and refused to end it. His response left room for doubt in her mind and implied that he wanted her to accept the situation the way it was. Kellita thought he was suggesting he could have a family and still "do the wild thing on the side." She was hurt and angry not only because she believed he had been unfaithful, but because he refused to apologize for his behavior and seemed to have no regard for her feelings. In an attempt to save their marriage, she asked him to seek counseling with her, but he refused.

After much thought, Kellita decided to hire a private investigator, and his report confirmed her suspicions. Even though she was expecting the news, she was devastated. When she confronted Donald during a heated argument, he finally confessed to the nature of the relationship and admitted that he was emotionally involved with a woman. Kellita asked him to end it, but he also refused that request.

At first Kellita was angry, but her anger soon turned to shame and finally to overwhelming feelings of betrayal and powerlessness. She continually tried to decide which feelings were relevant to the situation and eventually exhausted herself trying to manage her confusing, intense, and painful emotions. At times, "not feeling" seemed a better option.

Despite Kellita's realization that Donald's extramarital relationship had developed into an emotional attachment, she wasn't ready to give up, but the stress was affecting her emotional and psychological health, so she sought counseling. She thought about separation, but instead continued trying to find a way of reaching Donald and resolving the crisis in their marriage. During this coping phase, she relied on her religious beliefs and began to depend more heavily on her good friends for emotional support. Although this way of coping gave her more inner strength, she still had difficulty accepting its reality and the enormity of what it meant for her marriage. By the end of the first study, the couple had agreed to a trial separation, leaving Kellita in emotional limbo.

Some wives told me that their desire not to make these kinds of accidental discoveries is one reason they, at some point in the marriage, decided not to travel with their husbands. But since it is the wife who typically manages the finances and monitors expenses when her husband is on the road, she can still discover certain financial discrepancies and, like Kellita, inadvertently become aware of his involvement with another woman. If she decides not to monitor his traveling expenses, it may be either because she wants to trust her husband or because she doesn't want to know about his activities. She may nonetheless be vigilant and notice if things seem odd or disturbing, and she may follow up on her fears.

Suspicion work can involve some form of denial.[5] A wife may deny something that actually occurred or act as if it could not occur. During Douglas's

NFL career, Alyssa denied reality when she was reluctant to interpret what the clicking sound meant when she answered the landline, or when she wouldn't admit to herself what he was doing on the many evenings he wasn't at home. Responding to major stressors or sudden disruptive crises by trying to escape from or avoid experiencing their emotions is common for players' wives, a process Tanya described as "going numb" and Kellita characterized as "numbed out." Not feeling seems preferable to experiencing such emotional intensity.[6] Rather than allowing herself to express fear, rage, jealousy, or other strong emotions, she will intensify her efforts to be rational or practical. "I feel like sometimes I just was a machine, and I just blocked out everything so I could keep going," Kathleen explained during the first study. "I feel like I stepped out of my body. I opened myself up and I stepped out. And the emotional part, the feelings stayed in a closet, and the robot part, the physical part, did the work."

Although a woman's suspicions may be unfounded, her concerns will be stressful for her anyway if she defines them as justified. "You could drive yourself crazy looking for things," Alyssa said. "I can look at a situation and I can get very suspicious, and it's nothing." Recalling the early years in her marriage, Sheila said, "Every time he went on a road trip, I'm like, 'Oh, I know he's out with somebody. I know he is.' And then I just thought, 'This is dumb. I'm going to drive myself nuts. Unless he gives you a reason, don't think about it.' So that's basically been my philosophy."

The virtually universal use of suspicion work demonstrates these women's hypersensitivity to the possibility of their husbands having affairs. This hypersensitivity may result from many years of suppressing or coping with anxieties and fears through emotion work, and it highlights the limitations of suspicion work. If a wife is unable to effectively manage her anxieties and fears, or if denying emotion fails and the situation remains unresolved (perhaps through therapy or other methods of accepting reality), she may experience marital or emotional burnout or depression. She may read too much into situational clues and even exaggerate certain situations, real or imagined. If unchecked, this hypersensitivity can reinforce or increase a woman's fears or may eventually become a self-fulfilling prophecy: if her husband believes that she's convinced of his unfaithfulness, he may decide that he has nothing to lose if he has an affair.

As in Tanya's experience, the seeds of hypersensitivity may have been sown during the couple's courtship or in the early stages of their marriage when trust emerged as an important relational issue. This happened in the early years of Jill's marriage to Craig:

It was his first year with the team and they were staying at the hotel, and I called him and said "Hi." He said, "Oh, hi, you're here. I'll meet you down in the lobby." And he hung up. I called him back and I said, "Craig." He said, "Oh, hi." I said, "I just called you and you said you'll meet me down in the lobby." He said, "Oh." I said, "What's going on?" I mean, my heart was pounding. I was so upset. He said, "It's no big deal. It was one of the girls at the training camp. There's a couple of girls that are out there. They're ball girls." Well, I don't know what this was, but I caught him and I was fuming.

If the husband's behavior in some way caused the wife to redefine her trust in him, and if her suspicion continues to escalate despite her attempts to effectively manage it, trying to maintain trust may become an issue the couple is reluctant to acknowledge. A wife may become troubled when occupational changes occur, such as his sudden fame, his road-trip behavior, or his difficulty in adjusting to failures or retirement.

Some wives deal with their need to monitor or scrutinize their husbands by finding ways to accept how their husbands interact with interested women in public situations. Wives who engage in suspicion work often realize that if it's ineffective or their suspicions are unwarranted, their hypersensitivity may jeopardize or adversely affect their marital relationships. This may have something to do with knowing when to be suspicious, but it's the level of suspicion that influences how she interprets a clue.

If a wife married the professional athlete and not the man, the discovery of a clue to infidelity can have different meanings. She may decide that the other woman isn't a threat to her marriage. If this is the case, she is more likely to disregard it, to look the other way, or to forgive her husband. But the discovery has a different meaning if she believes that her marriage is at risk. Rather than give up the comfortable lifestyle or financial security, she may decide to have an affair of her own.

Coping with Marital Tension

In addition to using internal coping styles, the wives relied on re-entry routines and communication methods that involved their partners. As discussed throughout this book, transitions between road trips or when the husband returns home for the offseason can be especially challenging for couples, and many develop familiar re-entry routines that serve to ease him back into family life and reorient his wife and family to his presence. These routines may include discussions of topics related to his experiences on the road, and they may gradually or rapidly focus on female groupies and the other interested women and his awareness of or interaction with them. The couple's prioritization of this issue underscores a shared awareness of the culture of infidelity in his occupational world. Several wives pointed out that these topics are more effectively addressed if the couple can practice forms of communication that are nonconfrontational, nonjudgmental, and nondefensive. After this topic is introduced and discussed to the couple's (or wife's) satisfaction, it's dropped in favor of talking about the husband's game performances, road-trip experiences, public-event experiences, or family issues.

Some partners use humor as a way of dealing with stress or anxiety, and this can be an invaluable way of easing tensions around the issues of female groupies. "We joke about it all the time," Marsha explained during the first study. "We're always teasing. There's nothing in our marriage we don't discuss or joke about. It would bother me to be uncomfortable with talking about something in our marriage. Glenn comes home with some real good stories. He'll tell me some of the stories because it's obvious some of the guys screw around." Although the use of humor may be effective, this strategy also can be used to deceive the wife, as Marsha later learned. Lacking other effective coping strategies, couples may rely on the use of humor in an attempt to deal with these stressful issues, or it may be used as a form of denial or subterfuge or to cover for a shared reluctance to discuss the husband's temptations. Depending on the relationship and quality of communication, re-entry routines that include humor can pave the way for a husband to more readily admit that he had been unfaithful on the road.

> You talk about whatever happens. Like I said, the unknown is what hurts more and, knowing, you can deal with it. And regardless of what happens, if you can just talk about it, that's what I was trying to tell Lewis. I'm not saying I have the gift of gab, I'm not saying that we have to sit here and just talk about everything. But tell me what went on. It's not asking too much.
>
> —OLIVIA

Other wives strongly believe that interested women and the issue of affairs isn't a humorous topic and should never be a joking matter. "If I had to deal with it, I would not treat it in a light manner because it's not a light matter to me," Susan said. "No matter what my beliefs are, if I felt this was an issue and if it was important to me that this be a monogamous marriage, I would not deal with it lightly in any way, shape, or form. I think you need to treat serious subjects seriously." The use of humor isn't always useful; it can be a sensitive issue and difficult to discuss if a wife encountered some form of it in childhood or in past relationships.

Some wives may be in denial about the possibility that their husbands will be unfaithful, and they may prefer to not discuss it at all. Other wives believe that discussing the possibility of affairs could become a self-fulfilling prophecy and should never be discussed. Many wives won't raise the issue unless a specific incident involving another woman requires clarification or explanation; the less said, the better.

Tracee shared her views with me about the quality of communication in her marriage when discussing the presence of interested women:

> I think more of myself than to sit around and ask my husband who he's looked at. I don't relate to that. But if it's something that went on and he tells me about it, we talk about it. I've had times where I might feel there's nothing to say. Why say it? Why bring it up? If a woman approaches you and she's coming on to you in a certain way, I feel you should be able to handle it. I don't really want to know about it. But if she was out there and did something really queer or weird, tell me about it. There was one woman at a card show that had on a little miniskirt and half of a top or whatever, and she went up to one of the guys and said, "I really like the way you guys scratch yourself and spit. It really turns me on." You know, a real ding-dong. If something queer happened, I've had him tell me about them.

Without compatible communication styles and effective communication skills, sensitive marital issues may not be addressed adequately, and the marriage will suffer. In contrast to some wives who are uncomfortable discussing the presence of interested women or the issue of infidelity as re-entry topics, other wives find meaningful communication and productive discussions essential and reassuring because they can minimize their stress, anxiety, or fear of the husband's unfaithfulness. Effective communication also can clearly affirm their thoughts about whether some measure of boundary work in public life is necessary or has been successful. These women want to trust their husbands. They want to have faith in the husbands' judgment, and they want to try not to think too much about it. The quality of communication in their relationship can allow for this. But if a husband is reluctant to raise or discuss these fundamental issues when he returns home from the road and his wife is curious or concerned, she soon learns that it's up to her to try to keep the channels of communication open.

Setting Marital Boundaries

Most wives establish and enforce boundaries around marital fidelity and have developed strategies to minimize ambiguity about how they would react if they learned that their husbands have been unfaithful. Because of the value they place on their marriages and the love they have for their husbands, many wives believe that their judgment and decision making should be tempered with understanding. Their boundary work includes seeking knowledge about the circumstances around which the husband may or may not be given the benefit of the doubt, such as a level of inebriation that caused him to lose consciousness and forget what happened. Some wives are more willing to forgive their husbands for a one-time encounter, which they might describe as a "mistake" or temporary weakness, but are less willing to overlook a habitual tendency to have frequent affairs or involve themselves in any version of a long-term affair. "It depends on the nature of the affair," Jessica explained. "I just don't think I'd divorce him. It just depends on how ugly the whole thing got. The bottom line is he'd have to come up with a really good explanation. I mean, we got to figure it out. 'Well, what does this other person think of you? What do you want to do? Is this person more important to you? Do you want this marriage to work? Then stop and never do it again.'" For other wives, however, an affair of any type is completely inappropriate.

> I'd probably throw hot water in his face. . . . Hey, I don't know. I might have shot him. That's the truth, you never know. . . . I'd be highly pissed. . . . Raymond knows how I feel about it. He knows I'm not going to put up with anything like that.
>
> —LISA

Even after the boundaries have been clearly established, and after levels of trust are defined between the marital partners, an affair can still create problems, especially if trust issues existed before the affair. Although a one-time encounter may be ultimately forgivable, its discovery may cause a wife to feel betrayed and this loss of trust can disrupt the marital relationship so it's never the same again. Her respect for her husband may truly be tested.

She may ask herself, "If he did it once, will he do it again?" This woman believes that it's crucial for her husband to be the first to inform her if he has an affair, before she learns about it through mass media or another person, such as from another wife or someone on his team. Whether or not wives in this situation ultimately forgive their husbands, they clearly wanted to be the first to know the truth even if their worst fear was confirmed. "If I had a gut feeling, I'd just want to know," Jill insisted. "Just tell me so that I don't carry that feeling with me all the time. You know? It would eat at me. I mean, seriously, it would just eat at me. My worst fear, my worst fear, is to find out that he has been messing around and I didn't know it." Skylar said that public humiliation would be devastating. "I've always told him . . . 'Don't make a fool out of me.' . . . Don't let me find out that you're doing all this stuff behind my back, and find out from someone else, because I don't know that I would get over that. That's a different level of disrespect, and respect is a really big, important thing to me." Admitting that he had a one-time encounter doesn't guarantee that the husband won't have another affair, so his confession may not serve to calm or minimize a wife's fears but instead may add to her worries. Several women in the first study and the majority in the second group said that although they trusted their husbands, their trust could not be unconditional. For instance, if a brief fling implies previous affairs or develops further into a series of affairs or a long-term affair, she will likely draw the line.

Given the amount of marriage work a wife provides to her husband and his career, learning that he has been unfaithful can be emotionally devastating. The wives in both studies described a wide range of emotions they experienced or expected if they discovered that their husbands were having an affair, but anger was understandably the most universal. When actually confronted with the reality of infidelity, a wife commonly responds emotionally and perhaps physically to the news, and then adapts according to her definition of the situation. Emma recalled her initial response when she discovered that Mason had been unfaithful: "I remember I got up from the table and I went to the kitchen sink, and I threw up. And then I proceeded that month to lose thirty-three pounds. I was so sick from finding out that he had an affair."

As a way of trying to regain their equilibrium upon learning about an affair, or trying to prove that the husband is having an affair or had an affair, some wives left their homes on a temporary basis or said that they would do so if the situation ever happened to them. "I always uproot," Tanya said. "Every time I've ever found out, I've always left. I mean, I came back, but

I would always leave." Other wives said that they wouldn't leave home but would make their husbands leave.

The way a wife defines and copes with infidelity may depend on why she married in the first place. A wife who married the professional athlete may accept his affair(s) with the implicit understanding that the situation won't embarrass her publicly or lead others to suspect her complicity. The wives in the first study identified three main factors that would lead a wife who married the man to stay with an unfaithful husband: financial security, low self-esteem, and imminent divorce. Some wives truly value an affluent and comfortable lifestyle, and they may become dependent on the husband's career to provide it. A wife may grow accustomed to what many would consider a lavish lifestyle and the elevated status that comes with her husband's career success; it may give her and her children opportunities that wouldn't have been possible otherwise. Beth, who participated in both studies and whose husband went on to become a baseball coach, observed that this pattern had not changed in Cliff's occupational world over the years: "I would have to say that, in a glimpse of what I saw probably within the past year or two, there are still those women that, you know, 'I'm married to you. I have your children. You provide a great life. I know that you're not always faithful but, you know what, that doesn't matter because I'm not going to give up what I have.'" If a wife is afraid of losing everything, she may decide to be more forgiving. "I really can see why the wife's afraid to rock the boat," Susan said. "Because she thinks, 'Well, you know, I've got it okay here and things are going pretty well at home. Yeah, he's cheating on me occasionally, but is that so bad?' Well, for me, that would be everything. For her, maybe that's not so bad." A wife also may have limited occupational skills or opportunities to seek employment outside the home, and the realities of his career demands make it difficult, if not impossible, for her to achieve financial autonomy. "There's wives that I know that know that if they leave their husband they're going to have nothing," Nora said. As a result, a wife may be reluctant to end her marriage if she lacks the necessary means to provide for herself or her children, specifically if the couple is in debt, an unfortunate situation that appears to be fairly common among retired players and their families. She may have developed a relational or emotional dependence on her husband in addition to her financial dependence.

Low self-esteem also can explain why a wife would be reluctant to end her marriage after discovering that her husband has been unfaithful. She may have merged her identity with his and internalized the "we" partnership, and this may be an effort to manage or conceal deep-seated feelings of insecurity or powerlessness, a lack of confidence, or a fragile self-image. If so, she may worry that she isn't a good enough wife or mother and blame herself for her husband's unfaithfulness. Beth shared her opinion about how a wife's low self-esteem and feelings of insecurity caused her to enable her husband's infidelity:

> She's weak. Well, not that she gets walked on, like he wipes his feet on her, but that she somewhere has some weak link that keeps her from saying, "You're cheating on me. You're committing adultery, and I won't put up with it, and get out of my life. I don't need this." But a lot of girls, they don't want to get a divorce. They think that maybe we'll get over this part, and they think they'll get through this one affair, and then it won't happen again—that somewhere along the line she did something wrong . . . and that's why he had an affair.

A woman experiencing this emotional dilemma may have fewer inner resources, or lack an adequate support network, to effectively handle her husband's affair and may be unable to disengage from the distressful situation. Women who had a troubled childhood may have normalized infidelity as a fact of marital and family life.

Finally, a wife may not be concerned about or may seem to accept her husband's infidelity because the marriage is in trouble and divorce seems inevitable.

Several wives who married the man rather than the professional athlete reported that their deepest fear was that their husbands would become overly consumed with the role and would no longer resist, or even begin to encourage, female attention in retirement. Many men are reluctant to surrender their careers and the identity of a professional athlete, and the emotional position this puts them in as they transition into retirement can cause inappropriate behaviors to emerge later.

The issue of infidelity is certainly emotionally troubling and threatens marriages, but the implications for these women are more far-reaching. Affairs can lead to pregnancies outside of the marriage, which can yield unforeseen consequences for the marital couple's children or for the children of the extramarital couple. Additionally, as we discovered in the previous chapter, it's common for several teammates to simultaneously date the same woman. This and other types of extramarital behavior are a serious health concern that leads the wives to develop justifiable fears about becoming exposed to sexually transmitted diseases. These types of sexual practices underline the importance of the wives' boundary work, as Sharon discovered: "I had a million gynecologists. They all bullshitted me right through the roof with everything. It didn't even dawn on me until we had that blood test. Walt says, 'Well, I could have gonorrhea.' I'm like, 'How could you?' He says, 'Well, there's this one girl. . . . ' Bullshit. You know? I was so shocked and so naïve."

Discovering Infidelity

After Douglas had retired and their children moved away, which occurred during the first study, Alyssa looked forward to a renewed life together with her husband. Right away, however, she noticed that his nightlife activities increased and he became more emotionally distant in their sexual interactions. Often, when she answered the landline, she could hear the clicking sound of someone hanging up, and it became so annoying that she dreaded picking it up. During the second study, she told me that a few years later, while she was running a few errands on a rainy January afternoon, her worst nightmare came true right in front of her when she saw Douglas with a woman she didn't recognize:

> It was profound disrespect. I felt disrespected and I couldn't understand why something like this would happen. There was deceit, there was lying, there was a lot to it, because even when I suspected certain things and I asked about it, I wasn't given the truth. So to actually see it, to face it, to come upon it where there was no denying it, like this is it, you know, it was hard. I mean, it was hard. I was angry. But at least it made me know that I wasn't crazy. I knew that something was up, and I couldn't pinpoint it, and every time I would get something that I thought I could address, it was always knocked down like, "No, no, that's nothing, that's nothing, that's nothing." But still, I knew something was happening and because the whole dynamic had just changed, and there was just so much unhappiness and I kept trying to find out what was causing the unhappiness.

> You know, the saddest thing, and what would be the most devastating, is if you were keeping him happy at home and he still cheated and he got it on the road. I think all of us could say, "Oh, my husband will never cheat. I really believe in him." But you know what? You never know.
>
> —BETH

Alyssa and Douglas separated shortly thereafter and basically ended their relationship, but they didn't seek a divorce.

A few years after Raymond retired from his NFL career, Lisa learned that he was having an affair with a female friend that he had known for a number of years. Although they separated for several years, they didn't end their relationship or seek a divorce. Kellita and Donald also separated because of his unfaithfulness. Among participants in the second study, Tanya and Ryan, Jill and Craig, Nora and Wyatt, Emma and Mason, and Marsha and Glenn ended their marriages largely because of the husband's infidelity.

Marsha hadn't yet discovered Glenn's infidelity during the first study, but she shared with me how humiliated she would feel if she ever did catch him cheating on her: "I've told Glenn . . . one of the worst things is the embarrassment of knowing that other people know that you made a total fool out of me. . . . I sat here supporting you . . . through your game, and you were making a fool out of me the whole time." During the second study, Marsha said that Glenn admitted that he had been unfaithful to her and discussed the prevalence of interested women in the MLB world:

> When we went through our divorce and he literally said to me, "I can't believe I did this. I swore when we got married that I would never cheat on you. . . . It's just . . . these women are at you no matter where you are. Business cards are being passed out, they're offering whatever, and the guys are like, 'Ah, she'll never know.' You know, it's like a little bit of peer pressure, and then it's just—it's there."

Many of the divorces and the separation that occurred in the lives of the women in the second study occurred after the husband retired from his career. When we talked during the second study, Marsha had worked through the pain of divorce and was circumspect about the end of her marriage:

> We married very young and it takes a toll on people. But also it's a great life. It was a lot of fun. I really enjoyed it. I wouldn't have given it up for the world. I look back, and do I wish that we could have made it work? My marriage was important to me, and that was a huge loss to me. But I've done just fine. . . . I had to come to a certain point in my life to say, you know, that these aren't awful guys. I mean, these are not horrible men.

CONCLUSION

The Final Score

> **SKYLAR**
>
> Carter and I ended up being in a small group with young wives, and I could not stop crying, because just talking to them I was reliving a lot of the pain and trauma that they were having. I totally understood. I mean, it was like I just wanted to put my arms around them and say, "It's going to be okay.". . . It really got me because I have been out of the lifestyle for a little bit of time, and worked to get really healthier in my own personal life, and going back into that, I experienced trauma just talking to them about it. I thought, since we're out of it, it was fine, but I didn't realize how traumatizing it was. . . . There's some stress disorder stuff that comes out of it that you don't realize, because you keep swallowing it, and when you get out of it and get back in, you sort of see, oh my gosh, this is insanity.

Although the male-dominated, heterosexual sport marriage remains basically the same as it was a quarter of a century ago, some aspects are beginning to change for the better. For example, one major finding from the second group is that some segment of the recent generation of husbands seems to be more sensitive to and understanding of marital and domestic issues, most notably the joys and demands of parenting. Also, as mentioned in the introduction, a few labor and work-family changes in the occupational worlds of professional sport have occurred over the years. Despite these trends, however, the sport marriage as a marital institution basically remains the same. It continues to empower men and subordinate women.

Now that we have gained insight into the sport marriage, we can see that the prevailing stereotypes of these women are misleading, and, as the women's stories bring to light, their marriages are filled with complexities and paradoxes. The women in both studies had to make difficult choices, and even though some outside observers may criticize or question their decisions, they really believed that the trade-offs they made were necessary to make their marriages work. They deliberately prioritized their husbands' careers, marital stability, and family functioning over anything else, and most of them were unaware of what the trade-offs truly entailed until they were well into their marriages.

Overall, these women make conscious decisions about the roles they assume, yet their interpretations of their marital experiences are filled with ambiguities and contradictions. On one hand, most of the women I interviewed—even those who were eventually divorced—seemed satisfied with their marriages, either because they loved their husbands and were willing to do whatever it took to make the relationship work, or because they enjoyed the lifestyle that comes with being the wife of a professional athlete and were willing to put up with a lot to be able to have that experience. They took great pride in their ability to make their marriages work and meet the myriad challenges they confronted in their husbands' occupational world. They developed confidence in themselves and their carefully cultivated abilities, and they found a certain degree of fulfillment in meeting their marital and family obligations. On the other hand, they experienced gender and marital inequality that led to various forms of subordination and oppression. They talked to me about layers of pain, fear, anger, insecurity, neglect, and social and emotional isolation, but because of their priorities, they carefully concealed their thoughts and feelings from others. As we have seen, some tried to deny their true feelings even to themselves.

The unique nature of these marriages and the lifestyle inherent in their husbands' choice of career can separate the wives and their children from close friends and family members and make it difficult for women married to professional athletes to form reliable friendships that might provide some buffer from the stressful nature of their lives. In a perfect world, other women in the same situation would be an important source of emotional or other types of support, but developing trusting relationships with other wives can be fraught with difficulties. A woman can become isolated by her belief that few people understand the special challenges of her particular marital situation, and she typically doesn't confide in others about her personal and marital problems. She may fear that other wives, friends, neighbors, or outsiders will exploit her, share private details about her marriage, or otherwise violate her trust. They may even try to break up her marriage. When she does choose to share personal details, she's typically criticized for complaining. After all, doesn't she live in a glamorous world filled with lots of money and celebrities? "You're making millions of dollars, so put up with the problems" is a common view that may come lightly sprinkled with condemnation. But many stereotypical beliefs about a professional athlete's affluent quality of life are largely unfounded; not all professional athletes command the type of salary that provides an opulent lifestyle. Even if a wife is lucky enough to live the life that most people believe she does, multimillion-dollar salaries don't always bring happiness, and they don't necessarily compensate for a troublesome marriage. In reality, wealth can contribute to deep-seated tension in the sport marriage. It's fairly common for these husbands to use their high salaries to define their role in the marriage and expect their wives to be happy with their way of life without complaints or other expressions of dissatisfaction. Many professional athletes view their paycheck as a gift to their wives. They may use it as a shield against complaints, a way to absolve themselves of family responsibilities, or a means of controlling their wives. Many seem to expect their wives to trade happiness for financial security.

A wife's feeling of loneliness and alienation can be intensified by her husband's inability to support her in ways that matter to her. His workaholic commitment to his career predictably leaves her feeling neglected, unappreciated, and emotionally abandoned. She may have the expectation that when his career is over it will be his turn to support her in ways that are important to her, but this is typically not the case. He may continue to disappoint her in myriad ways.

The challenges these women confront largely result from the publicly visible and unpredictable nature of their husbands' profession, combined with the women's developing sense of self. As explained earlier, most of the women I interviewed were not initially prepared to deal with the accumulating pressures and demands of the sport marriage (the primary exception being those who had some experiences in minor league baseball). This doesn't mean that they were submissive or weak. On the contrary, as a group and individually, my close contact with these women over the years showed me that they were strong, capable, and resilient. Without exception, they eventually became aware that the thing they valued and excelled at had entrapped them to some extent, and many of the interviews in the first study included heartfelt epiphanies about the consequences of the choices they made. It's significant, then, that when revisiting their experiences in their husbands' postcareer years—by that point fully understanding the meaning of their experiences—several of women said that they wouldn't have chosen differently if they had the chance to do it all over again.

As I began my fieldwork in the first study, it was clear that the women didn't, at first, expect to gain much personally from their participation in the study. Several women told me that they were participating because they were distinctly aware of how the media disseminates and reinforces misinformation about women married to professional athletes, because they wanted to dispel pervasive and undeserved stereotypes, and because they wanted to correct misleading assumptions, all of which we could argue have steadily increased throughout the years. They believed, therefore, that their participation would "set the record straight" about how women experience their marriages to professional athletes. This is one of the main reasons I participated in media interviews about my findings and the sport marriage in general. Most of the women told me that they hoped that other women thinking about marriage to a professional athlete would in some way learn from their experiences. Although this may have been their primary motivation, participating in the first study also resulted in an unexpected benefit for many of the wives. It certainly was never my intent, but some wives became intensely introspective as a result of our interviews in the first study and took advantage of them as a process of self-discovery and personal growth. They took the opportunity to evaluate, gain insight into, and learn more about themselves, their marriages, and their husbands' careers.

For some, the interviews were a transformative process, evolving in unexpected ways during their participation. The women seemed to appreciate and value opportunities to talk openly about their buried memories and innermost thoughts and to express various emotions they otherwise routinely suppressed or denied. Sharing their stories was not always an easy or simple process, and it was at times challenging for the women and for me, yet they took the interviews seriously and even looked forward to them. Using the interviewing methods I discuss in appendix A, I spent hundreds of hours listening to their candid narratives. They were amazingly frank. They almost universally challenged and questioned themselves and made unflinching self-appraisals. Our times together were filled with emotional disclosures and profound realizations, and they soon discovered that they had much to gain personally from participating in the study. "My expectations changed a whole lot when we were doing the interviews," Susan told me. "I found that it was not only enjoyable but also helpful to voice these things." Some of the women gained considerable awareness about their lack of self-esteem. Olivia learned that she was stronger than she thought and that it was okay to feel the way she did about personal and marital issues. She felt much better about herself as a direct result of her participation in the study. "For the first time, I feel like I'm somebody," she confided. Many of the women said they were empowered in different ways. "The interviews gave me a perspective on what I was going through and how I deal with different things. I didn't know that I had a method," Tracee said. The women were sensitized not only to previously unacknowledged feelings and thoughts, but to the ways in which they confronted the unpredictable and stress-inducing nature of their husbands' careers, especially in coping with the needs of family life. For example, Jessica was able to come to terms with her feelings in discussing her denial and difficulty in coping with Andrew's release from his last NFL team and his subsequent retirement from the game. "I think the interviews took the rose-colored glasses off in terms of what was really going on," she said. When Paula struggled to understand what it meant to be a rookie MLB wife, she found the interviews useful. "Even with baseball, I feel like I've been in this longer than I have just because I have so much more information now. So it feels like I was introduced to it," she said. This new awareness and sense of self-renewal appeared to help them begin learning new skills for coping with stressful situations, achieving self-support, and pursuing self-improvement. As Kellita said, "I learned a lot about myself that I didn't think I would."

Many of the wives interpreted the interviews as therapeutic, and I believe their positive experiences resulted from the collaborative experience of being taken seriously as authors of their own stories, despite their relative obscurity in the shadow of their public husbands. In vivid contrast to the negative things they had to say about members of the media who interview or report on their husbands, to me they expressed gratitude. For most of them, it was the first time they had finally been able to share their most personal experiences openly and honestly, and they were relieved to be able confide in someone who had an interest in what they had to say without passing judgment or unfairly criticizing or trivializing their experiences, beliefs, attitudes, thoughts, or emotions.

Based on what they learned from the marital events in their lives, the women in the second study offered advice to women who are thinking about marrying or are already married to a professional athlete. Many of the wives cautioned women to first think hard about marriage to a professional athlete and warned that the sport marriage isn't for every woman. But if marriage is in the cards, a woman must learn as much as possible about her future husband; in particular, she should be curious about his family background and his sport and career aspirations. She should try to minimize any unrealistic beliefs and hopes. Her motivation to get married must not include the expectation that it will be an affluent or glamorous lifestyle. If her husband is already on a team, she might make arrangements to meet with some of the wives on his team, spend time with them, and find out what to expect. She should understand that her marriage will be her first priority, and that her husband's career will be his first priority. She must realize and accept the fact that he loves his career and that it will come first in his life, and if she thinks he will change or that she can change him, she will be disappointed. She should know that the sport marriage demands more from women than most other marriages; it will be physically, emotionally, relationally, and psychologically demanding. She might consider joint/individual counseling before marrying to establish a support base and better understand her strengths and weaknesses as a marital partner. She should be prepared to put the best part of herself into her marriage and try to resist temptations, such as exploiting the benefits of celebrity, desirable lifestyle, or wealth. She should be prepared for the worst, such as a husband who is unfaithful, sustains a career-ending or life-threatening injury, or simply can't establish a successful career and has trouble letting go of his dreams, especially in retirement.

The wives told me that a woman in the sport marriage must have her own identity and make every attempt to maintain it. She should always "be her own person" and believe in herself. Although she will have detailed knowledge of her husband's sport and his career, she should avoid getting too wrapped up in it, because when his career is over, what will she have? By that point in her life, she may have difficulty trying to figure out who she is and what she wants to do. If it's realistic, she should have an occupation or career separate from her husband's that gives her personal satisfaction, rather than basing her self-worth on her husband's identity, celebrity, or career. Creating a life for her and her children should include her husband as much as possible, but she shouldn't expect that he will always be available to her or his family.

Regardless of when she marries her husband, the women said, she should take the initiative to be aware of developments in her husband's career. She should, for example, have knowledge about his contracts, be aware of their finances, be sensitive to quality of life problems, and have equal input in all marital/family decisions. She should be ready to relocate at a moment's notice with little or no support. She should understand that she has her limitations and should not give in to expectations that she must do everything by herself. If she can afford it, she might consider hiring adequate domestic support.

As part of adapting to some of the realities in her husband's career, the wives cautioned other wives to avoid gossip, learn how to deal with rumors, be aware of groupies, be confident and judicious in their use of social media, accept long separations from their husbands, and accept that they will be alone a great deal of the time during their marriages. If a woman isn't comfortable with being alone for much of the year, the sport marriage isn't for her, they said. She should know that her husband will most likely not be with her to support her during pregnancy and childbirth, and she should be ready to begin a new chapter with her newborn baby without him around. To minimize stress, she must establish and maintain effective boundaries with troublesome groupies, teammates, in-laws, family members, well-wishers, friends, and team administrators. She would do well to remind her husband that she will find it reassuring if he stays in contact with her during the season, especially when he's on the road. Similarly, she should stay in contact with him, to let him know that she has things handled at home—even if she's struggling—so he can focus on his job. Some wives advised that couples should minimize separations and do whatever they can to avoid separations that are longer than two weeks. Whenever possible, the wife should attempt to limit opportunities for him to be on his own for extended periods by traveling with her husband during the season. In other words, they should avoid leading two separate lives; otherwise, when his career is over they may discover that they have grown apart.

A wife must avoid a false sense of financial security and plan for the future, the women insisted. She must keep in mind that her husband's career is, at best, a short-term profession that can end unexpectedly, so she should hire a financial advisor, use a budget, and save as much money as she can. She should avoid living beyond a modest lifestyle or establishing a lifestyle that is based on the mistaken belief that he will have a long career. His career may provide a permanent source of income after he retires, but only if the couple made financial provisions during his career. She must realize that if the marriage ends during the husband's career, or if his career ends before the marriage, she should be prepared to move on.

Finally, the wives advised other women to develop a sense of humor, which will get them through the worst of times. They also encouraged them to enjoy the ride while it lasts. They believe that it's an exciting life that offers amazing experiences, but they caution women to avoid getting caught up in the trappings of celebrity and a lifestyle that most do not have and may never have.

Some keys to establishing and maintaining an emotionally healthy and fulfilling sport marriage emerged as a result of the wives' advice. One of the keys is to practice direct and open communication—not just small talk, but serious discussions—especially if the wife is worried, annoyed, or stressed out. Effective communication will promote intimacy, trust, and satisfaction with the marriage. Unless her husband invites it, a wife should initially think twice about criticizing or offering him advice about his career.

Providing mutual support is another important key to a fulfilling sport marriage. A wife should realize that her husband depends on her support in good times and bad times. If a wife can establish a pattern of support during her husband's career, this pattern may benefit the marriage after his career is over. But the couple also should recognize that the wife is also deserving of her husband's support. He can support her, for example, by checking in regularly to see how she's doing, encouraging her own current and future dreams and aspirations, and providing regular opportunities to keep each other informed about what's happening in the family.

A wife should avoid getting caught up in things she can't control and avoid envy or jealousy and the desire to be perfect. She should trust her husband and, if necessary, be willing to forgive him. If he is unfaithful, she must be willing to work through it, resolve it, or be prepared to dissolve the marriage. If she has a religion, she should follow it, because she will need it.

We learned in the last chapter that the years were not kind to some of the women who participated in the first study, and their marriages ended in divorce or separation. Of the women who were divorced, Tanya ended her marriage toward the end of her husband's career, and Marsha and Jill ended their marriages some years after their husbands retired. Alyssa separated many years after her husband retired. Of the women who were still married, the average length of their marriages was thirty-two years. Courtney's marriage was the shortest at twenty-six years and Sheila's marriage was the longest at forty-one years. These women were pleased with their marriages and found greater happiness as the years went by. Most of the ten women were employed in various occupations or established their own careers and businesses. In contrast to the husbands who had careers in the other major team sports, the majority of husbands who were former MLB players were able to establish and sustain second careers and remained in the MLB world in various occupations, such as coaching.

Of the seven women who participated in the second study only, Emma ended her marriage after her husband retired and Nora ended her marriage toward the end of her husband's career, both primarily because of their husbands' infidelity. The remaining five women were reasonably satisfied with their marriages and had fully adjusted to their husbands' retirement. The average length of their marriages was twenty-one years; Callie's and Kaylee's marriages were the shortest at thirteen years and Alaina's marriage was the longest at thirty-one years.

Nearly all the women who were still married were interested in improving the quality of their relationships with their husbands, and several were or had been actively engaged in therapy,[1] either with or without their husbands. Perhaps if wives were able to develop and rely on useful support systems, their ability to cope with the various stressors might be more effective, and deeper levels of marital satisfaction might be achieved. The marriages that seemed to be the most satisfying were those in which the women had their own occupations, careers, or businesses and were more future-oriented. They had married their husbands before their careers were well underway and a few had some idea of what to expect as a player's wife, although most said that nothing could have prepared them for it. They had developed effective skills in coping with occupational/marital stressors, demands, and pressures. They were able to have mutual control and to resolve power issues with their husbands, had established useful communication styles, and were devout members of and received support from a religious community.

One thing that has become abundantly clear as a result of my research is that the role of wife in the sport marriage is a full-time, unpaid job that could be said to require lots of overtime. As long as a woman realizes that her husband's career will be the priority at least until he retires, and she's willing to shoulder the responsibilities, deal with myriad beliefs about how she should conduct herself, and cope with the potential personal costs that are part of the implicit or explicit marital agreement, she may enjoy the rewards of some exciting and unique experiences in any of the occupational worlds of professional sport. But she would do well to ask herself before taking the plunge, "Is it worth it to me?"

> If I had it all over to do again—I love my husband, but I would've kept walking. Because of the stress that it puts on you, the uncertainty, the never knowing about being faithful, or whatever. It's just a lot. It takes a special kind of woman to deal with it, because I know that friends, or coworkers, or whatever, couldn't deal with what I have to deal with. And, you know, you just get to a point where you have to weigh things, and that's what I do. I weigh things. I think, "Well, is this worth it?" Because I'm not going to have a normal life. It's not going to be your everyday white-picket-fence type thing.
> —NICOLE

APPENDIX A

Research Methodology

The foundation for this book is the long-term qualitative study I conducted between 1989 and 1993 and supplemented by the longitudinal data I collected in 2015–16. For the most recent study, I conducted follow-up interviews with ten of the women who participated in the first study. I also interviewed an entirely new group of women whose husbands or ex-husbands were more recently retired. The new group of women and the women from the first study who also participated in the second study substantially corroborated my original findings.

First Study

In the first study, I was guided by the grounded theory approach.[1] The fieldwork consisted primarily of in-depth interviews but also included participant observation, human documents (including letters and postcards), and print media accounts (including newspaper and magazine articles). This multiple-method approach to data collection resulted in a saturation that consistently substantiated the findings.[2] In addition, I kept a comprehensive journal of field notes documenting my observations, interactions, and experiences.[3] After three full years of immersion in the field, I spent another year conducting interviews as I gradually, and with greater difficulty than I had anticipated, exited from the field.

GAINING ACCESS

Selection of the women was based on those to whom I was able to gain access. Considering the importance placed on managing the public's perception of sport organizations and the players, in addition to the high risk of uninvited media scrutiny into the players' private lives, it's understandable that sport organizations act as gatekeepers to closely protect their privacy and the privacy of the wives and families. Moreover, it's understandable that husbands protect their own privacy and act as gatekeepers to protect the privacy of their wives and families. This, and the fact that most wives of professional athletes purposely isolate themselves and don't easily trust outsiders, made it challenging to enter their world. Considering that I was an outsider to restricted worlds—the exclusive occupational worlds of the husbands and the private world of their wives—gaining entry to the wives' world was a singular achievement that required patience, persistence, and time. I gained a deeper appreciation for this unprecedented opportunity after attempting to find and enlist new participants for the second study.

Despite the many obstacles and challenges in making the initial contact for the first study, the sampling processes provided a diverse group of participants in terms of age, race, ethnicity, social class, education, length of marriage, and length of the husband's career. Purposive and snowball sampling were only moderately successful,[4] so I didn't limit it to wives of active players. Eventually, thirty-nine wives of active players and eight wives of retired players participated, one of whom participated in the pilot study. The forty-seven wives had husbands employed by more than twenty-eight teams in the four major professional team sports: twenty-one wives of MLB players, twenty-one wives of NFL players, three wives of NBA players, and two wives of NHL players. A core group of fifteen wives finished the lengthy interview guide, constituting an intensity sampling.[5] Another thirty-two participants were not able to finish the interview guide for reasons such as change of residence, time constraints, loss of interest, or a husband's opposition to his wife's participation. Although the primary data came from the long-term participants, interviews with the short-term participants validated much of the primary data, and subsequent saturation confirmed the primary data.

When I entered the field, I thought my interview questions were adequate and up to the task of understanding the nature of the sport marriage. In our initial interviews, however, I realized that the questions were only scratching the surface of their lived experience and that I was not prepared to adequately understand the depth and meaning of their narratives in only one interview. I also discovered that the women were anxious to share their thoughts and feelings about their marriages in ways that far exceeded my expectations. In response to this awareness, I developed an interviewing method I came to think of as "sequential interviewing," and it became my primary approach to data collection in the first study. All long-term participants and many short-term participants were sequentially interviewed.

INTERVIEWING PROCESS

The interviewing began by exploring my general interest in the marital/life experiences and coping responses of the wives. I believe they responded as they did because of my interviewing approach: I regarded the women as the experts of their own lives, and this understanding emerged through a collaborative process of gathering information; we interacted as conversational partners.[6] I didn't consider them simply as objects of research, but as individuals with interesting stories to share. Although my field observations and field notes were detailed and informative, the data from the interviews consistently revealed information that data from field observations alone could not always reveal.[7]

This interviewing process had three distinct advantages. First, it gave me a much deeper understanding of the seasonal cycles of the women's marital lives as I tried to follow the "seasonal clocks" in the different occupational worlds of the NFL, MLB, NBA, and NHL. Second, it offered me the unusual opportunity to simultaneously document the women's previous experiences in addition to the emerging events taking place at the time. This allowed for a better understanding of how past experiences relate to present marital experiences, and it contributed to the development of collaborative partnerships. Third, it provided me with the matchless opportunity to learn how the wives constructed their career-dominated marriages in the highly visible occupational worlds of their husbands. I didn't anticipate, however, and didn't intend, that many of the wives would interpret the sequential and collaborative method of interviewing as having some therapeutic value.

A major disadvantage of sequential interviewing was that it required me to sustain access to wives who were always relocating. Their husbands' careers were in constant flux due to expected and unexpected trades, serious injuries, free agency issues, getting sent down to the minor leagues, not getting called up to the big leagues, getting cut from the team, and so forth. These and other occupational realities made keeping current with them immensely challenging.

The recorded interviews with the women ranged in length from thirty minutes to more than three hours and took place at different times and in a wide variety of settings and circumstances. In addition, I occasionally participated in group interviews[8] with some of the wives during crisis situations in their husbands' careers. Spontaneous interviews also occurred in various other fieldwork situations. I conducted phone interviews when face-to-face interviews were not possible. When possible, after completing the interview guide or after stopping at some point in the interview guide, and after varying periods of time, I also conducted follow-up interviews. Since I was included in the wives' everyday lives, I had occasion to observe interactions between the marital partners. Of course, knowing that I was interviewing their wives, it seems reasonable to assume that the husbands were on their best behavior around me; even so, I was able to observe certain patterns that were consistent with what the wives shared with me in our interviews.

Because of the unusual nature of the fieldwork, I learned other ways to be flexible in my research methods. I varied the interviewing techniques I used when it seemed appropriate and necessary to gain a rich data set. To clarify and corroborate the data collected from semistandardized and unstandardized interviews with the wives,[9] I conducted semistandardized and unstandardized interviews with nineteen other participants,[10] including ten husbands. The interviews with the husbands, which occurred individually or jointly with their wives, focused on occupational details about their careers. The interviews with nine other individuals, who had regular contact with wives and families of professional athletes, centered on their knowledge about occupational issues in the careers of professional athletes and about the sport marriage in general; they were unrelated to specific wives in the study. These individuals included one ex-wife of a retired NFL player, two wives of MLB coaches, a wife of an MLB trainer, a wife of an minor league baseball player, an assistant director of community affairs for an MLB team, a community relations director for an NFL team, a public relations staff member for an NFL team, and a former general manager of a stadium complex for MLB and NFL teams. These interviews were fortuitous; some of the individuals were sequentially interviewed and a few were helpful key informants. Combined with the forty-seven wives, a total of sixty-six individuals participated in the first study.

SUSTAINING ACCESS

During the study, I remained an outsider to the husbands' occupational world, but I was gradually accepted by the women into their private world as an insider with subordinate status. After earning the women's trust, establishing rapport, and developing reciprocity, they began to include me in their everyday activities, such as helping with domestic tasks, running errands with or for them, shopping or house hunting with them, and sharing meals with them and their families. They also extended invitations to family gatherings, games, social functions, team events, and civic activities, which I attended with their knowledge and, at times, as an acquaintance. The women allowed me to lend a sympathetic ear, be a sounding board, and share opinions. By listening to their sincere and compelling stories and observing them in many different situations, I acquired a deep understanding of how they experience their marriages. In addition to learning about their past in our interviews, I was in the extraordinary position of observing firsthand the personal dilemmas, anxieties, stressors, and crises in their lives as they unfolded during the study. As a male fieldworker of color, my race and ethnicity posed neither a perceptible disadvantage nor advantage in my cross-race/same-race interviews or collaborative partnerships with the multiracial group of women. Among the women of color, perhaps the shared meanings about race and ethnicity and the fact that we had more in common affected their view of me, and therefore their acceptance. Race, ethnicity, and social class were relevant and acknowledged as a common denominator in our interviews, but gender issues by far emerged more regularly as topics of fruitful and spirited discussions.

EXITING THE FIELD

Although the years I devoted to the collection of data in the first study were extremely productive, I had spent so much time, energy, and effort developing and managing collaborative partnerships with the wives and trying to anticipate all contingencies, it was difficult for me to leave the field. I naïvely assumed that I could easily stop the ethnographic work. I had become thoroughly fascinated with the process of learning new facts and significant details that provided other interpretations or more insight into the issues, patterns, and processes in sport marriages. Critical data that I believed could not be ignored or minimized was continually emerging, and because the interviews were so productive for all involved, I was reluctant to end them. Similarly, although the interviews had been concluded, many of the wives wanted to stay in contact to discuss their husbands, their husbands' careers, their marriages, or their personal changes, such as personal, marital, or employment issues; recent pregnancies and births; how their families were doing; or issues related to their husbands' retirement. As I gradually tried to leave, I discovered that staying in contact extended my stay in the field. As long as the wives needed to share their stories, I was prepared to listen to them. I also needed to follow media coverage of the NFL, MLB, NBA, and NHL. Several of the husbands were interviewed on news and sports talk television and radio programs or were featured in media stories. Many others regularly played in games that were broadcast on television and radio. As a result, I was often pulled back in by the never-ending media coverage of professional sports. As I followed the careers of the various husbands in this way, I documented and updated the wives' responses to the occupational fluctuations in their husbands' careers. Remaining in contact with the women generated essential data that would have been unobtainable otherwise, and it supplemented data gained from previous interviews and field observations. What emerged was an implicit methodological irony: the same skills, techniques, or strategies that make fieldwork effective can keep the researcher in the field longer than anticipated. Like other researchers, I thought that fieldwork could be phased out in several orderly ways. But my experiences provided a contradiction to this common teaching, and there were certain challenges that made it difficult for me to let go and move on.

During that four-year odyssey in the field, I traveled thousands of miles, lived out of a large suitcase, and visited roughly forty different cities (many on a regular basis) in different parts of the country. I became aware of the importance of making the interviews as pleasant and comfortable as possible for the wives, and I was anxious to do this. When this proved successful, it became important for me to rely on my own emotion work because I was often tired from traveling great distances, participating in one or even two interviews that day, or managing the challenging nature of fieldwork.

My decision to end the first study was prompted not only by the depletion of research funds and deadline pressures, but also by my eventual acknowledgment that data saturation had been achieved. Also, the cumulative demands of fieldwork had become physically and emotionally exhausting. As I said my final goodbyes and exited from their lives, I understood that there would always be another game, another season, another offseason, another stressful occupational event, or another stressful marital situation, but it was time to move on.

Second Study

Attempting to initiate the second study many years later, I confronted several anticipated and unanticipated difficulties. Despite my best efforts, I encountered problems in finding interested participants, including complex issues in accessing the women, failure of selected sampling methods, and the unsuccessful attempts of a cooperative key informant to identify potential participants. Consequently, I was ultimately grateful to find seventeen willing participants for the second study.

Of the women who participated in the first study, ten women participated in the second study. Those who contacted me in response to my outreach were eager to talk about how their lives unfolded, the challenges they faced during their husband's retirement, and what they had learned about life along the way. I have no way of knowing why the rest of the original participants I tried to contact didn't respond to my requests for a follow-up interview. They may have felt that their participation in the first study was satisfactory. Given the passage of time, changes in their lives, and problems associated with frequent relocations, my communication may simply have not reached them. It may have been lost in the confusion of busy lives. Additionally, in the current era of social media, heightened transparency in everyday life, an unrelenting 24/7 news cycle, continual media attention given to all phases of professional sports, and the ever-present possibility of privacy invasions, some may have chosen to remain silent this time around.

As mentioned earlier, I believe that the need for privacy also contributed to the difficulties I had in finding new participants for the second study. Of the many women I attempted to reach,[11] seven who were new to the project participated as members of the second group. The seven new participants were currently or formerly married to retired players whose careers ended since the completion of the first study, and they included three wives of NFL players, one wife and one ex-wife of NBA players, and one wife and one ex-wife of MLB players. Phone interviews,[12] in the form of standardized interviews,[13] served as the basic method of collecting data. Two different interview guides—one for returning participants and one for new participants—were used in this interviewing process. The initial interviews averaged approximately one to two hours. When necessary, I conducted follow-up interviews with a few of the women to finish the interview guides, which were all eventually completed. In the end, I was extremely fortunate to be able to interview the women who did contact me.

As a result of the myriad difficulties in finding participants for the second study, selection was once again based on those to whom I was able to gain access. The interview guides and data collection were influenced by predetermined categories, which I selected because of the findings in the first study. Although the data collected in the second study was limited to one method of gathering data, it contributed to another rich data set and generally confirmed my original findings. In particular, the second study provided additional data about the husband's retirement process and the relational issues that emerged during and after his retirement, and about other occupational issues in these career-dominated marriages. I look forward to delving more deeply into these and other marital issues that could not be addressed in this book because of various constraints.

APPENDIX B

Participants

Participant	Husband	Sport	First Study	Second Study
Alaina	Logan	NFL		X
Alyssa	Douglas	NFL	X	X
Amanda	Casey	NFL	X	
Arisa	Nathan	NFL	X	
Beth	Cliff	MLB	X	X
Callie	Sean	NFL		X
Chloe	Henry	MLB	X	
Courtney	Jack	MLB	X	X
Dana	Matt	MLB	X	
Donna	Keith	NFL	X	
Emma	Mason	MLB		X
Gwen	Osten	NBA	X	
Haley	Alex	MLB	X	
Jessica	Andrew	NFL	X	
Jill	Craig	NFL	X	X
Kalyn	Caleb	MLB	X	
Kathleen	Blake	MLB	X	X
Kaylee	Dylan	NBA		X
Keira	Max	NFL		X
Kellita	Donald	NFL	X	
Lisa	Raymond	NFL	X	
Marsha	Glenn	MLB	X	X
Mia	Liam	MLB	X	
Naomi	Todd	NHL	X	

Nicole	Aiden	NFL	X	
Nora	Wyatt	NBA		X
Olivia	Lewis	MLB	X	
Pam	Lucas	NFL	X	
Paula	Jason	MLB	X	X
Rhonda	Brent	MLB	X	
Robyn	Tyler	MLB	X	
Samantha	Ted	NFL	X	
Sandy	Adam	NFL	X	
Sharon	Walt	NHL	X	
Sheila	Frank	MLB	X	X
Skylar	Carter	MLB		X
Stacy	Dennis	MLB	X	
Susan	Bill	NBA	X	X
Tanya	Ryan	NFL	X	X
Tracee	Allen	MLB	X	

NOTES

Preface

1. Unless otherwise specified, I use the terms "professional athlete(s)" and "player(s)" to refer only to male professional athletes.

2. The social world perspective is used as the conceptual basis for the terms "occupational world(s)," "social world(s)," "subworld(s)," "world(s)," and the phrase "world(s) of." For discussions of this concept, see Strauss, "A Social World Perspective"; and Unruh, "The Nature of Social Worlds." The social world perspective can be applied to occupations and careers, so we can think of the occupational worlds of medicine, law enforcement, politics, religion, military, entertainment, transnational professions, firefighting, business, foreign service, professional sport, and so forth. As occupational examples, see Kidder, "Style and Action"; and Rosecrance, "The Invisible Horsemen." Combining the social world and feminist perspectives, we recognize the existence of male-dominated occupational worlds, or occupational worlds heavily influenced by male hegemony, where most women are relegated to subordinate roles or status. Applying the social world perspective, we can see that the larger social world of sport includes various subworlds, such as professional sports, intercollegiate sports, the Olympic Games, X Games, recreational sports, and extreme/lifestyle sports. Each subworld, in turn, can be regarded as a distinct social world. For example, the social world of professional sports includes the subworlds, or the players' occupational worlds, of professional team sports, including National Football League (NFL), National Basketball Association (NBA), National Hockey League (NHL), Major League Baseball (MLB), Major League Soccer (MLS), and individual sports, such as golf and tennis. Whether they are team or individual sports, each of these subworlds is a different social world in its own right (e.g., social world of professional golf).

Additionally, within this context, the social world perspective can be extended to include the social world of players' wives and the social world of groupies.

3. Plunkett Research, Ltd., "Sports Industry Statistics and Market Size Overview."

4. Ortiz, *A Sociological Dimension of Leisure*.

5. To avoid any potential confusion, the terms "husbands," "wives," "players," and variations thereof are used to identify unique categories of men and women and are not intended to label individuals. These terms are consistent with the established lexicon in the occupational worlds of professional sport and therefore can provide insight into the wives' subjective and experiential interpretations of and their thoughts and feelings about gender and marriage.

6. Ortiz, *The Effects of the Professional Athlete's Occupational Life-Style on the Wife*.

7. Distinguishing between the terms "story" and "narrative" is not uncommon (see Berger and Quinney, "The Narrative Turn in Social Inquiry"), but my use of the terms is interchangeable (see Polletta et al., "The Sociology of Storytelling"). The women's personal narratives are filled with vivid details, and I quote them liberally in the tradition of thick description (see Geertz, "Thick Description") to provide insight into storylines about specific events, situations, and perceptions they shared in our interviews. Their individual storytelling process included the various meanings they attached to their emotions, behaviors, thoughts, and memories (see Blumer, "The Methodological Position of Symbolic Interactionism") and to their socially constructed realities (see Berger and Luckmann, *The Social Construction of Reality*), and this provides a comprehensive understanding of their collective lived experience. For discussions about the nature of stories, narratives, and storytelling, see Berger and Quinney, "The Narrative Turn in Social Inquiry"; Chase, "Narrative Inquiry"; and Polletta et al., "The Sociology of Storytelling."

8. Ortiz, *When Happiness Ends and Coping Begins*.

9. For detailed discussion of selected cross-gender aspects of my ethnographic work with the wives, see Ortiz, "Muted Masculinity as an Outsider Strategy"; and Ortiz, "The Ethnographic Process of Gender Management."

10. For interpretations and discussions of hegemonic masculinity, see Connell, *Gender and Power*; Connell, *Masculinities*; and Connell and Messerschmidt, "Hegemonic Masculinity."

11. Goffman, *Behavior in Public Places*; and Goffman, *The Presentation of Self in Everyday Life*.

12. Lofland et al., *Analyzing Social Settings*, 69–70.

13. I have discussed my fieldwork experiences and ethnographic methods in a series of scholarly publications; see Ortiz, "Clinical Typifications by Wives of Professional Athletes," "How Interviewing Became Therapy for Wives of Professional Athletes," and "Leaving the Private World of Wives of Professional Athletes" in addition to works cited in note 9.

14. Kemper and Royce, "Long-Term Field Research."

15. For discussion of some of my media experiences, see Ortiz, "Breaking Out of Academic Isolation."

16. Throughout this book, when I refer to the "second group," these are the most recent interviewees who didn't participate in the first study. When I refer to the "second study," this includes all the women I interviewed in 2015–16.

17. For example, see Sanderson, "Professional Athletes' Shrinking Privacy Boundaries."

18. Saldana, *Longitudinal Qualitative Research*; also see, Cochran-Smith et al., "A Longitudinal Study of Teaching Practice and Early Career Decisions."

19. Distinct racial, ethnic, social class, and gender differences clearly exist in the lived experience of women married to professional athletes, and although these are relevant, specific analysis of these differences is beyond the limited scope of this book. My studies revealed that even though there are differences, the women shared similarities in their career-dominated experiences in the sport marriage and that the husbands' status as a professional athlete transcends these differences regarding the issues they collectively discussed during the studies. Perhaps these differences could be specifically examined by future researchers.

Introduction: Lifting the Veil of Silence

1. For example, see Harvey and Wiese, "The Dual-Career Couple."

2. For example, see Finch, *Married to the Job*; and Fowlkes, "The Myth of Merit and Male Professional Careers."

3. Finch, *Married to the Job*, 63, 163–64; Hochschild, "The Role of the Ambassador's Wife"; Lopata, *Occupation*; Callan and Ardener, eds., *The Incorporated Wife*; Strickland, "A Typology of Career Wife Roles"; Papanek, "Men, Women, and Work"; and Haas, "Families and Work." Papanek, in explaining her concept of the "two-person career," notes that the wife's involvement in a two-person (single) career includes her gainful unemployment, her hierarchical status in the husband's organization, and her public performances that benefit the husband's career. The husband's employer benefits from the wife's support and contributions, but the wife may not. Even though the husband and sport organization involvement may devalue or take for granted the wife's involvement in her husband's career, she is expected to "know her place." Although the player's wife is encouraged to participate in the two-person career, she must not become too involved or interfere with it. Fowlkes (*Behind Every Successful Man*, 80–91) noted this in discussing patterns of accommodation and noninterference among wives of physicians and academicians. More recently, Haas ("Families and Work") has referred to support in two-person careers as spousal career support.

4. Scholars have documented the lived experience of wives in various male-dominated occupational worlds. For example, see Peters-Golden and Grant,

"Physician's Spouse"; Taylor and Hartley, "The Two-Person Career"; Karaffa et al., "Perceived Impact of Police Work on Marital Relationships"; Dimiceli, Steinhardt, and Smith, "Stressful Experiences, Coping Strategies, and Predictors of Health-Related Outcomes among Wives of Deployed Military Servicemen"; Mederer and Weinstein, "Choices and Constraints in a Two-Person Career"; Pfefferbaum et al., "The Impact of the 1995 Oklahoma City Bombing on the Partners of Firefighters"; Fowlkes, *Behind Every Successful Man*; Hochschild, "The Role of the Ambassador's Wife"; Boss, McCubbin, and Lester, "The Corporate Executive Wife's Coping Patterns in Response to Routine Husband-Father Absence"; O'Connor, Nye, and Van Assendelft, "Wives in the White House"; Whip, "The Parliamentary Wife"; and Coles and Fechter, eds., *Gender and Family among Transnational Professionals*. No other scholar, however, has identified or applied the idea of a career-dominated marriage as a globally sanctioned work-family model, nor have they examined the sport marriage in depth.

5. Roehling, Moen, and Batt, "Spillover."

6. For example, see Golightly et al., "Early-Onset Arthritis in Retired National Football League Players"; Guskiewicz et al., "Association between Recurrent Concussion and Late-Life Cognitive Impairment in Retired Professional Football Players"; Lehman et al., "Neurodegenerative Causes of Death among Retired National Football League Players"; Mez et al., "Clinicopathological Evaluation of Chronic Traumatic Encephalopathy in Players of American Football"; Bey and Ostick, "Second Impact Syndrome"; and Manley et al., "A Systematic Review of Potential Long-Term Effects of Sport-Related Concussion."

7. Associated Press, "NFL, Ex-Players Agree to $765M Settlement in Concussions Suit."

8. For example, see Webner and Iverson, "Suicide in Professional American Football Players in the Past 95 Years"; and Omalu et al., "Chronic Traumatic Encephalopathy, Suicides and Parasuicides in Professional American Athletes."

9. Gender work is a specific application of *gender management*, which refers to a physical, a behavioral, or an interactional process. Couples rely on various interactive strategies in their use of gender work. A wife's gender work includes her efforts to perform marital and family roles in maintaining marital and family stability and functioning. Traditional notions of femininity generally guide her gender work, particularly in the support she seeks to provide to her husband both in private and public life. A husband's gender work includes his efforts to fulfill his interpretation of masculinity and self-expectations in performing occupational and domestic roles. This may include avoiding what he defines as feminine and constructing, displaying, or proving masculinity to himself and others. It involves his identity construction as a professional athlete and, as Goffman ("Role Distance," 106–7) suggested, his embracement of his occupational role. It also may serve as a response to occupational uncertainty and perhaps a sense of occupational powerlessness. Additionally, his gender work may include

his internalization and normalization of the spoiled athlete syndrome. The use of gender work, however, can create a dilemma for him. For example, he may have difficulty transitioning between his occupational role and his marital and family roles, and this can become a constant source of disappointment for many wives. The transition may be difficult because he is accustomed to proving his masculinity in occupational situations, but he may not define his gender work in the same way at home.

10. Goffman, "On Face-Work."
11. Carroll, "Spouses of High-Performing Men."
12. Coser, *Greedy Institutions*.
13. For example, see Munro, "Feminism."

1. Influences on the Sport Marriage

1. Hochschild refers to this process as emotion work. See chapter 2, note 9.

2. I use this term as a sensitizing concept (see Blumer, "What Is Wrong with Social Theory?") to describe a pattern of male entitlement and a set of genderized attitudes about power and control expressed by some male professional athletes, and to provide useful insight into the ways in which the husbands do gender work and control work (see chapter 4, note 2) in their marriages.

3. This term is a variation of what has been discussed elsewhere; see Kilmartin, *The Masculine Self*, 71–73, 215. Such stereotypical views of women, which this conceptualization may encompass, can reflect the ways some male athletes do gender work in their interactions with women, including intimate relationships. This dualistic attitude is evident, for example, among male athletes in locker-room conversations about women as sex objects and about their sexual exploits or conquests.

4. Goffman, *The Presentation of Self in Everyday Life*.
5. McPherson, "The Child in Competitive Sport," 258–61.
6. Fine, *With the Boys*; and Yablonski and Brower, *The Little League Game*.

7. For interpretations of overinvolved parents (which may loosely fit the description of "hovering parents" or "helicopter parents") and their participation in the athletic experiences of, for example, their sons in Little League baseball, see Chafetz and Kotarba, "Son Worshippers"; Fine, *With the Boys*; Skolnikoff and Engvall, *Young Athletes, Couch Potatoes, and Helicopter Parents*; and Yablonski and Brower, *The Little League Game*. Overinvolved mothers in sport families may be compared to or viewed as a variation of what has been characterized as "intensive mothering." For discussion of this parenting model, see Hays, *The Cultural Contradictions of Motherhood*; and Nelson, *Parenting Out of Control*.

8. For example, see Bissinger, *Friday Night Lights*.
9. Johnson and Rivers, *The Vance*, 148.
10. For example, see Benedict and Klein, "Arrest and Conviction Rates for Athletes Accused of Sexual Assault."

11. Psychoanalytic theory suggests that because mothers are the initial socializers for sons in a patriarchal society, men may idealize their mothers as a reflection of their attachment to them (Chodorow, *Feminism and Psychoanalytic Theory*). It may not be uncommon for a son to become dependent on his mother for various reasons, to resolve his dependence by repressing his love and attachment to her, and to identify with the patriarchal power of his father (Chodorow, *Feminism and Psychoanalytic Theory*; Connell, *Masculinities*; and Johnson, *Strong Mothers, Weak Wives*). In adulthood, a man may be attracted to a woman with whom he can express emotions he has suppressed and who has relational skills comparable to his mother, but with whom he can be the dominant partner (Chodorow, *Feminism and Psychoanalytic Theory*; and Johnson, *Strong Mothers, Weak Wives*). As part of the motherizing process, it may not be unusual for him to marry a woman he believes can replace his mother, caring for him and his children as he builds his career in professional sports.

12. Goffman, "The Nature of Deference and Demeanor."

13. For example, see Farole, "Sources of Stress for Major League Baseball Players' Wives"; Gmelch and San Antonio, "Baseball Wives"; and Mitchell and Cronson, "The Celebrity Family."

14. Other scholarly interpretations of the term *boundary work* exist; for example, see Lamont and Molnar, "The Studies of Boundaries in the Social Sciences"; and Nippert-Eng, *Home and Work*. My use of this term should not be confused with these and other versions. Instead, I refer to it as a specific application of *boundary management*, which is the process of constructing, establishing, and enforcing boundaries of preferred interaction and conduct in public situations in the occupational worlds of professional sport and in private situations in the marriage. Regarding the latter, for instance, wives combine boundary work and control work (see chapter 4, note 2) in their interactions with their husbands when they believe it is necessary to apply pressure to achieve some desired purpose in their relationship. The wives also rely on boundary work in their public interactions with overzealous fans or female groupies. Unwritten rules serve as the basis for the wives' boundary work in public situations. Couples also may mutually rely on some form of boundary work in private life when they are dealing with marital or occupational issues (during the motherization process, managing infidelity, dealing with life on the road, and so forth). Others in their worlds, such as teammates, flight attendants, or mothers-in-law, are capable of using boundary work in their private or public interactions with players' wives.

15. Cancian, "The Feminization of Love"; and Chodorow, *Feminism and Psychoanalytic Theory*.

16. For example, see Rubin, *Worlds of Pain*; and Weitzer, "Why We Need More Research on Sex Work."

17. For examples and perceptions of the good girl/bad girl duality among minor league baseball players and MLB players, see Gmelch and San Antonio, "Groupies and American Baseball." For examples of the good girl/bad girl duality among

rodeo cowboys, see Forsyth and Thompson, "Helpmates of the Rodeo"; and Gauthier and Forsyth, "Buckle Bunnies."

18. For example, see Trujillo, "Hegemonic Masculinity on the Mound," 297–98.

19. Chodorow, *Feminism and Psychoanalytic Theory*; and Rubin, *Worlds of Pain*.

20. For example, see Swidler, *Talk of Love*.

21. Cancian, *The Feminization of Love*.

22. My idea of organizational dominance is not the same as organizational control. Organizational dominance emphasizes certain factors and characteristics of sport organizations that the wives shared with me.

23. Although masculinity is a relatively neglected primary characteristic of total institutions, it can be a significant factor characterizing the membership of men in a total institution. My idea of an institutionalized brotherhood emphasizes men's rigid interpretations of masculinity, such as hegemonic masculinity. It underscores the basis of male empowerment in total institutions (see note 25), such as sport organizations.

24. For discussion of the sport ethic, see Hughes and Coakley, "Positive Deviance among Athletes."

25. For discussion of his concept of total institutions, see Goffman, "On the Characteristics of Total Institutions," 4–5. For a recent application of his concept in the world of English professional football (soccer), see Parker and Manley, "Goffman, Identity and Organizational Control."

26. Simmel, "The Sociology of Secrecy and of Secret Societies."

27. For example, see Jervis, *Relocation, Gender, and Emotion*, 23.

28. For example, see Ryan, "The Positive Reaction to Dwyane Wade's Extended Paternity Leave Signals a Cultural Shift."

29. For discussion of Simmel's concept of "social circles," see Simmel, "The Web of Group-Affiliations." For a recent application of his idea, see Stoetzler, "Intersectional Individuality."

30. Klapp, "Social Types"; and Klapp, *Heroes, Villians, and Fools*.

31. Cooley, *Social Organization*, 23.

32. For example, see Fair, "Constructing Masculinity Through Penetration Discourse"; and Schacht, "Misogyny On and Off the Pitch."

33. For example, see Messner and Stevens, "Scoring without Consent"; and Welch, "Violence against Women by Professional Football Players."

34. Goffman, *Stigma*.

35. For example, see Curry, "Fraternal Bonding in the Locker Room."

36. The omnipresence of the internet and social media has increased opportunities for infidelity in recent years. For example, see Mileham, "Online Infidelity in Internet Chat Rooms"; and Wysocki and Childers, "Let My Fingers Do the Talking." Online liaisons may have serious consequences for the sport marriage and marriages in general, and may contribute to the institutionalization of infidelity in the occupational worlds of professional sport.

37. My idea of the internalized "we" partnership builds on Papanek's ("Men,

Women, and Work," 856–57) discussion of the "vicarious achievement" typically experienced by wives as part of the two-person career, and Finch's (*Married to the Job*) references to the vicarious connection wives establish with their husbands. For example, see Mederer and Weinstein, "Choices and Constraints in a Two-Person Career," 336. In addition to the various occupational achievements of their husbands during their careers (for instance, World Series participants/champions [MLB], Super Bowl participants/champions [NFL], Most Valuable Player Award [NBA], All-Star selection [MLB and NBA], Pro Bowl selection [NFL], ESPY Award, product/brand endorsements, significant salary increases) and perhaps after their careers have ended (e.g., Hall of Fame induction), vicarious achievement in the sport marriage also includes the wife's heightened self-esteem and validation of her self-image, her self-sacrifice, and her vicarious identification with her husband and valued aspects of his career. The notion of the "we" partnership is not limited to the wives; mothers-in-law and fans also construct their variations of this idea. This suggests that there is a need to establish a vicarious identification with the husbands, or to vicariously experience the husbands' occupational achievements, by their wives, their mothers, and their fans.

38. Goffman, "Embarrassment and Social Organization."

39. For discussion of how wives are "absorbed" into the husbands' corporate career, see Kanter, *Men and Women of the Corporation*. Callan and Ardener (*The Incorporated Wife*) and Finch (*Married to the Job*) have discussed a similar process when wives are "incorporated" into their husbands' occupations.

40. For example, see Pavalko and Elder, "Women Behind the Men."

41. For a review of paid and unpaid care work, see England, "Emerging Theories of Care Work."

42. For his discussion of role embracement, see Goffman, "Role Distance," 106–7.

43. This could be a marital or occupational pattern in the sport marriage. It could apply to both partners who, in a sense, "wake up" years later and deal with what they discover. This marital or occupational pattern might be thought of as the "Rip Van Winkle Effect." See Irving, *Rip Van Winkle*.

2. In the Public Eye

1. For discussion of transnational/global migration or sport labor migration among professional athletes, see Agergaard and Ryba, "Migration and Career Transitions in Professional Sports." It's worth noting that both studies included women whose husbands followed the global or transnational migration patterns of other professional athletes seeking to initiate or continue their careers overseas.

2. For example, see Sanderson, "Professional Athletes' Shrinking Privacy Boundaries."

3. For example, see Cashmore, *Celebrity/Culture*; van Krieken, *Celebrity Society*; and Wenner, *Fallen Sports Heroes, Media, and Celebrity Culture*.

4. Connell, *Gender and Power*; and Goffman, *Gender Advertisements*, 1–9.

5. My use of the term *image work* differs from its use by other scholars; for example, see Prus, *Beyond the Power Mystique*. Image work is specifically related to my idea of *image management*, which involves attempts to express the "right" public image to fans and interested others in public life. Although the husbands also engage in image work, my focus is on the wives. This process includes interactive strategies that define, construct, establish, and present the physical appearance, demeanor, and personality that husbands, sport organizations, fans, and the media expect of women married to professional athletes. It involves a wife's awareness of appropriate public behavior and the necessity of avoiding any behavior that might embarrass or disgrace the husband or his team. Image work may be thought of as a public relations strategy that wives rely on as they attempt to "play" to the audience of fans in public situations, whether or not they accompany their husbands. In contrast to their self-image, working on their public image has more to do with their public self rather than their private self, which is reserved for private life. In some cases, a wife's public image can become an integral part of her self-image, and some wives may take their public image quite seriously; they may think of themselves as celebrities or may attempt to take advantage of their husbands' celebrity status. When this occurs, their image work can carry over into private life, which can offend others, upset others, or make others uncomfortable.

6. Stone, "Appearance and the Self."

7. Goffman, "On Face-Work." Face work is one of the essential aspects of image work. Image work is a contrast to and a dimension of face work, giving emphasis to the construction and management of the public image of the celebrity or celebrity spouse.

8. My use of the notion of identity work is consistent with Snow and Anderson's ("Identity Work among the Homeless," 1348) conceptualization as they apply it to identity construction and management in the context of, for example, situations, appearances, and groups.

9. For discussion of Hochschild's emotion management perspective and concept of emotion work, see Hochschild, "Emotion Work, Feeling Rules, and Social Structure"; and Hochschild, *The Managed Heart*.

3. Traveling with the Team

1. Because of the extensive data I was able to collect on the MLB wives' traveling experiences, chapter 3 focuses exclusively on the wives, husbands, teammates, players, and teams in the MLB world. Although a comparable number of MLB wives and NFL wives participated, most of the NFL wives chose not to travel

with their husbands (primarily because of the league's shorter travel schedule), and the data I was able to collect on the traveling experiences of NHL and NBA wives was limited by the participant sample. There is enough data, however, to suggest that NFL, NBA, and NHL wives have similar traveling experiences and face similar issues.

2. Some MLB teams sponsor at least one family trip per season, when wives and children are accommodated. In this case, teammates may be allowed input about when, where, and how this trip will take place, and the team will usually decide to include families on a "short trip" (six or seven games in two or three cities). Teams and players tend to prefer short trips, because they view families with energetic children as distracting, especially during tension-filled parts of the season. Establishing travel policy is just one example of how some managers and the players work together to establish exclusionary practices regarding the wives. As we will see, the travel secretaries also can take part in excluding wives from road trips.

3. Whether *code management* is self- or other-initiated, it involves adherence to the implicit code of conduct. *Code work*, as practiced by the husbands, wives, organizational management, and teammates, includes the use of various interactive strategies in road-trip situations that can involve code enforcement, code following, and code busting. Code enforcement includes exclusionary practices. It is often influenced by some form of boundary work and, in turn, can influence the use of code work. Code work is not limited to teammates or husbands as code enforcers. As code followers and code busters, the wives rely on their own code work when they respond to or challenge code enforcers. The code of conduct is often interpreted differently by the wife who travels only on family trips and the wife who travels with the team during the entire season, and her use of code work will reflect these interpretations. Therefore, the meaning of the code of conduct and its repercussions, and thus her code work, may vary with each wife.

4. For Simmel's classic idea of the "stranger," see Simmel, "The Stranger." For a subsequent conceptual approach, see Schuetz, "The Stranger." Applying Simmel's idea, a traveling wife is cast in the role of stranger, because although she is important to her husband, she isn't important to his team and will never be a member of it. Given her outsider and subordinate status as a spouse, she is a female stranger who is both accepted and rejected by the men on the team. For application of Simmel's notion of the stranger in the NFL world, see Fontana and Frey, "The Placekicker in Professional Football."

5. For example, see Forsyth and Thompson, "Helpmates of the Rodeo," 408.

6. For example, see Nash, "Bus Riding"; and Zurcher, "The Airplane Passenger."

7. For discussion of Goffman's idea of "nonperson," see Goffman, *Behavior in Public Places*, 84; Goffman, *The Presentation of Self in Everyday Life*; and Goffman, "The Nature of Deference and Demeanor," 67–68.

8. Teammates define the back of the plane as a safe region for their interac-

tions only, while the other passengers regard it as a back region and off-limits to them. For discussion of his idea of safe region, see Goffman, *Behavior in Public Places*, 160; and Goffman, *The Presentation of Self in Everyday Life*. For discussion of his concept of back region, see Goffman, *The Presentation of Self in Everyday Life*.

9. My idea of muted femininity is a form of gender work, an interactive process used not only by traveling wives to minimize aspects of femininity in private and public situations, but by other wives in the sport marriage, especially when relying on image work. I refer to the counterpart of this idea, muted masculinity, in the preface.

10. Mood sharing isn't limited to road-trip situations, and it isn't limited to couples in the MLB world. For MLB couples, returning on the same bus or plane after a road game is comparable to riding in the same car after a home game; both serve as cocoons of emotional decompression for the husbands. I extend Lofland's (*A World of Strangers*, 73) idea of the car serving as a cocoon of privacy for occupants in city life by suggesting that a wife's emotion work can be an integral part of these private moments with her husband. The bus and car are privatized spaces in which couples can release or express feelings that they suppress in public situations. Beth told me, for example, that when she and Cliff are alone in the car on the ride home after a game, Cliff was often moody or unresponsive to Beth. She shared his mood and understood his need to evaluate his performance, and she specifically avoided upsetting him by discussing sensitive family matters. She tried to read the situation and do her best to listen to Cliff when he was angry or dejected after a bad game, or to make herself available as a sounding board, or to silently provide emotional support if he didn't want to talk. She was careful not to criticize, admonish, correct, or tease him. Although there were many times when Beth wanted to express her own feelings, she wouldn't do so if they were contradictory to his. Instead, she suppressed her own emotions and displayed emotions that reflected and shared Cliff's emotions until they arrived home. Depending on the circumstances, and given the intensity of emotions, Beth may have become angry by the time they arrived home, and she may have needed time to decompress from the ride home. In these and other similar situations, if a woman's feelings are noticeably different from what she actually displays, she may experience what Hochschild (*The Managed Heart*, 90) refers to as emotional dissonance.

4. Star Power

1. For a classic discussion of power in marriages, see Blood and Wolfe, *Husbands and Wives*. For a more recent discussion, see Xu and Lai, "Resources, Gender Ideologies, and Marital Power." For discussion of control in marriages, see Stets and Hammons, "Gender, Control, and Marital Commitment."

2. Because applying power is a process, we cannot think of power without thinking of control. *Control management* involves gaining, negotiating, exerting, and enforcing power in situations, interactions, and relationships. It involves the use of resources, such as money, love, communication skills, parenting skills, social skills, level of education, or occupational status. *Control work* can be viewed as the genuine use of power and the specific application of control management. Control work refers to a process through which partners use interactive strategies in attempts to control resources or access to resources, each other, or a situation, or to cope with family, marital, and occupational stressors. In the sport marriage, partners try to achieve some desired outcome by making control attempts and applying control tactics. Without viable resources, control management, and thus control work, is usually not effective. When control work is combined with gender work, it can result in a more effective use of both.

3. Domestic control is a type of control work both partners use. A husband's domestic control reflects and emphasizes his domestic power when he's home during the offseason. A wife's domestic control reflects her domestic mastery—a valued resource—and emphasizes her domestic power, particularly during the season when the husband is absent. Domestic control can be very useful for a wife when coping with occupational or marital stressors.

4. Mead, *Mind, Self, and Society*.

5. Komter, "Hidden Power in Marriage."

6. Johnson, *Strong Mothers, Weak Wives*.

7. Papanek, "Men, Women, and Work," 862–63.

8. Trujillo, "Hegemonic Masculinity on the Mound," 298.

9. Hartley, "Letting Ourselves Go," 67–69. For example, see Bishop, Gruys, and Evans, "Sized Out."

10. For example, see Blumberg and Coleman, "A Theoretical Look at the Gender Balance of Power in the American Couple."

11. A player's wife is acutely aware that other women are interested in her husband because he is a professional athlete, but any attempt to use physical attractiveness as a source of indirect power (frequently manipulation) or personal power (usually sexual influence) through her use of persuasion (see Howard, Blumstein, and Schwartz, "Sex, Power, and Influence Tactics in Intimate Relationships"; and Johnson, "Women and Power") or impression management (Goffman, *The Presentation of Self in Everyday Life*) may prove to be fruitless. Any leverage her physical attractiveness may have provided is minimized or negated.

12. For example, see Cancian, "The Feminization of Love," 706; and Komter, "Hidden Power in Marriage," 205.

13. Komter, "Hidden Power in Marriage," 201.

14. Thoits, "Gender and Marital Status Differences in Control and Distress."

15. For discussion of how wives in the organizer role use control work as the

basis for coping with the occupational stressors in their husbands' careers, see Ortiz, "Constructing Dependency in Coping with Stressful Occupational Events."

16. The pattern of controlling mothers and passive fathers was more common than controlling fathers and passive mothers in the family backgrounds of most of the women in the first study, and several women emulated this pattern in their own marriages. It seems, however, that how a wife learned about control work and used it in her marriage was influenced by whichever parent exerted more control and how it was used in family relationships.

17. A husband's celebrity status, public image, high income, or occupation/career can influence his use of power and control, and these also are influential in how his wife constructs her identity. Through his use of power and control, she may come to believe he is acting in the best interest of her and their children. Her control work contributes to self-empowerment and enables her to cope with the pressures and stressors inherent in his career. As suggested by Szinovacz ("Family Power," 683), it's possible that one's self-image, self-esteem, or feelings of self-worth can play a part in one's need to have power. In this case, a wife's effective use of control work when she successfully copes with occupational stressors may fulfill her need to be in control.

18. For variations of this role, or what Hochschild and Machung describe as a gender strategy, see Hochschild and Machung, *The Second Shift*.

5. The In-Laws

1. For example, see Kivett, "Mother-in-Law and Daughter-in-Law Relations"; and Marotz-Baden and Cowan, "Mothers-in-Law and Daughters-in-Law."

2. For example, see Cotterill, *Friendly Relations?*; and Jackson and Berg-Cross, "Extending the Extended Family."

3. Chodorow, *Feminism and Psychoanalytic Theory*, 63.

4. For example, see Mitchell and Cronson, "The Celebrity Family"; and Winton, *Children as Caregivers*, 151–52.

5. When a mother spousifies her son, he serves as a substitute for the father. This usually occurs because the father is physically or emotionally absent from family life. He may be passive in family interactions or not involve himself in family life or be occupationally unsuccessful. As a dimension of the spousification process, the mother may experience a sense of vicarious achievement and pride through her son's athletic success in organized youth sport programs, to the point where she becomes the overinvolved mother. She intentionally or unintentionally fails to acknowledge the boundaries of her support for her son's participation in sports. In this case, the son is not only a substitute for the father, but a passive and compliant adult son who submits to his mother's controlling attitude. This intergenerational family pattern may repeat itself in the sport marriage when

the husband's serial, often sustained, absences can create what is essentially a single-parent household. Given this pattern of routine husband/father separation and absence, the player's wife may spousify one or more of her children, giving them equal status with her and serving as a substitute for the high-profile but absent husband.

6. In Goffman's discussion of anchored relations in public life (*Relations in Public*), he uses the term *tie-signs* to describe how people express the nature of their relationship, verbally and nonverbally, to others in public situations. I suggest that in the sport marriage, private situations also can be included because private situations involve an audience that includes each person in the relationship and those outside the relationship.

7. For example, see Lim, "Korean Immigrant Women's Challenge to Gender Inequality at Home," 44–46.

8. Subordination work is the direct use of *subordination management*, which is the interactive process that involves a person's use of strategies to manage subordination in relationships requiring deference. A wife in the sport marriage uses subordination work with her mother-in-law and husband, separately or jointly, and in public or private situations. Her subordination work includes various forms of emotion work in addition to constructing an identity that signals her intention to be a "good wife" in private life and a "good player's wife" in public life. As a consequence, it can result in a dilemma for her: she is deeply aware of her need to avoid jeopardizing her relationship with her mother-in-law, which can affect her marriage, but she also is concerned about jeopardizing her own sense of self and her marital and family priorities. Therefore, she may at times realize that it may be fruitless. Whatever the result may be, she understands that there may be a cost. Also, her husband may rely on a variation of subordination work in relationship to his mother, a pattern established early in family life.

9. For example, see Lim, "Korean Immigrant Women's Challenge to Gender Inequality at Home," 44–45.

10. For example, see Gallin, "The Intersection of Class and Age"; Kaneko and Yamada, "Wives and Mothers-in-Law"; and Kim, "Changing Relationships between Daughters-in-Law and Mothers-in-Law in Urban South Korea."

11. Gross and Stone, "Embarrassment and the Analysis of Role Requirements," 13.

12. The notion of role reversal has been examined and applied in the study of family and marital processes. For example, see Mayseless et al., "I Was More Her Mom than She Was Mine." Role reversal processes occur in parent-child relationships, mother-daughter relationships, and husband-wife relationships, but I offer a variation of and possibly a different approach to current perspectives of role reversal. In these sport families, a role reversal occurs when the mother-in-law takes the role of wife (primarily in public situations) and the wife

is placed in the role of mother. This is evident, expected, and even normalized in the sport marriage.

13. As Chafetz and Kotarba ("Son Worshippers," 239) observed, Little League mothers "win" when they feel like "good mothers" and, like these mothers, the wives "win" when they feel like "good wives," especially when their husbands "win."

6. A World of Groupies

1. Traditionally, the term *groupie* refers to a young woman who has intense interest in or inclination to participate in sexual activities with players. For example, see Crawford and Gosling, "The Myth of the 'Puck Bunny'"; Forsyth and Thompson, "Helpmates of the Rodeo," 409; Gauthier and Forsyth, "Buckle Bunnies," 349; Gmelch and San Antonio, "Groupies and American Baseball," 32–33. It is not the only label that applies to young women who show an inordinate interest in male professional athletes, although it has been typically used in the male-dominated world of rock music; for example, see Des Barres, *I'm with the Band*; Larsen, "It's a Man's Man's Man's World"; and Rhodes, *Electric Ladyland*. Other terms for these women are less flattering. Hip-hop stars describe them as chicken heads (Weitzer and Kubrin, "Misogyny in Rap Music") and police officers call them badge bunnies (Rabe-Hemp, "POLICEwomen or PoliceWOMEN"). As reported by Koppel (*The Astronaut Wives Club*), in the 1960s NASA's Mercury Seven astronauts referred to them as cape cookies. Female groupies have a long tradition in the MLB world, and according to Michelson (*Sportin' Ladies*), over the decades they have been labeled, for example, Annies, Shirleys, and bimbos. As discussed by Gauthier and Forsyth ("Buckle Bunnies") and Forsyth and Thompson ("Helpmates of the Rodeo"), they are buckle bunnies to rodeo cowboys. To minor league hockey players and NHL players, they are puck bunnies (Crawford and Gosling, "The Myth of the 'Puck Bunny'"). They also are self-identified by, for instance, Blasi (*Jock Itch*) as jersey chasers. Other labels mentioned by the wives include cleat chasers, stadium lizards, lot lizards, bleacher creatures, and worse. The term "groupie" reflects the subordinate status of these women in the occupational worlds of professional sport. I use it because it's part of the established lexicon in the occupational worlds of professional sport. The wives in both studies, however, routinely used it in their narratives to refer to specific types of both female and male fans whom they believe form sexual and nonsexual liaisons with players and players' wives. The term itself provides insight into the wives' perceptions and subjective interpretations about and lived experience involving groupies in general and female groupies in particular.

2. For example, see Des Barres, *I'm with the Band*; Larsen, "It's a Man's Man's Man's World"; and Rhodes, *Electric Ladyland*.

3. Koppel, *The Astronaut Wives Club*.

4. Klapp, "Social Types"; and Klapp, *Heroes, Villains, and Fools*.

5. Of course, other types of groupies in addition to those the wives described to me may exist. These could include, for example, male groupies who follow female professional athletes and female groupies who follow female professional athletes.

6. Nussbaum, "Objectification."

7. Stone, "Appearance and the Self."

8. Bartky, *Femininity and Domination*; and Saul, *Feminism*.

9. Connell, *Gender and Power*.

10. Goffman, *Gender Advertisements*, 1–9; and West and Zimmerman, "Doing Gender."

11. Montemurro and Gillen, "How Clothes Make the Woman Immoral."

12. For example, see Freitas et al., "Appearance Management as Border Construction"; and Montemurro and Gillen, "How Clothes Make the Woman Immoral."

13. For example, see Davidson and Helstein, "Queering the Gaze."

14. For example, see Hasinoff and Shepherd, "Sexting in Context."

15. For example, see Miguel, "Visual Intimacy on Social Media."

16. For example, see Smolak, Murnen, and Myers, "Sexualizing the Self"; and Ruckel and Hill, "Look @ Me 2.0."

17. For example, see Haslanger, "On Being Objective and Being Objectified."

18. Goffman, "The Nature of Deference and Demeanor"; and Stone, "Appearance and the Self."

19. Goffman, *The Presentation of Self in Everyday Life*.

20. Richardson, "Secrecy and Status"; and Simmel, "The Sociology of Secrecy and of Secret Societies."

21. For example, see Gmelch and San Antonio, "Groupies and American Baseball."

7. A Closer Look at the Culture of Infidelity

1. A player's wife who enables may believe that she can have a fulfilling marital relationship through her control work and will use manipulation as a control tactic, a pattern that became established early in their relationship when Tanya took on Ryan as her project. She believed that helping him to be as successful as he could be in his NFL career would create the stability in her marriage that she didn't have in her childhood. Also, in viewing him as a project, he would be a positive reflection of her in their everyday life because, as she told me, "If he looked good, I looked good."

2. For example, see Richardson, "Secrecy and Status."

3. Ibid.

4. Suspicion work is the explicit application of *suspicion management*, which is an individual and sometimes internal process specific to a wife's attempts to

deal with the fear that her husband is involved in extramarital relationships. Her efforts occur in the form of suspicion work and involve managing her level of trust in her husband to be faithful to her. I identify two strategies and frame them as motivating factors in a wife's interpretation of evidence related to her husband's unfaithfulness. There may be others, such as using the internet and social media to search for clues.

5. In this context, suspicion work can include two major forms of denial: *reality denial* and *evocative denial*. Each is the basis for some aspect of the wife's use of suspicion work. Reality denial involves denying something that actually occurred or acting as if it could not occur. Evocative denial is a specific type of emotion work used to manage reality denial. It involves denying any emergent emotion while attempting to be judicious. When reality denial becomes a form of conscious denial, evocative denial becomes a preventive stance toward situations the wife defines as extremely stressful, painful, or fearful. The idea of "not feeling" is a far more viable strategy in coping with certain situations, events, or issues wives want to avoid or do not want to experience emotionally. If evocative denial fails, the psychic cost may be *burn-up*, the short-term peak experience of an intensely experienced personal crisis, which can have psychological or emotional consequences. A special thank you to Arlie Hochschild for suggesting the idea of evocative denial in some of our many discussions about the findings from the first study.

6. For example, see Hochschild, *The Managed Heart*, 187–88.

Conclusion: The Final Score

1. For example, see Ritvo and Glick, "Family Problems and Sports Performance."

Appendix A: Research Methodology

1. Charmaz, *Constructing Grounded Theory*; Corbin and Strauss, *Basics of Qualitative Research*; and Glaser and Strauss, *The Discovery of Grounded Theory*.
2. Corbin and Strauss, *Basics of Qualitative Research*; and Patton, *Qualitative Research and Evaluation Methods*.
3. Emerson, Fretz, and Shaw, *Writing Ethnographic Fieldnotes*.
4. Berg and Lune, *Qualitative Research Methods for the Social Sciences*; and Patton, *Qualitative Research and Evaluation Methods*.
5. Patton, *Qualitative Research and Evaluation Methods*.
6. Rubin and Rubin, *Qualitative Interviewing*, 7.
7. Spradley, *The Ethnographic Interview*.
8. Frey and Fontana, "The Group Interview in Social Research."
9. Berg and Lune, *Qualitative Research Methods for the Social Sciences*.

10. Jonassohn, Turowetz, and Gruneau, "Research Methods in the Sociology of Sport," 187.

11. Countless women who were not part of the first study have contacted me via phone and email to express their interest in and to seek more information about my research. Many of these women also offered to be interviewed, so they were a primary participant source. In my effort to contact as many potential participants as possible, I worked with a key informant who was in a good position to recruit players' wives, but this effort was not successful. Some participants offered to contact women they thought may have an interest in participating, but despite their generous offers, this snowball sampling method failed. I also conducted various Google searches to find participants through websites, but this effort failed.

12. Sturges and Hanrahan, "Comparing Telephone and Face-to-Face Qualitative Interviewing."

13. Berg and Lune, *Qualitative Research Methods for the Social Sciences*.

BIBLIOGRAPHY

Agergaard, Sine, and Tatiana V. Ryba. "Migration and Career Transitions in Professional Sports: Transnational Athletic Careers in a Psychological and Sociological Perspective." *Sociology of Sport Journal* 31, no. 2 (2014): 228–47.
Associated Press. "NFL, Ex-Players Agree to $765M Settlement in Concussions Suit." August 29, 2013. http://www.nfl.com/news/story/0ap1000000235494/article/nfl-explayers-agree-to-765m-settlement-in-concussions-suit.
Bartky, Sandra L. *Femininity and Domination: Studies in the Phenomenology of Oppression*. New York: Routledge, 1990.
Benedict, Jeffrey, and Alan Klein. "Arrest and Conviction Rates for Athletes Accused of Sexual Assault." *Sociology of Sport Journal* 14, no. 1 (1997): 86–94.
Berg, Bruce L., and Howard Lune. *Qualitative Research Methods for the Social Sciences*. 8th ed. Boston: Pearson, 2012.
Berger, Peter L., and Thomas Luckmann. *The Social Construction of Reality: A Treatise in the Sociology of Knowledge*. Garden City, NY: Doubleday, 1966.
Berger, Ronald J., and Richard Quinney. "The Narrative Turn in Social Inquiry." In *Storytelling Sociology: Narrative as Social Inquiry*, edited by Ronald J. Berger and Richard Quinney, 1–11. Boulder, CO: Rienner, 2005.
Bey, Tareg, and Brian Ostick. "Second Impact Syndrome." *Western Journal of Emergency Medicine* 10, no. 1 (2009): 6–10.
Bishop, Katelynn, Kjerstin Gruys, and Maddie Evans. "Sized Out: Women, Clothing Size, and Inequality." *Gender & Society* 32, no. 2 (2018): 180–203.
Bissinger, H. G. *Friday Night Lights: A Town, a Team, and a Dream*. Cambridge, MA: Da Capo Press, 1990.
Blasi, Rosa. *Jock Itch: The Misadventures of a Retired Jersey Chaser*. New York: HarperCollins, 2011.
Blood, Robert O., and Donald M. Wolfe, *Husbands and Wives: The Dynamics of Married Living*. Glencoe, IL: Free Press, 1960.

Blumberg, Rae Lesser, and Marion Tolbert Coleman. "A Theoretical Look at the Gender Balance of Power in the American Couple." *Journal of Family Issues* 10, no. 2 (1989): 225–50.

Blumer, Herbert. "The Methodological Position of Symbolic Interactionism." In *Symbolic Interactionism: Perspective and Method*, 1–60. Englewood Cliffs, NJ: Prentice-Hall, 1969.

———. "What Is Wrong with Social Theory?" In *Symbolic Interactionism: Perspective and Method*, 140–52. Englewood Cliffs, NJ: Prentice-Hall, 1969.

Boss, Pauline G., Hamilton I. McCubbin, and Gary Lester. "The Corporate Executive Wife's Coping Patterns in Response to Routine Husband-Father Absence." *Family Process* 18, no. 1 (1979): 79–86.

Callan, Hilary, and Shirley Ardener, eds. *The Incorporated Wife*. London: Croom Helm, 1984.

Cancian, Francesca M. "The Feminization of Love." *Signs: Journal of Women in Culture and Society* 11, no. 4 (1986): 692–709.

Carroll, Jane L. "Spouses of High-Performing Men: A Profile of Marital Adjustment and Psychological Outcomes." In *High-Performing Families: Causes, Consequences, and Clinical Solutions*, edited by Bryan E. Robinson and Nancy D. Chase, 23–40. Alexandria, VA: American Counseling Association, 2001.

Cashmore, Ellis. *Celebrity/Culture*. 2nd ed. New York: Routledge, 2014.

Chafetz, Janet Saltzman, and Joseph A. Kotarba. "Son Worshippers: The Role of Little League Mothers in Recreating Gender." In *Studies in Symbolic Interaction*, vol. 18, edited by Norman K. Denzin, 217–41. Greenwich, CT: JAI Press, 1995.

Charmaz, Kathy. *Constructing Grounded Theory*. 2nd ed. Los Angeles: Sage, 2014.

Chase, Susan E. "Narrative Inquiry: Toward Theoretical and Methodological Maturity." In *The Sage Handbook of Qualitative Research*. 5th ed., edited by Norman K. Denzin and Yvonna S. Lincoln, 546–60. Los Angeles: Sage, 2018.

Chodorow, Nancy. *Feminism and Psychoanalytic Theory*. New Haven, CT: Yale University Press, 1989.

Cochran-Smith, Marilyn, Patrick McQuillan, Kara Mitchell, Dianna Gahlsdorf Terrell, Joan Barnatt, Lisa D'Souza, Cindy Jong, Karen Shakman, Karen Lam, and Ann Marie Gleeson. "A Longitudinal Study of Teaching Practice and Early Career Decisions: A Cautionary Tale." *American Educational Research Journal* 49, no. 5 (2012): 844–80.

Coles, Anne, and Anne-Meike Fechter, eds. *Gender and Family among Transnational Professionals*. New York: Routledge, 2008.

Connell, R. W. *Gender and Power: Society, the Person and Sexual Politics*. Stanford, CA: Stanford University Press, 1987.

———. *Masculinities*. Berkeley: University of California Press, 2005.

Connell, R. W., and James W. Messerschmidt. "Hegemonic Masculinity: Rethinking the Concept." *Gender & Society* 19, no. 6 (2005): 829–59.

Cooley, Charles Horton. *Social Organization: A Study of the Larger Mind*. New York: Scribner's, 1909.

Corbin, Juliet, and Anselm Strauss. *Basics of Qualitative Research: Techniques and Procedures for Developing Grounded Theory*. 4th ed. Los Angeles: Sage, 2014.

Coser, Lewis A. *Greedy Institutions: Patterns of Undivided Commitment*. New York: The Free Press, 1974.

Cotterill, Pamela. *Friendly Relations? Mothers and Their Daughters-in-Law*. London: Taylor & Francis, 1994.

Crawford, Garry, and Victoria K. Gosling. "The Myth of the 'Puck Bunny': Female Fans and Men's Ice Hockey." *Sociology* 38, no. 3 (2004): 477–93.

Curry, Timothy Jon. "Fraternal Bonding in the Locker Room: A Profeminist Analysis of Talk about Competition and Women." *Sociology of Sport Journal* 8, no. 2 (1991): 119–35.

Davidson, Judy, and Michelle Helstein. "Queering the Gaze: Calgary Hockey Breasts, Dynamics of Desire, and Colonial Hauntings." *Sociology of Sport Journal* 33, no. 4 (2016): 282–93.

Des Barres, Pamela. *I'm with the Band: Confessions of a Groupie*. New York: Beech Tree Books, 1987.

Dimiceli, Erin E., Mary A. Steinhardt, and Shanna E. Smith. "Stressful Experiences, Coping Strategies, and Predictors of Health-Related Outcomes among Wives of Deployed Military Servicemen." *Armed Forces & Society* 36, no. 2 (2010): 351–73.

Emerson, Robert M., Rachel I. Fretz, and Linda L. Shaw. *Writing Ethnographic Fieldnotes*. 2nd ed. Chicago: University of Chicago Press, 2011.

England, Paula. "Emerging Theories of Care Work." *Annual Review of Sociology* 31 (2005): 381–99.

Fair, Brian. "Constructing Masculinity through Penetration Discourse: The Intersection of Misogyny and Homophobia in High School Wrestling." *Men and Masculinities* 14, no. 4 (2011): 491–504.

Farole, Cheryl A. "Sources of Stress for Major League Baseball Players' Wives." *Journal of Performance Education* 1, no. 1 (1996): 77–99.

Finch, Janet. *Married to the Job: Wives' Incorporation in Men's Work*. London: Allen & Unwin, 1983.

Fine, Gary Alan. *With the Boys: Little League Baseball and Preadolescent Culture*. Chicago: University of Chicago Press, 1987.

Fontana, Andrea, and James Frey. "The Placekicker in Professional Football: Simmel's Stranger Revisited." *Qualitative Sociology* 6, no. 4 (1983): 308–21.

Forsyth, Craig J., and Carol Y. Thompson. "Helpmates of the Rodeo: Fans, Wives, and Groupies." *Journal of Sport & Social Issues* 31, no. 4 (2007): 394–416.

Fowlkes, Martha R. *Behind Every Successful Man: Wives of Medicine and Academe*. New York: Columbia University Press, 1980.

———. "The Myth of Merit and Male Professional Careers: The Roles of Wives." In *Families and Work*, edited by Naomi Gerstel and Harriet Engel Gross, 347–60. Philadelphia: Temple University Press, 1987.

Freitas, Anthony, Susan Kaiser, Joan Chandler, Carol Hall, Jung-Won Kim, and

Tania Hammidi. "Appearance Management as Border Construction: Least Favorite Clothing, Group Distancing, and Identity . . . Not!" *Sociological Inquiry* 67, no. 3 (1997): 323–35.

Frey, James H., and Andrea Fontana. "The Group Interview in Social Research." *Social Science Journal* 28, no. 2 (1991): 175–87.

Friedan, Betty. *The Feminine Mystique*. New York: Norton, [1963] 2013.

Gallin, Rita S. "The Intersection of Class and Age: Mother-in-Law/Daughter-in-Law Relations in Rural Taiwan." *Journal of Cross-Cultural Gerontology* 9, no. 2 (1994): 127–40.

Gauthier, DeAnn K., and Craig J. Forsyth. "Buckle Bunnies: Groupies of the Rodeo Circuit." *Deviant Behavior* 21, no. 4 (2000): 349–65.

Geertz, Clifford. "Thick Description: Toward an Interpretive Theory of Culture." In *The Interpretation of Cultures: Selected Essays*, 3–30. New York: Basic Books, 1973.

Glaser, Barney G., and Anselm L. Strauss. *The Discovery of Grounded Theory: Strategies for Qualitative Research*. Chicago: Aldine, 1967.

Gmelch, George, and Patricia Mary San Antonio. "Baseball Wives: Gender and the Work of Baseball." *Journal of Contemporary Ethnography* 30, no. 3 (2001): 335–56.

———. "Groupies and American Baseball." *Journal of Sport & Social Issues* 22, no. 1 (1998): 32–45.

Goffman, Erving. *Behavior in Public Places: Notes on the Social Organization of Gatherings*. Glencoe, NY: The Free Press, 1963.

———. "Embarrassment and Social Organization." In *Interactional Ritual: Essays on Face-to- Face Behavior*, 97–112. Chicago: Aldine, 1967.

———. *Gender Advertisements*. Cambridge, MA: Harvard University Press, 1979.

———. "The Nature of Deference and Demeanor." In *Interactional Ritual: Essays on Face-to- Face Behavior*, 47–95. Chicago: Aldine, 1967.

———. "On Face-Work: An Analysis of Ritual Elements in Social Interaction." In *Interactional Ritual: Essays on Face-to-Face Behavior*, 5–45. Chicago: Aldine, 1967.

———. "On the Characteristics of Total Institutions." In *Asylums: Essays on the Social Situation of Mental Patients and Other Inmates*, 1–124. Chicago: Aldine, 1961.

———. *The Presentation of Self in Everyday Life*. Garden City, NY: Anchor Doubleday, 1959.

———. *Relations in Public: Microstudies of the Public Order*. New York: Basic Books, 1971.

———. "Role Distance." In *Encounters: Two Studies in the Sociology of Interaction*, 85–152. Indianapolis, IN: Bobbs-Merrill, 1961.

———. *Stigma: Notes on the Management of Spoiled Identity*. New York: Simon & Schuster, 1963.

Golightly, Yvonne M., Stephen W. Marshall, Leigh F. Callahan, and Kevin Guskiewicz. "Early-Onset Arthritis in Retired National Football League Players." *Journal of Physical Activity and Health* 6, no. 5 (2009): 638–43.

Gross, Edward, and Gregory P. Stone. "Embarrassment and the Analysis of Role Requirements." *American Journal of Sociology* 70, no. 1 (1964): 1–15.

Guskiewicz, Kevin M., Stephen W. Marshall, Julian Bailes, Michael McCrea, Robert C. Cantu, Christopher Randolph, and Barry D. Jordan. "Association between Recurrent Concussion and Late-Life Cognitive Impairment in Retired Professional Football Players." *Neurosurgery* 75, no. 4 (2005): 719–26.

Haas, Linda. "Families and Work." In *Handbook of Marriage and the Family*. 2nd ed., edited by Marvin B. Sussman, Suzanne K. Steinmetz, and Gary W. Peterson, 571–612. New York: Plenum Press, 1999.

Hartley, Cecilia. "Letting Ourselves Go: Making Room for the Fat Body in Feminist Scholarship." In *Bodies Out of Bounds: Fatness and Transgression*, edited by Jana Evans Braziel and Kathleen LeBesco, 60–73. Berkeley: University of California Press, 2001.

Harvey, Michael, and Danielle Wiese. "The Dual-Career Couple: Female Expatriates and Male Trailing Spouses." *Thunderbird International Business Review* 40, no. 4 (1998): 359–88.

Hasinoff, Amy Adele, and Tamara Shepherd. "Sexting in Context: Privacy Norms and Expectations." *International Journal of Communication* 8 (2014): 2932–55.

Haslanger, Sally. "On Being Objective and Being Objectified." In *A Mind of One's Own: Feminist Essays on Reason and Objectivity*. 2nd ed., edited by Louise M. Antony and Charlotte Witt, 209–53. Boulder, CO: Westview Press, 2002.

Hays, Sharon. *The Cultural Contributions of Motherhood*. New Haven, CT: Yale University Press, 1996.

Hochschild, Arlie Russell. "Emotion Work, Feeling Rules, and Social Structure." *American Journal of Sociology* 85, no. 3 (1979): 551–75.

———. *The Managed Heart: Commercialization of Human Feeling*. Berkeley: University of California Press, 1983.

———. "The Role of the Ambassador's Wife: An Exploratory Study." *Journal of Marriage and the Family* 31, no. 1 (1969): 73–87.

Hochschild, Arlie, with Anne Machung. *The Second Shift: Working Parents and the Revolution at Home*. New York: Viking Penguin, 1989.

Howard, Judith A., Philip Blumstein, and Pepper Schwartz. "Sex, Power, and Influence Tactics in Intimate Relationships." *Journal of Personality and Social Psychology* 51, no. 1 (1986): 102–9.

Hughes, Robert, and Jay Coakley. "Positive Deviance among Athletes: The Implications of Overconformity to the Sport Ethic." *Sociology of Sport Journal* 8, no. 4 (1991): 307–25.

Irving, Washington. *Rip Van Winkle*. North Charleston, SC: CreateSpace, 2012.

Jackson, Jacqueline, and Linda Berg-Cross. "Extending the Extended Family: The Mother-in-Law and Daughter-in-Law Relationship of Black Women." *Family Relations* 37, no. 3 (1988): 293–97.

Jervis, Sue. *Relocation, Gender, and Emotion: A Psycho-Social Perspective on the Experiences of Military Wives*. London: Karnac Books, 2011.

Johnson, Miriam M. *Strong Mothers, Weak Wives: The Search for Gender Equality*. Berkeley: University of California Press, 1988.

Johnson, Paula. "Women and Power: Towards a Theory of Effectiveness." *Journal of Social Issues* 32, no. 3 (1976): 99–110.

Johnson, Vance, with Reggie Rivers. *The Vance: The Beginning and the End*. Dubuque, IA: Kendall/Hunt, 1994.

Jonassohn, Kurt, Allan Turowetz, and Richard Gruneau. "Research Methods in the Sociology of Sport: Strategies and Problems." *Qualitative Sociology* 4, no. 3 (1981): 179–97.

Kaneko, Yoshihiko, and Yoshiteru Yamada. "Wives and Mothers-in-Law: Potential for Family Conflict in Post-war Japan." *Journal of Elder Abuse & Neglect* 2, no. 1–2 (1990): 87–99.

Kanter, Rosabeth Moss. *Men and Women of the Corporation*. New York: Basic Books, 1977.

Karaffa, Kerry, Linda Openshaw, Julie Koch, Hugh Clark, Cynthia Harr, and Chris Stewart. "Perceived Impact of Police Work on Marital Relationships." *The Family Journal: Counseling and Therapy for Couples and Families* 23, no. 2 (2015): 120–31.

Kemper, Robert V., and Anya Peterson Royce. "Long-Term Field Research: Metaphors, Paradigms, and Themes." In *Chronicling Cultures: Long-Term Field Research in Anthropology*, edited by Robert V. Kemper and Anya Peterson Royce, xiii–xxxviii. Walnut Creek, CA: AltaMira Press, 2002.

Kidder, Jeffrey L. "Style and Action: A Decoding of Bike Messenger Symbols." *Journal of Contemporary Ethnography* 34, no. 2 (2005): 344–67.

Kilmartin, Christopher. *The Masculine Self*. 4th ed. Cornwall-on-Hudson, NY: Sloan, 2010.

Kim, Myung-Hye. "Changing Relationships between Daughters-in-Law and Mothers-in-Law in Urban South Korea." *Anthropological Quarterly* 69, no. 4 (1996): 179–92.

Kivett, Vira R. "Mother-in-Law and Daughter-in-Law Relations." In *Aging Parents and Adult Children*, edited by Jay A. Mancini, 17–32. Lexington, MA: Lexington Books, 1989.

Klapp, Orrin E. *Heroes, Villains, and Fools: The Changing American Character*. Englewood Cliffs, NJ: Prentice-Hall, 1962.

———. "Social Types: Process and Structure." *American Sociological Review* 23, no. 6 (1958): 674–78.

Komter, Aafke. "Hidden Power in Marriage." *Gender & Society* 3, no. 2 (1989): 187–216.

Koppel, Lily. *The Astronaut Wives Club: A True Story*. New York: Grand Central, 2013.

Lamont, Michele, and Virag Molnar. "The Study of Boundaries in the Social Sciences." *Annual Review of Sociology* 28 (2002): 167–95.

Larsen, Gretchen. "'It's a Man's Man's Man's World': Music Groupies and the Othering of Women in the World of Rock." *Organization* 24, no. 3 (2017): 397–417.

Lehman, Everett J., Misty J. Hein, Sherry L. Baron, and Christine M. Gersic. "Neurodegenerative Causes of Death among Retired National Football League Players." *Neurology* 79, no. 19 (2012): 1970–74.

Lim, In-Sook. "Korean Immigrant Women's Challenge to Gender Inequality at Home: The Interplay of Economic Resources, Gender, and Family." *Gender & Society* 11, no. 1 (1997): 31–51.

Lofland, John, David A. Snow, Leon Anderson, and Lyn H. Lofland. *Analyzing Social Settings: A Guide to Qualitative Observation and Analysis*. 4th ed. Belmont, CA: Wadsworth, 2006.

Lofland, Lyn H. *A World of Strangers: Order and Action in Urban Public Space*. New York: Basic Books, 1973.

Lopata, Helena Znaniecki. *Occupation: Housewife*. New York: Oxford University Press, 1971.

Manley, Geoff, Andrew J. Gardner, Kathryn J. Schneider, Kevin M. Guskiewicz, Julian Bailes, Robert C. Cantu, Rudolph J. Castellani, Micheal Turner, Barry D. Jordan, Christopher Randolph, Jiri Dvorak, K. Alix Hayden, Charles H. Tator, Paul McCrory, and Grant L. Iverson. "A Systematic Review of Potential Long-Term Effects of Sport-Related Concussion." *British Journal of Sports Medicine* 51, no. 12 (2017): 969–77.

Marotz-Baden, Ramona, and Deane Cowan. "Mothers-in-Law and Daughters-in-Law: The Effects of Proximity on Conflict and Stress." *Family Relations* 36, no. 4 (1987): 385–90.

Mayseless, Ofra, Kim Bartholomew, Antonia Henderson, and Shanna Trinke. "'I Was More Her Mom than She Was Mine': Role Reversal in a Community Sample." *Family Relations* 53, no. 1 (2004): 78–86.

McPherson, Barry D. "The Child in Competitive Sport: Influence of the Social Milieu." In *Children in Sport*. 2nd ed., edited by Richard A. Magill, Michael J. Ash, and Frank L. Smoll, 247–78. Champaign, IL: Human Kinetics, 1982.

Mead, George H. *Mind, Self, and Society: From the Standpoint of a Social Behaviorist*, edited by Charles W. Morris. Chicago: University of Chicago Press, 1934.

Mederer, Helen J., and Laurie Weinstein. "Choices and Constraints in a Two-Person Career: Ideology, Division of Labor, and Well-Being among Submarine Officers' Wives." *Journal of Family Issues* 13, no. 3 (1992): 334–50.

Messner, Michael A., and Mark A. Stevens. "Scoring without Consent: Confronting Male Athletes' Violence against Women." In *Paradoxes of Youth and Sport*, edited by Margaret Gatz, Michael A. Messner, and Sandra J. Ball-Rokeach, 225–39. Albany: State University of New York Press, 2002.

Mez, Jesse, Daniel H. Daneshvar, Patrick T. Kiernan, Bobak Abdolmohammadi, Victor E. Alvarez, Bertrand R. Huber, Michael L. Alosco, Todd M. Solomon, Christopher J. Nowinski, Lisa McHale, Kerry A. Cormier, Caroline A. Kubilus, Brett M. Martin, Lauren Murphy, Christine M. Baugh, Phillip H. Montenigro, Christine E. Chaisson, Yorghos Tripodis, Neil W. Kowall, Jennifer Weuve, Michael D. McClean, Robert C. Cantu, Lee E. Goldstein, Douglas I. Katz, Robert A. Stern, Thor D. Stein, and Ann C. McKee. "Clinicopathological Evaluation of Chronic Traumatic Encephalopathy in Players of American Football." *Journal of the American Medical Association* 318, no. 4 (2017): 360–70.

Michelson, Herbert A. *Sportin' Ladies: Confessions of the Bimbos*. Radnor, PA: Chilton, 1975.

Miguel, Cristina. "Visual Intimacy on Social Media: From Selfies to the Co-Construction of Intimacies Through Shared Pictures." *Social Media & Society* 2, no. 2 (2016): 1–10.

Mileham, Beatriz Lia Avila. "Online Infidelity in Internet Chat Rooms: An Ethnographic Exploration." *Computers in Human Behavior* 23, no. 1 (2007): 11–31.

Mitchell, Gary, and Harold Cronson. "The Celebrity Family: A Clinical Perspective." *American Journal of Family Therapy* 15, no. 3 (1987): 235–41.

Montemurro, Beth, and Meghan M. Gillen. "How Clothes Make the Woman Immoral: Impressions Given Off by Sexualized Clothing." *Clothing and Textiles Research Journal* 31, no. 3 (2013): 167–81.

Munro, Ealasaid. "Feminism: A Fourth Wave?" *Political Insight* 4, no. 2 (2013): 22–25.

Nash, Jeffrey E. "Bus Riding: Community on Wheels." *Urban Life* 4, no. 1 (1975): 99–124.

Nelson, Margaret K. *Parenting Out of Control: Anxious Parents in Uncertain Times*. New York: New York University Press, 2010.

Nippert-Eng, Christena E. *Home and Work: Negotiating Boundaries through Everyday Life*. Chicago: University of Chicago Press, 1995.

Nussbaum, Martha C. "Objectification." *Philosophy & Public Affairs* 24, no. 4 (1995): 249–91.

O'Connor, Karen, Bernadette Nye, and Laura Van Assendelft. "Wives in the White House: The Political Influence of First Ladies." *Presidential Studies Quarterly* 26, no. 3 (1996): 835–53.

Omalu, Bennet I., Julian Bailes, Jennifer Lynn Hammers, and Robert P. Fitzsimmons. "Chronic Traumatic Encephalopathy, Suicides and Parasuicides in Professional American Athletes: The Role of the Forensic Pathologist." *American Journal of Forensic Medicine and Pathology* 31, no. 1 (2010): 1–3.

Ortiz, Steven M. "Breaking Out of Academic Isolation: The Media Odyssey of a Sociologist." *The American Sociologist* 38, no. 3 (2007): 223–49.

———. "Clinical Typifications by Wives of Professional Athletes: The Field Researcher as Therapist." *Clinical Sociology Review* 12, no. 1 (1994): 48–68.

———. "Constructing Dependency in Coping with Stressful Occupational Events: At What Cost for Wives of Professional Athletes?" *Sociology of Sport Online* 5, no. 2 (2002): n.p.

———. "The Effects of the Professional Athlete's Occupational Life-Style on the Wife: An Exploratory Study of a Situational Approach to Geographic Mobility." Master's thesis, California State University, Fullerton, 1983.

———. "The Ethnographic Process of Gender Management: Doing the 'Right' Masculinity with Wives of Professional Athletes." *Qualitative Inquiry* 11, no. 2 (2005): 265–90.

———. "How Interviewing Became Therapy for Wives of Professional Athletes: Learning from a Serendipitous Experience." *Qualitative Inquiry* 7, no. 2 (2001): 192–220.

———. "Leaving the Private World of Wives of Professional Athletes: A Male Sociologist's Reflections." *Journal of Contemporary Ethnography* 33, no. 4 (2004): 466–87.

———. "Muted Masculinity as an Outsider Strategy: Gender Sharing in Ethnographic Work with Wives of Professional Athletes." *Symbolic Interaction* 26, no. 4 (2003): 601–11.

———. "A Sociological Dimension of Leisure: An Exploratory Study of Surfing as a 'Central Life Interest' of Surfers." Master's thesis, California State University, Long Beach, 1980.

———. "When Happiness Ends and Coping Begins: The Private Pain of the Professional Athlete's Wife." PhD dissertation, University of California, Berkeley, 1994.

Papanek, Hanna. "Men, Women, and Work: Reflections on the Two-Person Career." *American Journal of Sociology* 78, no. 4 (1973): 852–72.

Parker, Andrew, and Andrew Manley. "Goffman, Identity and Organizational Control: Elite Sports Academies and Social Theory." *Sociology of Sport Journal* 34, no. 3 (2017): 211–22.

Patton, Michael Quinn. *Qualitative Research and Evaluation Methods: Integrating Theory and Practice*. 4th ed. Thousand Oaks, CA: Sage, 2015.

Pavalko, Eliza K., and Glen H. Elder. "Women behind the Men: Variations in Wives' Support of Husbands' Careers." *Gender & Society* 7, no. 4 (1993): 548–67.

Peters-Golden, Holly, and Linda Grant. "Physician's Spouse: Privileged Role or Stigmatized Identity?" In *Research in the Sociology of Health Care: A Research Annual*, vol. 8, edited by Dorothy C. Wertz, 313–35. Greenwich, CT: JAI Press, 1989.

Pfefferbaum, Betty, Carol S. North, Kenneth Bunch, Teddy G. Wilson, Phebe Tucker, and John K. Schorr. "The Impact of the 1995 Oklahoma City Bombing on the Partners of Firefighters." *Journal of Urban Health: Bulletin of the New York Academy of Medicine* 79, no. 3 (2002): 364–72.

Plunkett Research, Ltd. "Sports Industry Statistics and Market Size Overview." Accessed October 4, 2018. https://www.plunkettresearch.com/statistics/Industry-Statistics-Sports-Industry-Statistic-and-Market-Size-Overview/.

Polletta, Francesca, Pang Ching Bobby Chen, Beth Gharrity Gardner, and Alice Motes. "The Sociology of Storytelling." *Annual Review of Sociology* 37 (2011): 109–30.

Prus, Robert. *Beyond the Power Mystique: Power as Intersubjective Accomplishment.* Albany: State University of New York Press, 1999.

Rabe-Hemp, Cara E. "POLICEwomen or policeWOMEN: Doing Gender and Police Work." *Feminist Criminology* 4, no. 2 (2009): 114–29.

Rhodes, Lisa L. *Electric Ladyland: Women and Rock Culture.* Philadelphia: University of Pennsylvania Press, 2005.

Richardson, Laurel. "Secrecy and Status: The Social Construction of Forbidden Relationships." *American Sociological Review* 53, no. 2 (1988): 209–19.

Ritvo, Eva C., and Ira D. Glick. "Family Problems and Sports Performance: The Role of Couple's Therapy in Treating Athletes and Their Families." *Physician and Sportsmedicine* 33, no. 9 (2005): 37–41.

Roehling, Patricia V., Phyllis Moen, and Rosemary Batt. "Spillover." In *It's About Time: Couples and Careers*, edited by Phyllis Moen, 101–21. Ithaca, NY: Cornell University Press, 2003.

Rosecrance, John. "The Invisible Horsemen: The Social World of the Backstretch." *Qualitative Sociology* 8, no. 3 (1985): 248–65.

Rubin, Herbert J., and Irene S. Rubin. *Qualitative Interviewing: The Art of Hearing Data.* 3rd ed. Los Angeles: Sage, 2012.

Rubin, Lillian Breslow. *Worlds of Pain: Life in the Working-Class Family.* New York: Basic Books, 1976.

Ruckel, Lindsey, and Melanie Hill. "Look @ Me 2.0: Self-Sexualization in Facebook Photographs, Body Surveillance, and Body Image." *Sexuality & Culture* 21, no. 1 (2017): 15–35.

Ryan, Shannon. "The Positive Reaction to Dwyane Wade's Extended Paternity Leave Signals a Cultural Shift." *Chicago Tribune.* November 13, 2018. http://www.chicagotribune.com/sports/ct-spt-dwyane-wade-paternity-leave-ryan-20181113-story.html.

Saldana, Johnny. *Longitudinal Qualitative Research: Analyzing Change Through Time.* Walnut Creek, CA: AltaMira Press, 2003.

Sanderson, Jimmy. "Professional Athletes' Shrinking Privacy Boundaries: Fans, Information and Communication Technologies, and Athlete Monitoring." *International Journal of Sport Communication* 2, no. 2 (2009): 240–56.

Saul, Jennifer Mather. 2003. *Feminism: Issues and Arguments.* Oxford, UK: Oxford University Press.

Schacht, Steven P. "Misogyny On and Off the Pitch: The Gendered World of Male Rugby Players." *Gender & Society* 10, no. 5 (1996): 550–65.

Schuetz, Alfred. "The Stranger: An Essay in Social Psychology." *American Journal of Sociology* 49, no. 6 (1944): 499–507.

Simmel, Georg. "The Sociology of Secrecy and of Secret Societies." *American Journal of Sociology* 11, no. 4 (1906): 441–98.

———. "The Stranger." In *The Sociology of Georg Simmel*. Translated and edited by Kurt H. Wolff, 402–8. New York: The Free Press, 1950.

———. "The Web of Group-Affiliations." In *Conflict and the Web of Group-Affiliations*, translated by Reinhard Bendix, 125–95. Glencoe, IL: The Free Press, 1955.

Skolnikoff, Jessica, and Robert Engvall. *Young Athletes, Couch Potatoes, and Helicopter Parents: The Production of Play*. Lanham, MD: Rowman & Littlefield, 2014.

Smolak, Linda, Sarah K. Murnen, and Taryn A. Myers. "Sexualizing the Self: What College Women and Men Think About and Do to Be 'Sexy.'" *Psychology of Women Quarterly* 38, no. 3 (2014): 379–97.

Snow, David A., and Leon Anderson. "Identity Work among the Homeless: The Verbal Construction and Avowal of Personal Identities." *American Journal of Sociology* 92, no. 6 (1987): 1336–71.

Spradley, James P. *The Ethnographic Interview*. New York: Holt, Rinehart, and Winston, 1979.

Stets, Jan E., and Stacy A. Hammons. "Gender, Control, and Marital Commitment." *Journal of Family Issues* 23, no. 1 (2002): 3–25.

Stoetzler, Marcel. "Intersectional Individuality: Georg Simmel's Concept of 'The Intersection of Social Circles' and the Emancipation of Women." *Sociological Inquiry* 86, no. 2 (2016): 216–40.

Stone, Gregory P. "Appearance and the Self." In *Human Behavior and Social Processes: An Interactionist Approach*, edited by Arnold M. Rose, 86–118. Boston: Houghton Mifflin, 1962.

Strauss, Anselm. "A Social World Perspective." In *Studies in Symbolic Interaction*, vol. 1, edited by Norman K. Denzin, 119–28. Greenwich, CT: JAI Press, 1978.

Strickland, W. Jay. "A Typology of Career Wife Roles." *Human Relations* 45, no. 8 (1992): 797–811.

Sturges, Judith E., and Kathleen J. Hanrahan. "Comparing Telephone and Face-to-Face Qualitative Interviewing: A Research Note." *Qualitative Research* 4, no. 1 (2004): 107–18.

Swidler, Ann. *Talk of Love: How Culture Matters*. Chicago: University of Chicago Press, 2001.

Szinovacz, Maximiliane E. "Family Power." In *Handbook of Marriage and the Family*, edited by Marvin B. Sussman and Suzanne K. Steinmetz, 651–93. New York: Plenum Press, 1987.

Taylor, Mary G., and Shirley Foster Hartley. "The Two-Person Career: A Classic Example." *Sociology of Work and Occupations* 2, no. 4 (1975): 354–72.

Thoits, Peggy A. "Gender and Marital Status Differences in Control and Distress: Common Stress versus Unique Stress Explanations." *Journal of Health and Social Behavior* 28, no. 1 (1987): 7–22.

Trujillo, Nick. "Hegemonic Masculinity on the Mound: Media Representations of Nolan Ryan and American Sports Culture." *Critical Studies in Mass Communication* 8, no. 3 (1991): 290–308.

Unruh, David R. "The Nature of Social Worlds." *Pacific Sociological Review* 23, no. 3 (1980): 271–96.

van Krieken, Robert. *Celebrity Society*. New York: Routledge, 2012.

Webner, David, and Grant L. Iverson. "Suicide in Professional American Football Players in the Past 95 Years." *Brain Injury* 30, no. 13–14 (2016): 1718–21.

Weitzer, Ronald. "Why We Need More Research on Sex Work." In *Sex for Sale: Prostitution, Pornography, and the Sex Industry*, edited by Ronald Weitzer, 1–13. New York: Routledge, 2000.

Weitzer, Ronald, and Charis E. Kubrin. "Misogyny in Rap Music: A Content Analysis of Prevalence and Meanings." *Men and Masculinities* 12, no. 1 (2009): 3–29.

Welch, Michael. "Violence against Women by Professional Football Players: A Gender Analysis of Hypermasculinity, Positional Status, Narcissism, and Entitlement." *Journal of Sport & Social Issues* 21, no. 4 (1997): 392–411.

Wenner, Lawrence A., ed. *Fallen Sports Heroes, Media, and Celebrity Culture*. New York: Peter Lang, 2013.

West, Candace, and Don H. Zimmerman. "Doing Gender." *Gender & Society* 1, no. 2 (1987): 125–51.

Whip, Rosemary. "The Parliamentary Wife: Participant in the 'Two-Person Single Career.'" *Australian Journal of Political Science* 17, no. 2 (1982): 38–44.

Winton, Chester A. *Children as Caregivers: Parental and Parentified Children*. Boston: Allyn and Bacon, 2003.

Wysocki, Diane Kholos, and Cheryl D. Childers. "'Let My Fingers Do the Talking': Sexting and Infidelity in Cyberspace." *Sexuality & Culture* 15, no. 3 (2011): 217–39.

Xu, Xiaohe, and Shu-Chuan Lai. "Resources, Gender Ideologies, and Marital Power: The Case of Taiwan." *Journal of Family Issues* 23, no. 2 (2002): 209–45.

Yablonski, Lewis, and Jonathan J. Brower. *The Little League Game: How Kids, Coaches, and Parents Really Play It*. New York: Times Books, 1979.

Zurcher, Louis A. "The Airplane Passenger: Protection of Self in an Encapsulated Group." *Qualitative Sociology* 1, no. 3 (1979): 77–99.

INDEX

affairs. *See* culture of infidelity
affluence, 39, 40
Alaina (participant): on basic marital understanding, 43–44; on game etiquette, 53, 57; on groupies, 165, 170; on hierarchy of players' wives, 32, 33, 34; on husbands and control work, 101–2; on in-laws, 131; on length of marriage, 209; on organizational dominance, 29; on public life/image, 50; on scope of domestic responsibilities, 16; on wives' control work at home, 113–14
alcohol/substance use, in public, 56
Alyssa (participant): on basic marital understanding, 40; on celebrityhood of husband, 60; on childhood, 119, 120; on culture of infidelity, 188, 191, 199–200; on groupies, 162, 176–77, 178; on husbands and control work, 104–5; on in-laws, 152–53; on institutionalized brotherhood, 37; on secondhand identity, 66–67; on separation, 208
Amanda (participant): on culture of infidelity, 185; on sexual subordination, 111–13
appearance. *See* physical appearance expectations, of wives; young female groupies
apprentice veteran wives, 31

Arisa (participant): on basic marital understanding, 43; on childhood, 119; on husbands and control work, 105, 106; on in-laws, 132; on motherization, 23; on spoiled athlete syndrome, 19
authority figures, 103
autograph seekers, 52, 57–60, 61, 62, 66, 74

bar groupies, 161–62. *See also* nightclub groupies
bench players, 30–31
Beth (participant): on autograph seekers, 59; on basic marital understanding, 38–39, 41; on childhood, 117–19; on culture of infidelity, 197, 198, 199; on groupies, 161, 166, 172; on hierarchy of players' wives, 33–34; on in-laws, 130, 133–34, 136, 144, 146, 147–48, 153; on mood sharing, 231n10; on secondhand identity, 65, 66, 67–69; on travel code of conduct, 82, 84, 91
big-league attitude, 60–61
bonds: mother-son, 14, 20, 21, 128-29, 135-39, 146, 150-53; teammates, 35, 36, 37, 87, 95, 179; wives, 32
booster clubs, 165–66
boundaries: sport organization prescriptions for players, 35–38; of total institutions, 29

boundaries of exclusion. *See* culture of infidelity; traveling with team, and code enforcement; wives as outsiders

boundary work/boundary management: with autograph hounds, 58–59; defined, 226n14; with family time, 72–73; with in-laws, 134–35, 137, 141, 143–45, 152; with motherization by husband, 25–26; and public expectations, 48, 61–62; setting marital boundaries, 25, 139, 145, 150, 195–99; walking-ahead strategy, 58. *See also* groupieism and boundary work

breast flashing, 161

business acumen, of wives, 43

businessman groupies, 159

bus travel, code of conduct, 85–86

Callie (participant): on game etiquette, 55, 56; on groupies, 160, 164, 173; on guarding private life, 69; on in-laws, 140, 150, 152; on institutionalized brotherhood, 36; on length of marriage, 209

camp groupies, 157, 163–64, 191–92

career-dominated marriages, 1–16, 201–10; impacts on marital and family life, 6–9; normalization of conformity, 11–12; player workaholic approach to careers, 7–8; serious health challenges, 5–6; two-person career idea, 39–45, 223n3, 228n37; wives and gender work, 6, 224n9; wives' self-management strategies, 9, 11

care work, 43, 106

celebrity status: of franchise players, 31; and image work of wives in public, 60–62; media treatment of, 46–48; as motive for marriage, 39; and quasi-celebrityhood of wives, 62–64; and spoiled athlete syndrome, 21–22. *See also* public life and image work by wives

cheerleaders, 20, 74–75, 168–69

childhood influences on wives. *See under* star power and control work

children: as focus of identity work of wives, 66; intrusion of father's celebrity status on, 72; mother as primary parent, 6. *See also* family life; mother-son bond

Chloe (participant): on adapting to exclusion, 74; on guarding private life, 69

code busters, 79–80, 86, 95–98

code of conduct, and travel. *See* traveling with team, and code enforcement

code work/code management: defined 230n3; and gender relations, 80; and mood sharing, 85–86; and moral responsibilities, 91–92. *See also* traveling with team, and code enforcement

cohabiting girlfriends, 32

college sports, 8, 21, 32

control work/control management: defined, 232n2. *See also* star power and control work

counseling and therapy, 181, 189–90, 191, 206, 209

Courtney (participant): on culture of infidelity, 184; on guarding private life, 69; on length of marriage, 208

culture of infidelity, 15, 38; ability to trust and suspicion work, 187–92, 237nn4–5; affairs of wives, 187, 192; communication, marital tension, and re-entry routines, 192–95; and competitive physical attractiveness of wives, 110–11; discovery of infidelity, 199–200; faithful husbands as conspirators, 88–89, 92–93, 96; institutionalization/normalization of, 37–38, 81, 179, 198; patterns of infidelity, 185–87; setting marital boundaries, 195–99; sex talk as common among players/wives, 183–84; as tradeoff for benefits of sport marriage, 39; wives as conspirators, 88, 90–92, 180–81, 184–85, 236n1. *See also* groupieism and boundary work; secrets; traveling with team, and code enforcement; wives as outsiders

Dana (participant): on code busting, 95, 97; on game etiquette, 55; on motherization, 23; on postponement of own career goals, 6; on sense of abandon-

ment, 1–2; on travel code of conduct, 86, 90
denial: regarding extramarital activities, 173, 193–94; and suspicion work, 190–91, 237n5
depression, 5, 24, 116, 191
divorce: avoidance of, during career, 126–27; due to infidelity, 180–81, 200, 208–9. *See also* trial separations
domestic control, defined, 14, 232n3. *See also* star power and control work
domestic workers, 7
Donna (participant): on celebrityhood of husband, 60, 61; on culture of infidelity, 187; on groupies, 171, 176; on guarding private life, 72; on secondhand identity, 64, 65, 66, 67
dress codes. *See* physical appearance expectations, of wives

early childhood influences on wives. *See* star power and control work
eating disorders, 111–13
Emma (participant): on basic marital understanding 44; on code busting, 96, 97–98; on culture of infidelity, 182, 183–84, 196, 200; on divorce, 209; on groupies, 157, 162, 178; on hierarchy of players' wives, 34; on in-laws, 131; on organizational dominance, 29; on public life/image, 52; on secondhand identity, 65–66; on travel code of conduct, 78, 79–80, 82, 83, 92, 94–95; on wives' control work at home, 115–16
emotional dissonance, 231n10
emotional distance, 109
emotional instability, and spoiled athlete syndrome, 21–22
emotion work: burnout, 191; forgiveness, 197; and mood sharing, 85–86, 231n10; suppression of emotions in public, 52, 53–54, 58–59, 73–74, 75; suppression of emotions with husbands, 108–9, 115; suppression of emotions with in-laws, 128–29, 133, 144, 147. *See also* "right" emotions; star power and control work; "wrong" emotions; *and specific emotions*

entitlement, sense of, 21, 60–61
errant behavior, 21–22
eternal boyhood. *See* spoiled athlete syndrome
evocative denial, 237n5
exclusion of wives. *See* wives as outsiders
extramarital relationships. *See* culture of infidelity; groupieism and boundary work; traveling with team, and code enforcement
eye candy, 65

face work, 52–53. *See also* public life and image work by wives
fame. *See* celebrity status
family-free careers, 6, 113
family groupies, 157, 158–59
family life: family/domestic responsibilities of players, 7, 37, 150, 201–2, 203; during offseason, 70–73; as priority for wives, 39–40; wives as controllers of, 102. *See also* children; in-laws and subordination work; star power and control work
fans: concerns over players' injuries, 62–63; and expectations of wives, 110; experience as part of "we" partnership, 63–64, 74; and game spectator behavior, 54–55, 57; as reinforcers of spoiled athlete syndrome, 104–5; seeking selfies, 57, 62
fast-food sex mentality, 38
fathers-in-law, 130–31. *See also* in-laws and subordination work
female groupies: fast-food sex mentality, 38; and good girl/bad girl duality, 26–27; at hotel bars, 87; tasteful dress of wives to distinguish from, 52; at teammate-bonding activities, 37; wives in competition with, 110
female partners, 20, 87–88, 178, 185–86
female sexuality, and virgin-prostitute syndrome, 26–28, 109, 225n3
Feminine Mystique, The (Friedan), 2
femininity: compliance and good girl image, 80; good girl/bad girl duality, 26, 109, 110; muted, 84–85, 231n9; and pre-

senting the right image, 49; of young female groupies, 160–61
fiancées, 32
financial security, as motive for sport marriage, 38–39, 197, 203
first-round draft picks, 32
fishbowl situations. *See* privacy issues
flight attendants, 78, 82, 83, 84–85, 185
fourth-wave feminism, 10
Friedan, Betty, 2
futurizing, as coping strategy, 116

game etiquette, 53–57, 147–49
gatekeepers, 211–12. *See also* mothers-in-law, as family gatekeeper
gay male groupies, 159, 160
gender work/gender management, defined, 224–25n9
gender work, of players, 20, 35–38
gender work, of wives, 6, 224n9
girlfriends, 32, 87
God complex, 21
good girl/bad girl duality, 26–27, 109, 110
"good wife" image, 49
gossip, among wives, 81, 90–91, 146, 148, 157
grandma groupies, 165–66, 176
groupieism and boundary work, 14–15; groupieism defined, 156–57; and husband passivity/indifference, 154–56, 171–72, 173–77; invisible groupies, 164–70; setting boundaries, 171–79; and tie-signs, 174, 176; visible groupies, 157–64. *See also specific groupie types*
groupies (term), 235n1
Gwen (participant): on culture of infidelity, 186; on game etiquette, 53–54; on groupies, 158, 166, 167–68, 169, 170; on guarding private life, 70; on husbands and control work, 105; on in-laws, 128–29, 130–31, 133, 134, 136, 140–42, 145, 149, 150, 151; on institutionalized brotherhood, 35; on motherization, 22

Haley (participant): on need for flexibility in marriage, 10–11

hegemonic masculinity: and early-life sports, 20; gay male groupies seen as threat to, 160; normalization of extra-marital sexual relations, 179; occupational normalization of, 3; supported by institutionalized brotherhood, 35–38, 227n23; and virgin-prostitute syndrome, 26–28, 109, 225n3. *See also* culture of infidelity; groupieism and boundary work
hierarchy of players' wives, 4–5, 28, 30–35, 54; affluence and salary levels, 33; and code busting, 95–96; display of status symbols, 35; and husband's team status, 13, 98; lack of status for unmarried female partners, 32
hotel groupies, 161–62
hotels, code of conduct, 35, 87–89, 95–96, 97
hypersexualization of wife, 109

identity work, 65–66, 168, 229n8
image work/image management, defined, 229n5. *See also* public life and image work by wives
impression management, 168, 232n11. *See also* public life and image work by wives
induced labor, in childbirth, 30
infidelity. *See* culture of infidelity
injuries. *See* occupational injuries
in-laws and subordination work, 14, 128–29, 137; building daughter-in-law/mother-in-law relationships, 132–35; financial support of in-laws, 131–32; improvement in relations, 152–53; living with in-laws, 142–44; mother-son bond and husband passivity, 129, 135–36, 140–42, 151; parental/marital role reversals, 150–51, 234n12; power struggles and desire to "win," 151–52; in private life, 139–46; in public life, 146–48; survival of subordination, 138–39, 234n8
inner circles, of social circles, 32, 168
institutionalized brotherhood, 28, 35–38, 85, 97, 179, 184, 227n23

invisibility. *See* social invisibility
invisible groupies, 164–70

jersey chasers. *See* young female groupies
Jessica (participant): on basic marital understanding, 43; on childhood, 120-21; on control and emotional dichotomy, 124-25; on culture of infidelity, 195; on participation in study, 205
Jill (participant): on childhood, 120; on culture of infidelity, 187, 191–92, 196, 200; on divorce, 208; on groupies, 173; on husbands and control work, 99–101, 102, 107; on motherization, 22, 26
journeyman players, 30–31

Kalyn (participant): on childhood, 119; on spoiled athlete syndrome, 22; on wives' control work at home, 114
Kathleen (participant): on control and emotional dichotomy, 123; on culture of infidelity, 191; on game etiquette, 55; on travel code of conduct, 90; on wives' control work at home, 116
Kaylee (participant): on basic marital understanding, 41; on culture of infidelity, 183; on guarding private life, 72; on husband's control work during offseason, 107; on length of marriage, 209; on wives' control work at home, 114
Keira (participant): on basic marital understanding, 43; on control and emotional dichotomy, 126; on groupies, 163; on hierarchy of players' wives, 34–35; on public life/image, 50
Kellita (participant): on culture of infidelity, 188–90, 191, 200; on guarding private life, 70; on participation in study, 205; on public life/image, 53; on secondhand identity, 67

Lisa (participant): on adapting to exclusion, 74–75; on culture of infidelity, 38, 185, 186–87, 195, 200; on groupies, 154–55, 159, 161, 169, 170, 172, 174; on guarding private life, 70; on husband's opioid addiction, 6

long-term affairs, 185–87, 196
loyalty, implicit competition for, 81, 93–94. *See also* institutionalized brotherhood

Major League Baseball (MLB): challenges of seasonal relocations and schedules, 7; disparity in salaries, 33; paternity leave policies, 30; post-retirement careers, 208; travel schedules, 78 (*see also* traveling with team, and code enforcement)
male dominance. *See* hegemonic masculinity
male groupies, 157, 159–60
male subordination, to mother, 151
management, defined, 9
manipulation, as control tactic, 116–17
marital infidelity. *See* culture of infidelity
marital teamwork. *See* "we" partnership
marquee players, 30–31
marriage work, 3, 63–64
married-couple groupies, 157–58, 167
Marsha (participant): on autograph seekers, 58, 59; on celebrityhood of husband, 61; on childhood, 120–21; on culture of infidelity, 193, 200; on divorce, 200, 208; on groupies, 161, 167, 169, 173–74; on guarding private life, 70, 71, 72–73; on motherization, 23, 24, 25–26; on public life/image, 50; on quasi-celebrityhood of wives, 62–63; on secondhand identity, 65; on travel code of conduct, 79, 85, 87, 88, 93; on unwritten rulebook, 11; on wives' control work at home, 115
masculinity. *See* hegemonic masculinity; muted masculinity
media: misquotes in articles, 71; myths regarding wives, 9–10, 110; sex scandals, ix, 38, 165, 185, 187; treatment of celebrities, 46–48. *See also* social media
Me Too movement, 10
Mia (participant): on childhood, 120
mistresses, 184, 186. *See also* long-term affairs
mood sharing, 85–86, 231n10

moral codes, for positive role models, 4
mother-in-law groupies, 146–47
motherization of the wife, 19, 22–26, 121, 180, 226n11, 226n14; and offseason, 107; role of mother-in-law in, 22, 150–51; and sexual relationship, 26–28, 109–10
mother overinvolvement, 21–22, 121, 129
mothers-in-law, as family gatekeeper, 134–35. See also in-laws and subordination work; mother-son bond
mother-son bond, 20–21, 128–29. See also in-laws and subordination work; spousification of children
muted femininity, 84–85, 231n9
muted masculinity, xi, 231n9
MVP status, 34

Naomi (participant): on celebrityhood of husband, 60; on public life/image, 52–53
narcissism, and male entitlement, 21
National Basketball League (NBA): training camp course on groupies, 155–56; travel schedules, 78
National Football League (NFL): risks for debilitating health issues, 5–6; team spirit nights, 37; travel schedules, 78
National Hockey League (NHL): travel schedules, 78
neglect, sense of, 75–76
Nicole (participant): on husbands and control work, 104; on reflective assessment, 210
nightclub groupies, 37–38, 161–63, 180–81
Nora (participant): on adapting to exclusion, 73–74; on basic marital understanding, 42, 43; on control and emotional dichotomy, 123–24; on culture of infidelity, 182, 183, 197, 200; on divorce, 209; on game etiquette, 54; on groupies, 155–56, 167, 169, 174, 175; on guarding private life, 69–70, 72; on public life/image, 50

occupational activities of wives, 66–69, 208, 209
occupational influences, on sport marriage: hierarchy of players' wives, 4–5, 30–35; institutionalized brotherhood, 35–38, 227n23; organizational dominance, 28–30, 227n22
occupational injuries, 5–6, 8; declining to report, 36; emotional support during, 43; fan concerns over, 62–63; and game etiquette, 54
Olivia (participant): on autograph seekers, 58; on culture of infidelity, 188, 193; on groupies, 156, 161, 164, 170, 174, 178; on in-laws, 134, 139, 145, 146–47; on participation in study, 205; on public life/image, 46–48; on travel code of conduct, 82, 89–90, 91–92; on virgin-prostitute syndrome, 28
one-time encounters, 185, 195–96
opioid addiction, 5–6
organizational dominance, 28–30, 78, 79, 81, 227n22. See also career-dominated marriages
organizational groupies, 165, 166, 168–69, 170, 173, 176
outsiders, wives as. See wives as outsiders
overinvolved mothers, 21, 22, 121, 129, 225n7, 233-34n5
overinvolvement. See parental overinvolvement, in sport-oriented families

Pam (participant): on guarding private life, 71
pampering, in sport-oriented families, 20–21. See also spoiled athlete syndrome
parental leave, 30
parental overinvolvement, in sport-oriented families, 20, 103, 121. See also in-laws and subordination work; spoiled athlete syndrome
participants in study, details about, 218–19
passivity of husbands/players. See groupieism and boundary work; in-laws and subordination work; star power and control work
paternity lawsuits, 38
patriarchy: cultural trends beyond, xiii, 2, 10; and domestic roles, 126; and female

subordination, 151, 179; and fourth-wave feminism, 10; and motherization, 226n11. *See also* hegemonic masculinity
Paula (participant): on groupies, 178; on in-laws, 132, 135, 138, 140, 142–43, 144, 145, 151, 152–53; on participation in study, 205; on public life/image, 49, 51
pecking order. *See* hierarchy of players' wives
perfectionism, 124
performance-enhancing drugs, 5–6
physical appearance expectations, of wives, 49–52, 65, 110–11
plane travel: code of conduct, 82–84; flight attendants as insiders, 78, 82, 83, 84–85, 185
power and control. *See* control work/control management; hegemonic masculinity; in-laws and subordination work; subordination work/subordination management
pregnancies, of groupies, 170, 185, 198
privacy issues: changing media boundaries, 48; during offseason, 69–73; protection of family, 40; at restaurants, 61, 71–72; and risks of using domestic workers, 7; sense of vulnerability and security, 71; sport organization protection of players, 29
private self vs. public self, 48, 52–53, 66, 104
professional athletes: as expendable, 8; workaholic approach to careers, 7–8
pseudo friends, 167, 168, 170
pseudo wives, 167–68
public life and image work by wives, 13; and acceptance of secondhand identity, 49, 64–69; adaptation to exclusion, 73–76; and addressing groupie behavior, 171–72; attendance at games and related events, 49; and autograph seekers, 52, 57–60, 61; and game etiquette, 53–57; guarding private life, 69–73; and husbands' ability to control wives, 175; and husbands' celebrity status, 60–62; and in-law relationships, 146–48; nonassertion of control by wives, 123–24; presenting the right image, 49–53; and quasi-celebrityhood of wives, 62–64
public relations, by wives, 43–44
public self vs. private self, 48, 52–53, 66, 104
puss mail, 163

quasi-celebrityhood of wives, 62–64
queen bees, 34

reality denial, 237n5
reality television, 10
re-entry routines, 192–95
relocation events, 4, 7, 42, 44, 145–46, 206–7
research methodology: access to participants, 211–12, 214–16; first study, 211–16; interviewing process, 212–13; second study, 216–17
resentment: in children due to lack of family privacy, 72; of closeness of brotherhood relations, 37; about exclusion of wives, 75–76; during retirement years, 45; over sole responsibility for family during seasons, 125, 126; of star treatment of husband, 73; over travel code of conduct, 95, 98
retirement years: challenges for players, 40; changes in control patterns, 126–27; changes in roles, 44; consequences for NFL players with TBIs, 5; continuance of celebrity status, 60; continuance of culture of infidelity, 198, 199–200; debt-ridden, 197; and divorce, 126–27, 169; employment goals of wives, 7; mental health issues, 5; overdependency on wives, 115–16; regrets of wives during, 44–45; transitions to other male-dominated occupations, 8, 108–9
revolving-door girlfriends, 32
Rhonda (participant): on adapting to exclusion, 75–76; on celebrityhood of husband, 61, 62; on childhood, 120; on control and emotional dichotomy, 124; on groupies, 174; on guarding private life, 70–71, 72; on husbands and control work, 104; on in-laws, 142; on public

life/image, 48–49, 51, 60; on secondhand identity, 67; on sexual subordination, 110; on spoiled athlete syndrome, 20–21; on suppression of emotion, 17–18; on virgin-prostitute syndrome, 27, 28; on wives' control work at home, 117

"right" emotions, 85, 144

road-trip rules. *See* traveling with team, and code enforcement

Robyn (participant): on code busting, 96; on control and emotional dichotomy, 124–25; on game etiquette, 57; on guarding private life, 70; on husbands and control work, 102, 107–8; on motherization, 25, 26; on quasi-celebrityhood of wives, 63; on travel code of conduct, 83, 84, 87, 89, 91, 94; on wives' control work at home, 115, 117

role reversals, 150–51, 234n12

rookie players, 30–31, 37, 156, 169

rookie wives, 31, 32–35, 51, 56–57, 80, 114

Samantha (participant): on spoiled athlete syndrome, 19–20

Sandy (participant): on childhood, 121; on control and emotional dichotomy, 124; on in-laws, 130, 133, 134, 135, 138, 144–45; on virgin-prostitute syndrome, 27

seasonal groupies, 157, 163, 170

secondhand identity, 49, 64–69

secrets: conspiracy of silence in sport organizations, 29, 81; group boundaries and silence among teammates, 36, 38, 186; mother-in-law gatekeeping of, 135. *See also* culture of infidelity; gossip, among wives; groupieism and boundary work; traveling with team, and code enforcement

self-esteem, of players, 55, 164

self-esteem, of wives: and divorce, 197–98; and expectations of physical appearance, 110; and secondhand identity, 64–65; and sense of being in control, 123, 233n17

self-management strategies, defined, 9

self-sexualization, 163

senior veteran wives, 31

separations, marital. *See* divorce; trial separations

sexism of sizism, 110

sexting, 163, 182–83

sexual conquest. *See* culture of infidelity

sexualization of wives, 74–75

sexually transmitted diseases, 198–99

sexual objectification of female groupies, 160, 163

sexual subordination of wives, 109–11

sex workers, 27, 38, 87, 177

Sharon (participant): on childhood, 118; on control and emotional dichotomy, 127; on culture of infidelity, 198–99; on husbands and control work, 102–3; on motherization, 24–25; on sexual subordination, 109–10

Sheila (participant): on basic marital understanding, 39; on control and emotional dichotomy, 122; on culture of infidelity, 188, 191; on game etiquette, 53, 55; on husband's control work during offseason, 108–9; on in-laws, 141, 152; on length of marriage, 208; on organizational dominance, 30; on travel code of conduct, 83, 84, 86, 88, 89, 90, 91; on virgin-prostitute syndrome, 26, 27

short-term affairs, 185–87

"sitting on the bubble," 8

Skylar (participant): on celebrityhood of husband, 61; on control and emotional dichotomy, 125; on culture of infidelity, 182, 184–85, 196; on game etiquette, 55–56; on groupies, 176, 177–78; on guarding private life, 71; on hierarchy of players' wives, 31, 34; on in-laws, 137–38, 140; on motherization, 24; on public life/image, 50; on stress disorder symptoms, 201; on travel code of conduct, 81, 82, 83, 91; on wives' control work at home, 113

slump busters, 160

social circles: blabbers of secrets, 90–91 (*see also* gossip, among wives); challenges of trusting relationships, 201–2; and pseudo friends, 168; and pseudo wives, 167–68; queen bees, 34; refusal to join, 66; and social media, 32; during travel with team, 81. *See also* hierarchy of players' wives

social invisibility: of groupies, 165; of wives, 53, 63, 75, 82, 88, 89–90. *See also* wives as outsiders

social media: exposure of groupie interactions, 173; and public scandals, 71; selfies with fans, 57, 62; sexting, 163, 182–83; social circle interactions, 32; use of, by groupies, 163, 182–83; wives' reactions to, 64

social world perspective, 221n2

spectators. *See* fans

spoiled athlete syndrome, 19–20, 40, 44, 104–5, 108, 115–16, 224n9; childhood origins and mother's role in, 20–21; defined, 225n2; and material comfort, 39; vs. shared sense of entitlement, 60; and virgin-prostitute syndrome, 26; wife's role in, 22

sport ethic, 29, 36

sport marriage, influences on, 17–19; motivations to marry, 38–45; occupational influences, 28–38; personal influences, 19–28

sport organizations: cheerleaders, 20, 74–75, 169; and groupies, 155–56, 164, 168–69, 235n1; institutionalized brotherhood, 35–38, 227n23; public relations expectations of players and wives, 62–64; reinforcement of support role of wives, 63; security measures in hotels, 164; as total institutions, 28–29; travel policies for wives, 78–79, 230n2; travel secretary role in culture of infidelity, 81; unwritten rules for wives, 29–33; wives as outsiders, 29–30, 74–75

spousification of children, 130–31, 146, 150–51, 233n5. *See also* in-laws and subordination work; mother-son bond

Stacy (participant): on adapting to exclusion, 74, 75; on autograph seekers, 59; on basic marital understanding, 41–42; on code busting, 95, 96, 97; on control and emotional dichotomy, 123, 124, 126–27; on groupies, 171, 172–73, 175, 177; on husbands and control work, 103; on quasi-celebrityhood of wives, 62; on secondhand identity, 65; on travel code of conduct, 77–78, 80, 83–84, 85, 88, 98

stalking, 178

star college athletes, 32

star players, 21–22, 30–31, 34

star power and control work, 14, 99–100; childhood influences on wives, 113–21, 233n16; control as compensation for powerlessness, 101–2; emotional dichotomy for wives, 122–27, 233n17; and exclusion of wives, 73–76; husbands and passive control work, 102–6; husbands' control during offseason, 107–9; manipulation as control tactic, 116–17; normalization of control, 117–21; and retirement, 126–27; sexual subordination of wives, 109–11

status hierarchy. *See* hierarchy of players' wives

steady girlfriends, 32

strangers, wives as. *See* traveling with team, and code enforcement; wives as outsiders

subordination work/subordination management: avoidance in male gender work, 36; defined, 234n8; male dominance and female, 2, 3, 13, 36–37; self-reinforcement of, 80; sexual subordination of wives, 109–11. *See also* in-laws and subordination work

subworlds, 221n2

surrogate wives, 149

Susan (participant): on autograph seekers, 58; on control and emotional dichotomy, 126; on culture of infidelity, 182, 193–94, 197; on groupies, 158, 162, 174–75, 177; on participation in study, 204–5; on public life/image, 51–52; on secondhand identity, 67

suspicion work/suspicion management, 187–92; defined, 237nn4–5

Tanya (participant): on culture of infidelity, 180–81, 191, 196–97, 200; on divorce,

208; on guarding private life, 71; on husbands and control work, 236n1; on virgin-prostitute syndrome, 28

team groupies, 165, 166, 169–70

tested veteran wives, 31

therapy. *See* counseling and therapy

tie-signs, 133, 174, 176, 234n6

total institutions, 28–29, 227n23

Tracee (participant): on adapting to exclusion, 73; on culture of infidelity, 194; on groupies, 160, 172; on participation in study, 205

training camps, 8, 155–56, 163–64

traveling with team, and code enforcement, 13–14, 77—78; code busters, 95–98; code of conduct, 79–81; guardians of the code, 89–94; in hotel bars and nightspots, 35, 87–89, 94, 95–96, 97; perpetuation of the code, 98; on planes and buses, 78, 82–86, 185; repercussions for code busting, 79–80, 86, 94–95, 97; teammate exclusion or undermining of wives, 79–84, 230n2, 230n4. *See also* culture of infidelity

trial separations, 181, 190, 199–200, 208. *See also* divorce

two-person career, 39–45, 223n3, 228n37

unfaithfulness, 22, 40. *See also* culture of infidelity; groupieism and boundary work

unmarried female partners, 3, 32

unwritten rules for wives, 11–12, 29–33, 49–51. *See also* physical appearance expectations, of wives; traveling with team, and code enforcement

validation, vicarious: through husband's achievements, 151–52; through son's achievements, 130, 151–52, 233n5. *See also* star power and control work

verbal abuse, in sport-oriented families, 20

veteran players, 8, 30–31, 82, 88, 95–96

veteran wives, 12, 31–35, 51, 98

vicarious wives, 167

violent behavior, 9; normalization of, 36; and spoiled athlete syndrome, 21, 22

virgin-prostitute syndrome, 19, 26–28, 109, 110, 225n3

visible groupies, 84–85, 157–64

vulnerability, sense of, 71, 115

WAGs (wives and girlfriends), 9

walking-ahead strategy, 58

wannabe wives, 167–68

"we" partnership, 41–45, 55; affirmation via marriage work, 63–64; continuance in mother-son bond, 150–51; fan experience of, 63–64, 74; and game etiquette, 55; internalization by wives, 41–42, 122–23, 197–98; and vicarious achievement, 227–28n37. *See also* wives as outsiders

wife face, 52–53, 64, 72, 73–74

wife groupies, 165, 166–67

wifely duty, 109, 183–84

"wife of" identity, 3, 39–40, 61, 64–69. *See also* "we" partnership

wives as outsiders, 29–30, 73–74; in husband's family, 135, 152; in husband's occupational world, 30, 36, 74–75; and institutionalized brotherhood, 35–37; in marriage, 30, 75–76; and travel, 80, 84, 96, 230n2, 230n4

work, defined, 9

workaholic approach to male careers, 7–8

work-family model, 224n4; balance, 3; changes, xiii, 201

working-class male groupies, 159–60

"wrong" emotions, 53–54, 58–59, 144

young female groupies: appearance of, 161; behaviors of, 161–63, 177–78; characteristics of, 157, 160–61, 168; types of, 161–63; unattractive, as slump busters, 160. *See also* organizational groupies; team groupies

STEVEN M. ORTIZ is an associate professor of sociology at Oregon State University.

SPORT AND SOCIETY

A Sporting Time: New York City and the Rise of Modern Athletics, 1820–70
  Melvin L. Adelman
Sandlot Seasons: Sport in Black Pittsburgh   *Rob Ruck*
West Ham United: The Making of a Football Club   *Charles Korr*
Beyond the Ring: The Role of Boxing in American Society
  Jeffrey T. Sammons
John L. Sullivan and His America   *Michael T. Isenberg*
Television and National Sport: The United States and Britain
  Joan M. Chandler
The Creation of American Team Sports: Baseball and Cricket, 1838–72
  George B. Kirsch
City Games: The Evolution of American Urban Society and the Rise of Sports
  Steven A. Riess
The Brawn Drain: Foreign Student-Athletes in American Universities
  John Bale
The Business of Professional Sports   *Edited by Paul D. Staudohar
  and James A. Mangan*
Fritz Pollard: Pioneer in Racial Advancement   *John M. Carroll*
A View from the Bench: The Story of an Ordinary Player on a Big-Time
  Football Team (*formerly* Go Big Red! The Story of a Nebraska
  Football Player)   *George Mills*
Sport and Exercise Science: Essays in the History of Sports Medicine
  Edited by Jack W. Berryman and Roberta J. Park
Minor League Baseball and Local Economic Development   *Arthur T. Johnson*
Harry Hooper: An American Baseball Life   *Paul J. Zingg*
Cowgirls of the Rodeo: Pioneer Professional Athletes   *Mary Lou LeCompte*
Sandow the Magnificent: Eugen Sandow and the Beginnings of Bodybuilding
  David Chapman
Big-Time Football at Harvard, 1905: The Diary of Coach Bill Reid
  Edited by Ronald A. Smith
Leftist Theories of Sport: A Critique and Reconstruction   *William J. Morgan*
Babe: The Life and Legend of Babe Didrikson Zaharias   *Susan E. Cayleff*
Stagg's University: The Rise, Decline, and Fall of Big-Time Football at Chicago
  Robin Lester
Muhammad Ali, the People's Champ   *Edited by Elliott J. Gorn*
People of Prowess: Sport, Leisure, and Labor in Early Anglo-America
  Nancy L. Struna
The New American Sport History: Recent Approaches and Perspectives
  Edited by S. W. Pope
Making the Team: The Cultural Work of Baseball Fiction   *Timothy Morris*

Making the American Team: Sport, Culture, and the Olympic Experience
    Mark Dyreson
Viva Baseball! Latin Major Leaguers and Their Special Hunger
    Samuel O. Regalado
Touching Base: Professional Baseball and American Culture in the
    Progressive Era (rev. ed.)   *Steven A. Riess*
Red Grange and the Rise of Modern Football   *John M. Carroll*
Golf and the American Country Club   *Richard J. Moss*
Extra Innings: Writing on Baseball   *Richard Peterson*
Global Games   *Maarten Van Bottenburg*
The Sporting World of the Modern South   *Edited by Patrick B. Miller*
Female Gladiators: Gender, Law, and Contact Sport in America
    Sarah K. Fields
The End of Baseball As We Knew It: The Players Union, 1960–81
    Charles P. Korr
Rocky Marciano: The Rock of His Times   *Russell Sullivan*
Saying It's So: A Cultural History of the Black Sox Scandal   *Daniel A. Nathan*
The Nazi Olympics: Sport, Politics, and Appeasement in the 1930s
    Edited by Arnd Krüger and William Murray
The Unlevel Playing Field: A Documentary History of the African American
    Experience in Sport   *David K. Wiggins and Patrick B. Miller*
Sports in Zion: Mormon Recreation, 1890–1940   *Richard Ian Kimball*
Sweet William: The Life of Billy Conn   *Andrew O'Toole*
Sports in Chicago   *Edited by Elliot J. Gorn*
The Chicago Sports Reader   *Edited by Steven A. Riess and Gerald R. Gems*
College Football and American Culture in the Cold War Era
    Kurt Edward Kemper
The End of Amateurism in American Track and Field   *Joseph M. Turrini*
Benching Jim Crow: The Rise and Fall of the Color Line in Southern College
    Sports, 1890–1980   *Charles H. Martin*
Pay for Play: A History of Big-Time College Athletic Reform
    Ronald A. Smith
Globetrotting: African American Athletes and Cold War Politics
    Damion L. Thomas
Cheating the Spread: Gamblers, Point Shavers, and Game Fixers in College
    Football and Basketball   *Albert J. Figone*
The Sons of Westwood: John Wooden, UCLA, and the Dynasty That Changed
    College Basketball   *John Matthew Smith*
Qualifying Times: Points of Change in U.S. Women's Sport   *Jaime Schultz*
NFL Football: A History of America's New National Pastime
    Richard C. Crepeau
Marvin Miller, Baseball Revolutionary   *Robert F. Burk*

I Wore Babe Ruth's Hat: Field Notes from a Life in Sports   *David W. Zang*
Changing the Playbook: How Power, Profit, and Politics Transformed
   College Sports   *Howard P. Chudacoff*
Team Chemistry: The History of Drugs and Alcohol in Major League Baseball
   Nathan Michael Corzine
Wounded Lions: Joe Paterno, Jerry Sandusky, and the Crises in Penn
   State Athletics   *Ronald A. Smith*
Sex Testing: Gender Policing in Women's Sports   *Lindsay Parks Pieper*
Cold War Games: Propaganda, the Olympics, and U.S. Foreign Policy
   Toby C. Rider
Game Faces: Sport Celebrity and the Laws of Reputation   *Sarah K. Fields*
The Rise and Fall of Olympic Amateurism   *Matthew P. Llewellyn
   and John Gleaves*
Bloomer Girls: Women Baseball Pioneers   *Debra A. Shattuck*
I Fight for a Living: Boxing and the Battle for Black Manhood, 1880–1915
   Louis Moore
The Revolt of the Black Athlete: 50th Anniversary Edition   *Harry Edwards*
Pigskin Nation: How the NFL Remade American Politics   *Jesse Berrett*
Hockey: A Global History   *Stephen Hardy and Andrew C. Holman*
Baseball: A History of America's Game   *Benjamin G. Rader*
Kansas City vs. Oakland: The Bitter Sports Rivalry That Defined an Era
   Matthew C. Ehrlich
The Gold in the Rings: The People and Events That Transformed the
   Olympic Games   *Stephen R. Wenn and Robert K. Barney*
Before March Madness: The Wars for the Soul of College Basketball
   Kurt Edward Kemper
The Sport Marriage: Women Who Make It Work   *Steven M. Ortiz*

REPRINT EDITIONS

The Nazi Olympics   *Richard D. Mandell*
Sports in the Western World (2d ed.)   *William J. Baker*
Jesse Owens: An American Life   *William J. Baker*

The University of Illinois Press
is a founding member of the
Association of University Presses.
_____

University of Illinois Press
1325 South Oak Street
Champaign, IL 61820-6903
www.press.uillinois.edu